P9-DYO-278

CECIL COUNTY
PUBLIC LIBRARY
301 Newark Ave.
Elkton, MD 21921

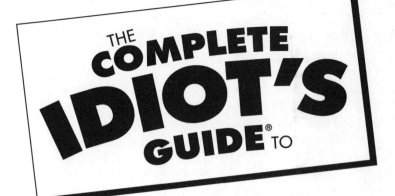

THE COMPLETE IDIOT'S GUIDE® TO

Vegetable Gardening

by Daria Price Bowman and Carl A. Price

ALPHA

A member of Penguin Group (USA) Inc.

ALPHA BOOKS

Published by the Penguin Group

Penguin Group (USA) Inc., 375 Hudson Street, New York, New York 10014, USA

Penguin Group (Canada), 90 Eglinton Avenue East, Suite 700, Toronto, Ontario M4P 2Y3, Canada (a division of Pearson Penguin Canada Inc.)

Penguin Books Ltd., 80 Strand, London WC2R 0RL, England

Penguin Ireland, 25 St. Stephen's Green, Dublin 2, Ireland (a division of Penguin Books Ltd.)

Penguin Group (Australia), 250 Camberwell Road, Camberwell, Victoria 3124, Australia (a division of Pearson Australia Group Pty. Ltd.)

Penguin Books India Pvt. Ltd., 11 Community Centre, Panchsheel Park, New Delhi—110 017, India

Penguin Group (NZ), 67 Apollo Drive, Rosedale, North Shore, Auckland 1311, New Zealand (a division of Pearson New Zealand Ltd.)

Penguin Books (South Africa) (Pty.) Ltd., 24 Sturdee Avenue, Rosebank, Johannesburg 2196, South Africa

Penguin Books Ltd., Registered Offices: 80 Strand, London WC2R 0RL, England

Copyright © 2009 by CWL Publishing Enterprises, Inc.

All rights reserved. No part of this book shall be reproduced, stored in a retrieval system, or transmitted by any means, electronic, mechanical, photocopying, recording, or otherwise, without written permission from the publisher. No patent liability is assumed with respect to the use of the information contained herein. Although every precaution has been taken in the preparation of this book, the publisher and authors assume no responsibility for errors or omissions. Neither is any liability assumed for damages resulting from the use of information contained herein. For information, address Alpha Books, 800 East 96th Street, Indianapolis, IN 46240.

THE COMPLETE IDIOT'S GUIDE TO and Design are registered trademarks of Penguin Group (USA) Inc.

International Standard Book Number: 978-1-59257-907-5
Library of Congress Catalog Card Number: 2008943246

11   10   09   8   7   6   5   4   3   2   1

Interpretation of the printing code: The rightmost number of the first series of numbers is the year of the book's printing; the rightmost number of the second series of numbers is the number of the book's printing. For example, a printing code of 09-1 shows that the first printing occurred in 2009.

Printed in the United States of America

Note: This publication contains the opinions and ideas of its authors. It is intended to provide helpful and informative material on the subject matter covered. It is sold with the understanding that the authors and publisher are not engaged in rendering professional services in the book. If the reader requires personal assistance or advice, a competent professional should be consulted.

The authors and publisher specifically disclaim any responsibility for any liability, loss, or risk, personal or otherwise, which is incurred as a consequence, directly or indirectly, of the use and application of any of the contents of this book.

Most Alpha books are available at special quantity discounts for bulk purchases for sales promotions, premiums, fund-raising, or educational use. Special books, or book excerpts, can also be created to fit specific needs.

For details, write: Special Markets, Alpha Books, 375 Hudson Street, New York, NY 10014.

Publisher: *Marie Butler-Knight*
Editorial Director: *Mike Sanders*
Senior Managing Editor: *Billy Fields*
Acquisitions Editor: *Michele Wells*
Senior Production Editor: *Megan Douglass*
Copy Editor: *Emily Garner*

Cartoonist: *Steve Barr*
Cover Designer: *Kurt Owens*
Book Designer: *Trina Wurst*
Indexer: *Tonya Heard*
Layout: *Chad Dressler*
Proofreader: *Laura Caddell*

Contents at a Glance

Contents

Appendixes

Foreword

I'm certain more people would garden if they felt confident in succeeding. And I don't mean throwing a few marigold or zinnia seeds onto a patch of bare soil and seeing them compete with a jungle of weeds to produce a splash of color, regardless of rainfall or soil fertility. I mean the deeply more satisfying form of gardening that produces edible results—luscious cantaloupes with chin-dripping flavor, meaty tomatoes where one slice can cover an entire slice of bread, raspberries the size of strawberries, strawberries the size of peaches, and bell peppers up to 10 inches long—crunchy, nutritious, and delicious. Surely there are few gardening accomplishments in life more satisfying than planting an Early Cascade tomato in your garden and harvesting a hundred or more red, ripe billiard ball–size fruits in a single season, or serving to a guest at dinner the blemish-free Buttercrunch lettuce he or she just admired on a tour of your garden.

That's why I recommend this book. It inspires confidence, assures success, and explains clearly and convincingly how to enjoy a bountiful harvest of not only the most worthwhile vegetables to grow, but also fruits, berries, and herbs.

Daria Price Bowman and Dr. Carl A. Price are a daughter-and-father partnership I greatly admire, for in this collaboration Daria brings to bear a practical approach, a lively writing style, and organizing ability, while her father is a wealth of information about the science of gardening. As a retired professor of plant biochemistry at Rutgers University for 40 years, Dr. Price knows the scientific reasons why certain basic gardening practices like composting and disease treatments work, even if the remedy itself is simple. Both are life-long gardeners, and although they advocate an organic remedy as the first line of defense, they know when to turn to science when all else fails.

Many garden books have been aimed at beginners, but these are largely focused on flower gardening, and many are gimmick books, advocating some sensational method of gardening with exaggerated claims like "weed free" and "no work." The information in this book, on the contrary, offers choices and clearly explains how to succeed whether you want to garden in traditional straight rows, plant in blocks, or harvest abundant produce from raised beds or containers. It's all here—clearly explained with special helpful sidebars such as Prof. Price's Pointers and others.

Every dietary study, it seems, confirms the wisdom of eating more fruits and vegetables and using herbs for seasoning for a healthy, long life. Broccoli is known to have anti-cancer properties; we are told that blueberries can reverse the process of aging; carrots can improve eyesight; garlic is associated with a healthy bloodstream; and vegetable fiber cleanses the colon of impurities.

Of course, fruits and vegetables and even herbs can be obtained from the produce section of the supermarket, but the longer a vegetable stays on the shelf or travels in transit from field to point-of-purchase, the more it loses freshness, crispness, and flavor. Moreover, flavor is lost in many fruits and vegetables by being picked too early so as to survive long journeys, even if they're flavorful varieties to begin with. But more often they're not those special home-garden varieties with a reputation for top flavor; rather they are commercial grower varieties, bred mainly for appearance and the ability to ship safely, without bruising. Indeed, few home garden varieties ever make it to the local produce counter simply because flavor is fairly far down on the list of priorities for commercial growers.

So here is a book written with the novice home gardener in mind, impartial in its advice, with step-by-step instructions to guide you every step of the way, whether you are keen to have a small garden the first year or a plot big enough to feed a family of four from the last frosts of spring through the first frosts of autumn and even until snow covers the ground. Follow its advice, and I believe you can be a successful gardener the very first season.

Derek Fell

Derek Fell is an award-winning author of gardening books and magazine articles, with more than 60 books to his credit, including *Vegetable Gardening with Derek Fell* (Friedman/Fairfax) and *Herb Gardening for Beginners* (Friedman/Fairfax). He has won more awards from the Garden Writers Association than any other person.

Introduction

Gardening takes many forms. Some gardeners get joy from raising dwarf conifers. Others find pleasure in planting peonies. Growing a vegetable garden is probably the most popular of all gardening styles, and it's not difficult to understand why. After all, when we till the earth, plant seeds, and harvest food to feed our family and friends, we are repeating tasks humans before us have done for thousands of years.

In this book, you get everything you need to know to create a garden of vegetables, fruits, and herbs. We offer very basic information that may be new to the novice, along with plenty of in-depth advice for the more experienced gardeners. Although there are no guarantees, after reading this book and following the techniques and procedures outlined on these pages—along with plenty of sunshine, adequate rainfall, and a sprinkling of good luck—you should be able to enjoy a bountiful harvest of home-grown vegetables.

How This Book Is Organized

The Complete Idiot's Guide to Vegetable Gardening is divided into six parts. Each addresses a different aspect of growing vegetables and herbs and offers a few fruits in the home garden.

Part 1, "Why Grow Food When the Grocery Store Is So Close By?" takes a broad look at why, when grocery stores are so convenient, you'd want to grow your own vegetables. Of course, it all has to do with things like health—both your own and the planet's—quality, and freshness, not to mention saving money, having a steady or at least seasonal source of hard-to-find foods, the fun of it, and the sense of accomplishment it brings. This part of the book also helps you decide what kind of garden you want to make, how big it will be, what it will look like, and even how much help you might need. We include sections on gardening with kids, growing organically, and making the most of small spaces.

In **Part 2, "Essential Planning,"** we get into some of the important basics of gardening, including an overview of what tools you most likely need to have, where to put your garden, how to do the proper planning on graph paper, translating your plan to a plot, and exploring some design schemes that may appeal to you. We also look at some of the smaller, but no less important, details like fencing options, paths and walkways, environmental factors, and architectural elements of your property.

Part 3, "Getting Ready to Plant," gets down and dirty. It's in these five chapters that you learn all about the science of gardening, including the importance of soil and the biology of plants. It's fairly complicated stuff, but we break it down into easy-to-understand tidbits. Part 3 also takes you step by step through creating garden beds where plants will thrive and the process for sowing seeds both indoors and directly in the garden, as well as how to transplant tender new seedlings.

Part 4, "What to Plant," is essentially a catalog of dozens of garden edibles and chock full of what you need to know to grow them. We cover everything from the basics like lettuce, tomatoes, corn, and beans to peppers, peas, eggplants, leafy greens, and the *Brassica* family (cabbages and their relatives). Farther into Part 4, you "get back to your roots" with information on root vegetables like turnips and parsnips and others like onions and potatoes whose edible parts also grow underground. We also include a chapter on herbs, another on some vegetables that may be less familiar, along with a few exotic veggies, and one on fruits typically grown along with vegetables.

Part 5, "Keeping It Growing," is all about maintenance: how and why to weed; the essentials of irrigation, pruning, trimming, and deadheading; and troubleshooting.

Finally, in **Part 6, "Reaping the Rewards,"** you learn how and when to harvest the edibles you've grown and then what to do with them when they're in your harvest basket. Canning; freezing; drying; and making jams, jellies, and pickles are some of the options you learn about. There's also a section on sharing the bounty of your garden. Part 6 ends with a look at the world of seed saving, taking care of tools, keeping records, and planning the next gardening season.

At the end of the book you'll find two appendixes of further resources so you can continue learning about gardening and growing your own food.

Some Other Important Stuff

With the hope of making this book easy to read and conveniently organized for finding what you need to grow beautiful vegetables, we've added sidebars throughout that provide additional information:

 **Food for Thought**

Find advice, tips, anecdotes, and even a little garden lore in these boxes.

 **Compost Pile**

Don't skip these boxes. They offer gentle warnings and advice on what *not* to do.

Garden Guru Says

In these boxes, find bits and pieces of horticultural information, techniques, and cultural practice that will, we hope, improve your expertise in the garden.

Prof. Price's Pointers

In these boxes, Prof. Price explains scientific, technical, historic, or academic aspects of gardening and gives definitions of some new terms.

Acknowledgments

We would like to thank a few folks who made the original of this book, and this new edition, possible. First, John Woods of CWL Publishing Enterprises, the packager of this book, was able to get past his previous experiences with Daria's writing habits and invited her to write this book and then asked her to tackle its new version.

Daria also owes much to her wonderful husband, Ernie Bowman, who keeps everything running smoothly when she's deep into a project; and to her daughters, Samantha and Cassie, who offer encouragement and express pride in their mom. Daria is grateful to her colleagues at Coldwell Banker Hearthside Realtors, where she makes her living, for putting up with her messy office and being grumpy, even though it didn't take all that long this time.

Daria is, above all, grateful to her father, Carl A. Price, the Prof. Price of this book. She's forever indebted to him for his good counsel and endless consultations, his research and rewrites. His contributions to this book were huge and essential.

Trademarks

All terms mentioned in this book that are known to be or are suspected of being trademarks or service marks have been appropriately capitalized. Alpha Books and Penguin Group (USA) Inc. cannot attest to the accuracy of this information. Use of a term in this book should not be regarded as affecting the validity of any trademark or service mark.

Part  Why Grow Food When the Grocery Store Is So Close By?

Not everyone needs or cares to know the history or the science behind gardening, but we find that kind of stuff fascinating. While researching this book, we were able to fill in some rather large gaps in our own knowledge banks, especially about the origins of agriculture. We hope you find this history interesting, too.

And Prof. Price has provided us with some really essential information about fruits and vegetables, and the science of how plants grow. But there's really only a little academic stuff here, so don't worry.

Growing Your Own Food

In This Chapter

- ◆ The growth of agriculture
- ◆ Learn why fresh produce is so satisfying
- ◆ Specialty and hard-to-find items you might want to grow
- ◆ What does *organic gardening* really mean?
- ◆ Easy ways to save money when you grow your own produce

Nothing is more basic than food. The earliest humans learned this the hard way, chasing after bison and bears with nothing but a big rock to kill them. It didn't take long—only a few thousand years—for our ancient ancestors to figure out that life is easier with a steady source of food, and the only way to have a truly reliable supply is to *grow* it. Thus agriculture was born. With agriculture came farming and gardening, and the rest is history.

In this chapter, we look at how our long-ago relatives tamed plants and carried them from continent to continent, developing new ways to garden along the way. And we see why growing produce has become one of America's favorite pastimes.

A Little History

About 12,000 years ago, human beings had had enough of their primitive hunting and gathering existence. They had, by that time, discovered fire and come to the realization that cooked food was a lot tastier than raw food. These early men and women had also learned how to craft crude cooking vessels out of bark, seashells, tortoise shells, and eventually clay and metal. Some of the smarter members of the human clan had cleverly devised food combinations that met their bodies' nutritional needs and had begun to mix meat and fish with collected fruits, roots, leaves, and seeds in their new cookware, making tasty soups and stews.

Because the hunting and gathering lifestyle was difficult and unpredictable, the very smartest folks developed ways to make plants grow in convenient places. (They also domesticated animals, but that's another book.) So around 10000 B.C.E. in what is now the Middle East, agriculture was born and soon spread to the Western Mediterranean and points north and east.

> **Prof. Price's Pointers**
>
> To sustain life, humans must consume foods that contain sugars (carbohydrates), proteins (nitrogen components), lipids (fats), micronutrients (minerals and vitamins), and fibers. All these essential nutritional elements are available by consuming a variety of plant species.

Over the next 10,000 years, farmers began to cultivate new food plants all over the world. In 7000 B.C.E., walnuts and beans were first planted. 6000 B.C.E. was a big year for corn. Grapes, oranges, and watermelons got their cultivation start around 4000 B.C.E. By 3000 B.C.E., barley, peas, carrots, onions, fava beans, and apples became part of the farmer's repertoire.

The vegetables and fruits we grow and eat today are either Old World or New World plants. From a historical perspective, Christopher Columbus gets the credit for introducing most of the New World plants to Europe.

New World foods include the following:

Beans	Pumpkins
Corn	Squash
Peanuts	Strawberries
Peppers	Sunflowers
Pineapples	Tomatoes
Potatoes	

Old World foods include these:

Beets	Okra
Broccoli	Onions
Carrots	Peas
Eggplant	Radishes
Lettuce	Yams

It's hard to believe that at one time, lettuce, peas, and radishes were rare and exotic. Today, we take even some of the most esoteric foods we eat for granted. When I (Daria) was growing up in the 1950s and 1960s, lemongrass might have been available in San Francisco, but the produce manager at the A & P in Arlington, Massachusetts, probably never heard of it. In the late 1970s, when I taught a class in Mexican cooking at the YMCA, I had to order cilantro by mail from a specialty house in New York. Now it's carried in most grocery stores.

With modern commerce, we are able to enjoy foods from every corner of the globe. And with the huge number of seed and plant growers and vendors, just about everything is available to grow yourself.

Fresh Is Best

If you've never picked a tomato from the vine and taken a bite right there in the garden, you don't really know what fresh food is. Harvesting edible plants and consuming them immediately is one of life's most sensual pleasures.

When I was a very young child, my family had a favorite summertime ritual—while Mom started a big pot of water on the stove, Dad and the kids would drive a short distance to a neighborhood farm where the farmer would let us pick our own corn. We would shuck the ears while Dad drove, and by the time we got home, the water would be boiling on the stove. In went the corn and, a few minutes later, we sat down to feast. That's as fresh as it gets.

With recent nutrition research proving that canned, frozen, and otherwise processed fruits and vegetables might be just as good, or even better, for us than their fresh counterparts, should we be less interested in growing our own? Absolutely not!

While most of us might assume that our homegrown foods might be more healthful, one of the reasons we are willing to do all the work that goes into producing produce is because fresh fruits and vegetables taste so much better.

Concern for carbon emissions from transporting food around the world, and pollution from overuse of nitrogen-based fertilizers from some growing practices are also big factors in people's motivation to grow their own food. Many environmentally conscious folks are turning to locally grown, organic foods to reduce pollution and help reduce their carbon footprint. Some strict locavores, like Colin Bevin, a.k.a. No Impact Man, strive to consume products raised within a 100-mile radius of their homes.

Prof. Price's Pointers

Fresh fruits and vegetables are undeniably wholesome and healthful, but eating them raw isn't necessarily the healthiest approach. According to a study published in 2000 by the American Chemical Society, the antioxidant levels of carrots increased dramatically immediately after being cooked to the point of mushiness. Research done in 2002 at Cornell University showed that the antioxidant value of tomatoes increases significantly when the tomatoes are cooked. In fact, many canned or frozen vegetables (but not broccoli, according to a 2008 scientific paper) and fruits have more nutritional or disease-prevention value than their raw counterparts.

It's a Matter of Taste

People garden for many reasons, but one of the primary motivating factors is taste. Homegrown vegetables and fruits taste far superior to anything you can buy in a store. Sure, roadside stands and farmers' markets sell great stuff, but nothing is as fresh as right out of your own garden.

Gardening gives you the opportunity to experience foods in a different way from what you're used to. You know where the fruits and vegetables come from, what went into growing them, how they've been handled, and how fresh they are. You can plan meals based on what's ripe right now. And you can choose to grow those things you savor most without being at the mercy of a produce manager's whim.

Food for Thought _____

The natural sugars in fruits and vegetables give them the flavors we like so much. After harvest, when the fruit is removed from the plant, those sugars quickly convert to starch that has a different and less stimulating taste. The longer the fruit sits before you eat it, the less sugar is available to produce the flavor.

Of course, there are limitations. The grocery store can offer asparagus and artichokes most of the spring and summer as they come in from various places around the world. The home gardener has one season—and that's often all too brief. But the joys of some other vegetable whose time to shine has come might be enough consolation.

Squash blossoms aren't typical grocery store fare, but if you grow your own zucchini, you can harvest these beautiful blooms to serve sautéed, lightly breaded and fried, or stuffed.

©iStockphoto.com

Specialties of the House

One of the best rewards of gardening is the opportunity it gives you to grow something special, something different from the ho-hum veggies found in every grocery store. For just a few dollars, you can become a specialist in Asian or Mexican vegetables. With a handful of herb plants and a little research, suddenly you are an expert on subtle seasonings or herbal remedies.

Growing your own food plants is so versatile, too. With successive plantings, you can add new things midseason or stop planting something that didn't work out well. You can change your approach from year to year.

Here are some specializations you might want to consider:

◆ A wide variety of one type of plant (beans, squash, cabbages, etc.)

◆ Baby and dwarf vegetables

◆ Produce for pickling

◆ Salad fixings (including 10 types of lettuce)

◆ Asian stir-fry foods

◆ Onions and their relatives

◆ Peppers (from hot to sweet)

◆ Heirloom vegetables

◆ Pumpkins or melons

◆ Fancy potatoes

◆ Tomatoes

◆ Latino cooking ingredients

◆ Herbs for French cuisine

◆ Medicinal herbs

Garden Guru Says

Most vegetables we eat are actually fruits—the ripened ovaries of a plant's flowers. Tomatoes, zucchini, and corn are all fruits of the plants on which they grow. Melons and strawberries are also fruits.

One of the great things about gardening is the flexibility it gives you to try growing new things or the same old thing but with a new method.

A Look at Organic Gardening

There are organic gardeners, and there are Organic Gardeners. Those truly committed to creating and maintaining a completely organic garden should understand that it requires more than simply forgoing pesticides and herbicides. Having an organic garden means you embrace an entire set of standards. In fact, there's a process for becoming certified as organic.

The USDA points out that the "principle guidelines for organic production are to use materials and practices that enhance the ecological balance of natural systems, and that integrate the parts of the farming system into an ecological whole."

Here are some basic organic gardening rules:

◆ Select a location that's appropriate for the plants you will grow.

◆ Prepare the soil with organic material.

◆ Choose disease-resistant varieties of plants.

◆ Rotate crops to avoid infestations and soil depletion.

◆ Compost your plant material and debris.

◆ Use compost and other organic material to enhance soil.

◆ Use nonchemical approaches to disease and insect control.

◆ Conserve water.

◆ Avoid use of power equipment.

We look more extensively at organic practices later in this book.

Protecting the Environment

Whether or not you're planning to garden organically, it's a good idea to understand why so many people are interested in this concept.

A major source of water pollution in the United States is fertilizer residues in storm water runoff. A great deal of that fertilizer comes from farms, but also from lawn and garden applications by homeowners. In addition, research indicates that most home-owners use far more than the recommended amounts of herbicides and pesticides when they treat their gardens and lawns. Careless watering is another problem in many parts of the country where several years of drought have strained supplies.

Careful use of resources and products is an intelligent way to approach gardening, whether or not you're willing to comply completely with organic principles.

Take, for example, David Benner, a gardening friend who lectures and writes about his gardening practices. He has one of the most Earth-friendly gardens you can imagine. While he specializes in shade plants, moss, and native flowering shrubs, his techniques would translate well to vegetable gardens.

Food for Thought

Consider this equation: you buy 10 young tomato plants for $2 a piece and each plant yields about 20 pounds of tomatoes. Calculated at $1.99 per pound, the price you might pay at a local farm stand, your $20 investment gives you about $400 in fresh, delicious tomatoes—enough to eat fresh all summer long with a few left over for canning or drying.

David removed every last square inch of grass from his property so he would no longer have to use a noise- and air-polluting lawn mower. He composts all his garbage and garden debris and uses the rich results to amend the soil and feed the plants. He faithfully conserves water and encourages native plants that require less water than exotic imports. David grows only those plants that are appropriate to the climate and conditions in his garden.

Protecting the Hyper-Allergic

Allergies are a problem for millions of people. For some, an allergy might be little more than an annoyance, but for others, an allergy to a food or environmental factor can be life threatening.

For those who have serious environmental allergies, especially allergies to insecticides, pesticides, and herbicides, growing foods organically or with an organic approach might be one of the few ways to have some control over quality of life.

Money in Your Pocket

Fussy consumers spend lots of money on organic or unusual vegetables at specialty stores, roadside stands, and farmers' markets. And they pay hefty prices for the very best stuff. Artichokes go for $2 or $3 apiece. A tiny sprig of rosemary is $2.99. And the mesclun? Try $12 a pound—if you can find it. Even plain old no-frill vegetables can be as costly as chicken or beef.

There is a better way. Growing your own produce can save you money. A friend of mine raises fancy mixed lettuces in a flat on her terrace. Her $9 investment in seeds, the seed tray, and potting mix rewards her with gourmet salad for two for most of the summer.

In addition to growing your favorite vegetables and fruits, why not grow the most expensive ones? Most won't cost any more to grow than the low-cost varieties.

Here are some of the more expensive types you might want to try:

Arugula	Fancy potatoes
Baby and dwarf vegetables	Herbs
Cherry and grape tomatoes	Radicchio
Fancy leaf lettuces	White eggplant

String beans are relatively inexpensive, but dainty French filet beans cost a fortune. The zucchini is practically given away by midsummer, so grow tiny, trendy, patty pan squash instead. And even if you can afford to pay for squash blossoms, try finding them even at the fanciest of green grocers.

When you grow your own produce from seed, the savings become even greater. Take, for example, fancy mesclun salad mix. These beautiful little salad greens can be prohibitively expensive, especially for everyday salads. But Johnny's Selected Seeds (www.johnnyseeds.com), for example, sells a gourmet mesclun mix for $4.30, with 1,200 seeds that will produce so much of the delicate, delicious stuff, you'll be giving it away to grateful friends.

Some wonderful fruits and vegetables have a relatively high initial investment, but they have a big payoff down the road. Asparagus, artichokes, and strawberries all should be started from plants rather than seed. It could cost $100 or more to start an asparagus patch, but 5 years later when you're still picking those exquisite shoots, you'll know it was worth every penny. Plus, if you take the time to can, freeze, or dehydrate the bounty, gardening can save you lots of money.

The Least You Need to Know

- ◆ Growing your own vegetables and fruits yields a steady supply of your favorites.

- ◆ You can create a specialty garden to supply your passion for particular types of cooking or flavoring.

- ◆ Fresh vegetables taste best, but their nutritional and disease-prevention qualities might not be quite as high as their canned or frozen counterparts.

◆ It's important to really understand what organic gardening means before you give yourself that label. But if strictly organic is too far a reach, keep in mind that even your smallest Earth-friendly efforts are worthwhile.

◆ Growing your own vegetables and fruits can greatly extend your food budget.

Chapter 2

What Kind of Garden Do You Want?

In This Chapter

♦ The timing of gardens

♦ The benefits of square-foot gardening

♦ Growing a little of this, a little of that

♦ Growing a garden of culinary delights, herbs, or medicinals

♦ Who to call when you need help

In this chapter, we look at what sort of garden you might want to create and check out how much time it will take to achieve the type of garden you want. Is your garden going to be one that gives you a smorgasbord of vegetables or focus on just a few culinary favorites? Are the medicinal and curative powers of herbs your special interest? Or does the idea of growing your own organic produce appeal to you? When considering these types of gardens, how much can you realistically handle? In addition to looking at the issues behind these questions, we also look at the highly specialized concept of square-foot gardening.

Later chapters cover, in much more detail, the techniques for growing various fruits and vegetables. In this chapter, we focus on the general types of gardens you might want to grow.

Time Is of the Essence

Gardening is America's favorite pastime—with the emphasis on *time*. Unlike other hobbies and avocations like golf, stamp collecting, or flea marketing, gardeners can only take time off in the off-season. And even then there's still garden-related stuff to do. When you commit to growing plants, you have to tend to their needs or they die. That's a basic fact of life!

So how much time does it take to grow a garden?

The reality is, it takes as much as you're willing to give. That's not being flip. You can grow a few plants, such as herbs, in a couple little pots on a windowsill or on the terrace with minimal time commitment. Count on ½ hour to put them in pots and a couple minutes each week to keep them watered and fertilized. That's it. No fuss, no muss.

If, on the other hand, your plan is to grow enough food to feed your family all year with some left over to sell at a little stand at the end of the driveway, you might want to consider quitting your day job and redefining your "job" as "gardener."

To get an idea of what you have to do to establish an extensive vegetable garden in a space that might have previously been your lawn, check out the following to-do list.

1. Test the soil.

2. Remove sod.

3. Turn the soil.

4. Remove rocks and roots.

5. Amend the soil.

6. Install irrigation.

7. Install fencing.

8. Create furrows, rows, mounds, and so on.

9. Buy seeds and plants.

10. Plant seeds and plants.

11. Put in trellises, plant cages, or stakes.

12. Water seeded and planted areas.

13. Thin seeded areas.

14. Weed furrows, rows, mounds, and so on.

15. Mulch.

16. Continue to water.

17. Continue to weed.

18. Deal with bugs.

19. Harvest.

20. Remove dead plants.

21. Turn the soil.

22. Plant cover crop.

The size and type of garden you want dictates how much time you should spend on gardening and on how many of these steps you need to take. Not every garden requires each one of these steps, but you get the picture.

Even if you've never gardened before, you can estimate how much time it will take you to do some of these tasks. When you have a number in mind, double it. Things always take much longer than you had planned. If you think you can afford that kind of time, go for it!

Square-Foot Gardening

About 25 years ago, a fellow by the name of Mel Bartholomew created a method of gardening based on the traditional French-intensive way of growing edibles in back-yards. The premise is that plants don't really need as much room as we tend to give them, and they'll do quite well when they're all crammed in together, as long as you make good preparations for them. This is a terrific approach for people who like things neat and tidy and are willing to do a fair amount of preparation work in the beginning.

Prof. Price's Pointers

The foundation for French-intensive gardening, which was the inspiration for square-foot gardening, is perfectly prepared soil. The long, narrow beds (to fit in the long, narrow backyards) were dug down at least 2 feet deep. Then the soil was amended with rich compost and humus and tilled to a light, fluffy consistency to allow for good root growth.

Square-foot gardens are usually done in raised beds that take a bit of time and, sometimes, cash to construct. But once installed, maintenance is less time-consuming.

To reduce the environmental impact of building a square-foot garden, you can look for recycled or left-over wood online, ask local contractors for extras, or ask for scraps at a lumber yard. If you're concerned about chemicals, you might want to avoid pressure-treated wood; and because railroad ties may have been soaked in kreosote, avoid these when creating raised vegetable beds.

Turn to Chapter 12 for more on square-foot gardening.

A Taster's Garden

A taster's garden is the type of garden that appeals to most people. You plant a few basic things like tomatoes, green peppers, and basil. And maybe you add eggplant, onions, and kale. You might even try broccoli, watermelon, and butternut squash. A little of this and a little of that is the idea; you don't want too much of any one variety. A taster's garden is a great way to get your hands dirty for the first time.

Food for Thought

If your space and time are limited, plant your taster's garden in a collection of pots on your deck or patio. You might have to leave out the watermelon and butternut squash, but you could add more herbs, and perhaps peas, beans, lettuce, and hot peppers.

Even a small garden like a taster's garden requires many hours of preparation and maintenance. When it's established (the initial preparation, fencing, irrigation, and other structural aspects complete), you can experiment with different plants each year, adding more of the vegetables you really like, eliminating those that don't work so well for you, and trying a few new things.

If you're a total beginner, the taster's garden is the best approach to try first.

A Garden of Culinary Delights

Those gardeners who love to cook and love to eat should plant a garden of culinary delights. In these gardens, you can grow your favorite gourmet treats. Sure, you can find these special things at a green grocer's, in specialty markets, or even your local supermarket, but they're *so* much tastier when they're freshly picked just before being added to the pot. And depending on their rarity, the prices you might have to pay in a market might be exorbitant.

Given unlimited garden space and time on my hands, my garden of culinary delights would include the following:

Artichokes	Poblano chiles
Arugula	Radicchio
Asparagus	Rainbow Swiss chard
Edamame	Shallots
Eggplant	Snow peas
Garlic	Sorrel
Herbs	Specialty potatoes
Jicama	Strawberries
Leeks	Tiny beets
Lettuce	Tomatillos
Okra	Tomatoes
Patty pan squash	

These are the fruits and vegetables I like best. Some of them, such as the specialty potatoes, rainbow Swiss chard, and delicate leaf lettuces, cost a fortune in markets. So I would grow lots of them to gorge on for the brief time they're in season.

If you want to try your hand at herbs, basil, parsley, dill, rosemary, sage, thyme, chervil, cilantro, and chives are good choices. If you're trying lettuce, go for all the frilly, delicate leaf varieties. And for tomatoes, try big juicy ones, tiny grape types, and a few interesting heirlooms and Italian plum varieties.

Unfortunately, I don't have the time or space to grow all these things, so I have to select the things that make sense for the way I garden now. That limits me to a few of the herbs (basil, parsley, dill, and coriander), the lettuces, and a couple tomato plants. If I'm feeling really ambitious, I would add arugula and sorrel. Then I just have to rely on my more prolific gardening friends to include me in their dinner parties—I'll bring the salad! Remember, you have to consider both time and space when deciding what you'll choose to prioritize with your culinary gardens, or with any garden.

Herb and Medicinal Gardening

For many gardeners, especially those with limited time and space, a garden devoted to herbs is enormously satisfying. An herb garden also enables you to explore the nuances of folk and herbal remedies.

We take a detailed look at herb gardening in Chapter 16.

Growing Seasonal Treats

Gardeners who specialize in flowering perennials strive to have something in bloom throughout the growing season. It takes considerable horticultural skill to plan a successful succession of blooms. Gardeners who grow vegetables might also have a succession of harvests in mind when they create their gardens. A few examples are shown in the following table.

Plant	Harvest Season
Arugula	late spring through early summer, fall
Basil	late spring through fall
Beans	late spring through mid-summer
Beets	late spring through mid-summer
Broccoli	mid-spring through early summer
Corn	late spring through mid-summer
Dill	late spring through late summer
Eggplant	mid-summer through fall
Garlic	late spring through early summer
Kale	mid-summer through late summer
Leeks	mid-summer, late summer

Plant	Harvest Season
Lettuce	mid-spring through fall
Melons	late spring through early summer
Oregano	mid-spring through fall
Potatoes	late spring, early summer
Pumpkins	late summer through fall
Radicchio	fall
Radishes	mid-spring through fall
Raspberries	late summer
Sage	mid-spring through fall
Scallions	late spring
Spinach	mid-spring through late spring
Strawberries	late spring through mid-summer
Thyme	mid-spring through fall
Tomatoes	late spring through late summer
Zucchini	late spring through early summer

Please note that this set of harvest times is approximate and based on conditions in my own Pennsylvania garden. Harvest seasons are different in other parts of the country. Representatives from your county extension office, local CSA, or garden center can advise you.

By starting seeds indoors, using a cold frame (like a little greenhouse; more on this later), buying established plants, and planting several varieties of the same vegetable or fruit, you can stretch out the harvest and enjoy a wide variety of edibles for many months. And if you live in warm climates such as California or Florida, you already have nearly year-long growing seasons, although not all plants will thrive, or even grow at all, under those conditions.

Tutti-Frutti Gardens

We could write a whole book on the topic of fruit trees, and a number of fruits would be good for edible gardens. Check out Chapter 18 for more detailed information about growing fruits such as strawberries, rhubarb, melons, and ground cherries.

Hiring Help

A friend wanted an organic vegetable garden in her backyard for some very good reasons: she wanted to serve her family fresh, organic food, and it was important to her that her children understood that food comes not just from the grocery store but from the beautiful bounty of nature's gifts. But she didn't have the time nor the skill set to plant or tend to the type of garden she wanted. So she hired a woman with a small company called The Turnip Truck who provides that highly specialized service.

You might not need someone to handle the whole job for you, but some aspects of starting or tending a garden might require more time, skill, or physical strength than you have. In such cases, call in the turnip truck!

Some ideal jobs for hired hands include initial tilling, installing irrigation systems, putting up fences, pulling weeds, laying down mulch, spreading manure, and turning the garden at the end of the season.

Compost Pile _____

If paying for a little help fits your budget, be sure your hired help know what they're doing. Local teens or other inexperienced gardeners might be willing to help with weeding, watering, and other chores in your garden, but they may need you to instruct them carefully. It's disheartening for everyone when a new hired hand proudly shows off his hours of labor only to be told that the weeds he pulled out were actually the new asparagus plants that cost you $100!

The Least You Need to Know

- Part of the fun of gardening is deciding what kind of garden suits your lifestyle and your tastes.

- Carefully consider the time you need for the style of garden you plan, and be realistic when evaluating your commitment to the type of garden you choose.

- It's always a good idea to start small when you're new to gardening.

- Hire help if you need it.

Do It in Style

In This Chapter

- ◆ Planting gardens in urban or small spaces
- ◆ Growing suburban gardens
- ◆ Very large gardens
- ◆ Introducing your kids to gardening
- ◆ Landscaping with vegetables

You know you want to plant a garden of some sort, and you've come up with a list of the plants you'd like to grow. You have some idea of what type of garden it's going to be and whether or not you'll use organic methods. Now it's time to get really serious. How is it going to work? Who's going to do the work? Do you want to just make a few horticultural attempts without a big commitment? Or is this something you're really drawn to in a big way?

In this chapter, you review all your options and learn how to create a garden with style.

Gardens in the City and Other Small Spaces

Not every gardener is blessed with an acre of ground. Millions of Americans live in apartments, condominiums, townhouses, and flats where the outdoor spaces might be strictly regulated or even nonexistent. Yet erstwhile gardeners who live in these dwellings still yearn to get their hands dirty just like anyone else. And for many, there's no reason why they shouldn't have an opportunity to grow at least a little bit of their own food.

Compost Pile

Lead from car and truck exhaust can poison produce grown in urban gardens, so when gardening in pots or other containers in the city, use fresh soil in the pots every year. Also, be sure to wash your harvest thoroughly before you eat it.

I've always marveled at the ingenuity of city gardeners. From my friends' eleventh-floor apartment on New York's Upper East Side, I can see a huge variety of plants growing in containers on windowsills and rooftops. In other parts of the city, fire escapes become mini jungles of flowers and produce during the summer months. At the retirement community where my mother lived, the residents use their balconies to re-create tiny versions of the gardens they left at their former homes.

Where you find a balcony, rooftop, fire escape, or windowsill, you can find room for a plant or two.

Life on the Ledge

Windowsill gardening is an indoor and an outdoor affair, but for the purposes of this chapter, let's concentrate on the great outdoors because to produce produce, most plants require far more sun than is available to them indoors. (One exception is greenhouse gardening, which is another book entirely. Herbs are the other exception. They are relatively easy to grow on an indoor windowsill.)

By necessity, most windowsill gardens are home to small plants that are comfortable growing in window boxes. Herbs are the most likely candidates, especially the more compact and lower-growing types like parsley, basil, marjoram, coriander, and oregano. (See Chapter 16 for more information on herbs.) An ample window box can provide enough space to grow things like leaf lettuces, sweet and hot peppers, eggplant, bush beans and peas, and strawberries. Look for dwarf varieties of other plants, too. Avoid root vegetables and sprawling plants like melons, squash, and cucumbers.

Several types of window boxes are available to choose from, including those made of cedar or plastic. On very wide masonry sills, like the ones on apartment buildings, cast cement, or reconstituted stone planters are an option. You should select whichever size and material works best for your windowsill.

Garden Guru Says

Go deep! Vegetables require a minimum soil depth of 9 inches to thrive in a window box or other planter.

Whatever material window box you choose, be sure it has excellent drainage. Select containers that have enough drainage holes to allow water to pass through quickly, or add more holes. Cover the holes with pieces of broken terra-cotta pots or use a handful of Styrofoam peanuts in the bottom of the pot over the holes to keep soil from leaking out.

Be sure your window boxes are securely attached to either the windowsill or the wall to protect passersby (and your insurance carrier) from any disasters. On wide sills, rest the box on the sill and fasten it with screws or bolts through the bottom of the box. On shallow sills, attach brackets to the wall and screw or bolt them to the bottom of the container. And always be considerate when watering. No one wants to a take an unscheduled shower in window box drippings!

Fire Escape Gardens

I love fire escape gardens. They are one of the most hopeful, life-affirming things I know of. The people who grow plants in the gritty environment of the urban streetscape exhibit great creativity and optimism. It's not easy to make things grow under these conditions, but they keep trying. Even the most ambitious fire escape garden will be limited in size. But with some careful planning, you can still grow some incredible edibles.

There's something about a fire escape garden that calls for found-object containers, especially giant olive oil cans (the kind used in restaurants), 2-pound coffee cans, milk cartons, and plastic water jugs with the tops cut off. I once saw tomatoes growing in milk crates lined with black plastic garbage bags. How creative!

The biggest problem facing fire escape gardeners is sunlight, or lack thereof. If the space gets fewer than about 5 hours of full sunlight a day, you'll have a really hard time growing plants. Consider growing ferns and flowers such as impatiens instead.

Plastic milk crates lined with garbage bags are an unusual but effective alternative to pots.

Balcony Bounty

For many folks, the only outdoor space they can call their own is a bit of balcony. This is where they park the hibachi, a lounge chair, and, if they have any horticultural leanings, a few plants in pots. There's no reason why a balcony can't become a mini farm for those so inclined.

Balcony gardeners can usually grow their plants in a combination of planters, hanging baskets, and window boxes attached to the railings. With a little ingenuity, even the smallest space can accommodate a wide variety of edible plants.

Garden Guru Says

Whether you're limited by space or not, sometimes smaller spaces are smarter choices, especially if you are an inexperienced gardener.

Basics in a Barrel

It's possible to grow a nice variety of edible plants in an old whiskey barrel or two. You've probably seen these barrels. They're cut in half across the middle, making planters about 2½ feet across and about 2 feet deep. Whiskey barrels are not completely water tight, but you should still drill 2 or 3 holes in the bottom for good drainage.

Food for Thought

New whiskey barrels are available at many garden centers, but you could also recycle other containers. Soni Pitts, who gardens outside her apartment building in Asheville, North Carolina, purchased old plastic Rubbermaid bins at a Goodwill store, punched holes in the bottom for drainage, filled them with good soil, and successfully planted carrots and beets. Yard sales, Freecycle (www.freecycle.org), and Craigslist (www.craigslist.org) are also good sources for reusable containers like trash cans, washtubs, or even diaper pails.

What can you grow in a barrel? Here are a few good combinations:

- 1 tomato, 2 peppers, 1 eggplant, 1 basil, and 1 parsley.

- 3 basil, 1 oregano, 3 bean plants with a climbing support, leaf lettuces, and mini carrots or radishes.

- 3 herb plants (parsley, basil, and cilantro, for example).

- 1 hot pepper, 2 cilantro, 1 lemongrass, and 3 snow pea plants on a climbing support. When the peas are done, put in a tomato plant.

- 2 parsley, 2 basil, 1 dill, 1 cilantro, 1 thyme, 1 rosemary, 1 oregano, and 1 chive.

- 6 dwarf strawberry plants.

- 1 large variety tomato plant and 3 basil.

- 1 cherry or grape tomato plant, leaf lettuces, and 15 scallion sets.

These are just a few of the many combinations of vegetables and herbs that grow well in a large container like a whiskey barrel. After you've tried it, you'll figure out what plants work best for you.

Garden Guru Says _____

To grow climbing peas or beans in a pot, they need something to climb. The easiest "something" is a support made of bamboo stakes. Insert three tall bamboo or fiberglass stakes equally spaced around the inside of the pot. Be sure the stakes are pushed all the way to the bottom of the pot. Secure the tops of the stakes with twine or a rubber band, forming a tepee. The plants will climb the stakes on their own.

Keep in mind that you can use several whiskey barrels or other containers without increasing your workload significantly. And there's no reason why you can't try some larger plants like pumpkin, cabbage, zucchini, or even cucumber. Just look for dwarf or bush varieties.

The key to success for large container gardening is adequate irrigation. Irrigation, fertilizer applications, and succession planting are all discussed later in the book.

Gardening in Suburban Spaces

The vast majority of Americans live in the suburbs, where properties range from small lots measured in feet to multiple-acre spreads. It's in the backyards of these homes that most of us garden.

Suburban landscaping is probably the largest segment of the gardening industry, with vast quantities of consumer dollars spent on foundation plantings and lawn care. It's reasonable to expect to pay up to 15 percent of the price of a new home on a landscaping package. And real estate agents can tell you that a badly landscaped house won't command as high a price as its well-done counterpart.

But where does the vegetable garden fit into this picture? In most cases, it's an afterthought. It doesn't need to be. A successful backyard garden should be carefully planned so it's integrated into the landscape. We talk about how to do this in Chapters 5, 6, and 7.

Doing It Big!

My first vegetable garden was an enormous affair, at least the size of a football field. My friend and I prepared it completely by hand and planted it with every vegetable we could think of.

That summer, we spent all our free time sowing, weeding, watering, and harvesting. I took a class on canning at the county extension office and filled hundreds of jars with tomatoes and pickles. My husband and I had enough frozen green peppers to last 5 years! And the zucchini bread—after a while friends stopped coming to the door if they saw me arrive with a little package wrapped in aluminum foil! I could never tackle a garden that large again, but it was worth all that effort for the incredible sense of accomplishment.

If you have the time, the space, and the cash for start-up expenses, doing it up big can be very rewarding. But if you've never gardened before, this is not the best route to follow.

Why do it big? Your reasons could vary depending on your circumstances. Maybe you want to grow your own organic food so you know everything that goes on and in it. Maybe you just love the taste of fresh vegetables or want to grow some produce for local restaurants or markets. Maybe you love canning and preserving foods and want to grow your own fresh fruit to preserve. Or maybe you just enjoy spending summer days outside in the sun and the dirt, making things grow.

Something for the Kiddies

My earliest experiences with gardening weren't quite hands-on. Instead, what I remember is watching my father dig holes in the garden and move plants from here to there. I can also remember him growing tomatoes in a large plot at the far end of our big suburban backyard. I can't recall many details except that he regularly pinched back some of the flowers on the tomatoes to force them to grow larger fruits. And I'm sure he explained the physiological reasons for doing that in great detail. I loved every minute of it, because it allowed us to be together.

One of the best reasons to involve your kids in gardening is that it does give you more precious time together. And if you make the experience fun rather than a chore, you might help your children develop a lifelong interest. In addition, many parents have found that children who might normally shun vegetables are more willing to at least give them a try if they've had a hand in growing, or at least picking, them.

It doesn't take much to create a kid-friendly garden. Here are just some of the gardening themes you might use to interest kids:

◆ A spaghetti sauce or pizza garden with tomatoes, peppers, onions, basil, and oregano plants

◆ An alphabet or name garden, with a plant for each letter of the alphabet, or one for each letter in the child's name (S = squash; A = arugula; M = mint)

◆ A giant tepee (made with 8- to 10-foot bamboo poles in a circle attached at the top with twine) with peas and beans planted at the base of the poles (They grow up the poles and cover them, making an enclosure.)

◆ Vegetable plants outside a playhouse or at the base of a climbing set

◆ A section of your vegetable garden just for the kids and planted with their favorite vegetables

◆ A series of pots and containers decorated and planted by your kids on the deck with favorites

◆ A collection of dwarf, miniature, and "baby" vegetables; or a "giant" garden featuring extra-large varieties of pumpkins, tomatoes, watermelons, and cabbages

Most children have relatively short attention spans, so it's really important that their gardens are low maintenance. And don't expect the kiddies to get too excited about preparing the soil or weeding. They'll be most interested in planting seeds and seedlings and harvesting. Watering can be fun, especially if it's done in a bathing suit and everyone gets wet!

Garden Guru Says

Several seed companies have special collections designed for children, with easy-to-grow, colorful, and fun plants. Check out Burpee Seeds (www.burpee.com), Kitchen Garden Seeds (www.kitchengardenseeds.com), and Renee's Garden (www.reneesgarden.com). Kitchen Garden Seeds has one collection called the "Oddly Strange Vegetable Garden," which might be especially appealing to children.

Children can learn so much from the experience of starting plants from seed. Try quick-to-germinate plants like radishes, carrots, peas, and beans to start from seed. For tomatoes, peppers, and eggplant, start out with young plants.

A tepee garden can be a magical place. Try planting dwarf sunflowers around the perimeter for color. (You can also harvest the seeds.) And with an inexpensive grass mat and old pillows inside, it makes a great hideout.

If you have the room, try some real kid-pleasing plants like corn, watermelon, and pumpkin. They need a lot of space but are very easy to grow. A heavy mulch (see Chapter 19) will keep weeding at a minimum. After all, there's nothing like weeding to take the fun out of gardening for a kid.

Produce Among the Posies

While most folks think of vegetables, herbs, and fruits as simply plants to grow for food, many gardeners—including me—like to use these plants as ornamental additions to beds, borders, and planters.

A friend of mine who gardens in a tiny yard mixes vegetables with flowers throughout his garden. One time he trained a strong vining tomato up a trellis and across an arbor. The tomatoes hung below the vine, just waiting to be picked. It was beautiful, if unusual.

I first saw extensive use of edibles in ornamental gardens when I visited England. At one small row house just outside London, the owner grew rhubarb in giant raised planters and chives in pots on top of a wall. At Tintinhull House, one of the great

National Trust properties in the southwest, fennel was used as a decorative accent in a perennial border. I also saw artichokes used decoratively.

Recently, I was given a 6-pack of baby kale plants. Because the big planters on my terrace only had a few lonely geraniums in them, I stuck two kale plants in each one. By mid-July, the huge blue-green kale leaves had made a pretty, if eccentric, foil to the fuchsia-colored geraniums. And I was able to harvest the kale leaves all summer.

If you think a vegetable is pretty, then by all means add it to the flowerbeds. Or try some of these tucked among the blooms:

Arugula	Okra
Chives	Purple basil
Curly parsley	Purple beans
Hot peppers	Sage
Kale	Strawberries
Leaf lettuce	Swiss chard

The Least You Need to Know

- ◆ You can grow your own vegetable garden in any size space, whether it's a container on a small terrace or the back 40.

- ◆ Get kids involved in gardening by letting them plant their favorite vegetables (especially if they're quick-growing, to hold their interest).

- ◆ Vegetable plants can be used as ornamental plants in your flower beds and among your landscaping.

Part 2

Essential Planning

This is a pretty long section because there's so much ground to cover. In the next several chapters, we go over the basic information you need to start and maintain your garden.

Chapter 4 is all about the tools of your new trade. After reading Chapter 5, you should have a pretty good idea of where you'll put the garden and how large a garden you can actually handle. Chapter 6 features the steps you might take to plot out a garden. The work itself can get kind of tedious, but you really should pay attention to this chapter because it will save you time and even money in the end. Chapter 7 is a bit more fun because we look at some of the design options for vegetable gardening, including cute cottage style, formal European-style vegetable garden designs, and even a bit on the feng shui of gardens.

CECIL COUNTY
PUBLIC LIBRARY
301 Newark Ave.
Elkton, MD 21921

4

Tools of the Gardening Trade

In This Chapter

- ◆ A brief history of gardening tools
- ◆ Spades versus shovels
- ◆ Selecting essential hand and cultivating tools
- ◆ The best gloves for the task at hand
- ◆ The real dirt on wheelbarrows and garden carts

The very earliest gardening tool was nothing more than a stick. An early woman decided that planting seeds was easier when she made a hole in the ground with the pointy end of stick instead of her hands. (Remember, at this point men were still out in the forest throwing rocks and spears at wild animals while women were growing crops and raising children.)

We've come a long way since that stick. Gardening tools are big business, and the choices are nearly limitless. This chapter helps you determine the tools you simply can't do without and those that make gardening tasks just a little easier. And you'll learn about some of the frills and extras. (If you're looking for tools and equipment for irrigation, turn to Chapter 19. For tool care and maintenance, go to Chapter 25. And for a look at machinery for tilling, flip to Chapter 9.)

Dig This

Starting around 9000 B.C.E., people began planting seeds rather than just gathering them. (Remember the evolution from hunter/gatherer to farmer we learned about in Chapter 1?) First came that digging stick, followed soon after by a rudimentary wooden hoe. Those early hand tools sufficed for about 5,000 years, until a bright farmer figured out how to harness an ox to pull a plow fashioned from a wooden hoe attached to a stone-age cutting tool similar to an *adze*. (Keep that word handy for crossword puzzles.)

Another few thousand years passed. Around 650 B.C.E., a precocious R&D type developed iron tools—a major breakthrough. The Romans made more innovations and transformed the plow into a heavier, more versatile tool. The tool trade remained more or less stagnant for a thousand years or so until the steam engine was invented and adapted for farming. Not long after that, the gasoline engine was developed and power tools came on the scene.

Food for Thought

A 60,000-year-old digging stick found in Africa might be the oldest surviving relic of its kind.

Wood and metal gardening tools became more refined in the seventeenth and eighteenth centuries, and by the nineteenth century they began to look much like the tools we use today. The materials of today's gardening tools are more sophisticated—cast aluminum and fiberglass, for example—but the shapes are pretty much the same.

Let's Call a Spade a Spade

The uninitiated might use the words *spade* and *shovel* interchangeably. But just try doing spadework with a shovel, and you'll soon learn the difference. Shovels have a larger bowl in the blade to move more of whatever material you're moving. Spades usually have straight-sided blades and are designed to cut through turf and soil. Use a spade to dig deep and straight down; use a shovel for larger areas and to move the soil out of the hole.

The garden spade can be long-handled or short, with a long or short blade. The blade end might be curved, slightly pointed, or cut straight. Although all kinds of spades might be used interchangeably, some shapes and styles work better for certain tasks. For example, a long-handled spade is useful for digging rocks or roots out of a bed.

A spade with a rectangular blade is great for edging beds and making straight cuts through sod.

The difference between a spade and a shovel isn't all that subtle.

poacher's spade   garden shovel

Garden Guru Says _____

If I had to restrict my tool collection to only one digging implement, I would choose my classic English poacher's spade from the Smith & Hawken catalog (which is, sadly, no longer available; a similar rabbiting spade is available from gardenhardware.com). This small, short-handled spade got its name because rabbit poachers on early English estates favored it. The long (5½×10½-inch) powder-coated steel blade has a sharp, slightly curved end that makes it ideal for planting or transplanting large annuals, perennials, and small shrubs. It's great for cutting through sod, edging beds, and digging out tap-rooted weeds. And it's especially useful in tight, fully planted spaces or even large planters.

Shovel It On

Shovels are great for digging new beds after the sod has been removed, for creating planting holes for large shrubs, and for general digging in loose soil.

In addition to digging, shovels are good for shoveling—moving stuff like soil, compost, mulch, or manure from one spot to another. The best shovel for moving large quantities of material is one with a squared-off blade because it has a wider entry point for scooping.

Fork It Over

The garden or spading fork is another useful—and sometimes essential—digging tool. The fork is built like a spade or shovel, except it has tines instead of a blade. The fork is especially helpful when soil is hard or compacted. It's also easier to dig in clay soils with a garden fork than with a spade or shovel.

Don't confuse pitchforks with spading forks, though. Pitchforks are used like shovels to move stuff, like hay or dried manure clumps, from one place to another. They're not for digging.

You Can Handle It

Spades, shovels, and garden forks have either long or short handles. Generally, the shorter the handle, the easier the tool is to use, especially in confined spaces like established growing beds. But a longer handle gives you more leverage, which is helpful for moving heavy things like wet soil or a root ball.

Long-handled spades, shovels, and forks tend to have straight handles much like a broomstick. The shorter versions frequently end in a D or a Y shape. These open handles create a space to grip the tool and add an extra bit of leverage. In terms of efficiency and utility, there really isn't much difference between the D and the Y, so select the one that feels best in your hand.

The Y- or D-shape handles on these spades are typical of short-handled types. Choose the one you find most comfortable.

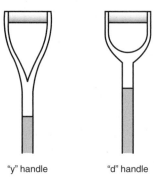

"y" handle   "d" handle

The Material World

Spade and shovel blades and fork tines are made of metal, usually either stainless steel or carbon steel. Stainless doesn't rust, which means stainless-steel tools don't need a lot of maintenance. Some of the carbon-steel tools, like those sold by Smith & Hawken and Kinsman Garden Supply, are made of carbon steel with either an enamel or powder coating. My poacher's spade, for example, is powder-coated and it hasn't rusted yet, after 10 years of heavy use.

I'm told that soil won't stick to stainless steel when you dig, but I've yet to find one the soil doesn't stick to at least a little. But don't worry about it too much. I've never found having soil stick to my spade to be a problem.

Some of the best digging tools have a powder coating over the steel (a kind of baked-on finish) that protects the steel and seems to prolong the life of the tools.

> **Garden Guru Says**
>
> The very strongest spades, shovels, and forks are made from forged steel rather than sheet steel. If you're looking for strength in particular, be sure to ask about the strength of the material before you purchase one of these tools.

Spade, shovel, and fork handles are usually made of wood. Less-expensive tools might be made with any one of several woods, but the best, most durable tools have handles made of ash, often with a metal strap. Some handles are made of fiberglass, which is a pretty sturdy material as well.

Hoes, Rakes, and Other Infamous Characters

Hoes and rakes are the workhorses of the tool trade. When the soil has been thoroughly dug and moved around, the hoes, rakes, cultivators, and weeders go into action. These are generally long-handled tools made of the same materials as spades and shovels.

Hoes

The hoe is the ancient tool that came into being right after the digging stick. No more than a sharp-edge blade of metal attached to a long handle, the hoe is primitive but essential. Use it to chop through the soil and push it around a bit. You can also use your hoe to weed between individual plants or rows of vegetables and to break up the surface of the soil around plants so water and fertilizers can penetrate into the roots.

The basic hoe has some specialized offspring: a *warren hoe* has a heart- or arrow-shape blade and is used for making furrows or rows. An *eye hoe* has a circular hole at the top center of the blade. It's useful in hard-packed soil or soil with lots of thick roots. A *circle hoe* has a circular blade. It can get in close to roots, and it's also useful in rocky soil. The blade comes in several sizes.

The *Dutch hoe* is also called the *scuffle hoe;* it has a flat blade with a horseshoe-shape shank, and is used to cut through weeds in a push-pull motion. A *collinear hoe* has a small, very sharp, replaceable blade for weeding. And a *grub hoe* is a very heavy-duty hoe with a sharply angled blade. It's used for tough digging like trenches.

Rakes

The garden rake is a classic tool. Think of Beatrix Potter's illustrations of Farmer McGregor chasing Peter Rabbit with a rake in his hand.

Unlike the fan-shape rakes used for collecting leaves, garden rakes have long handles and a head with short, steel tines set perpendicular to the handle. This essential tool is used to move a thin layer of soil around the surface of beds; to separate stones; to loosen roots and light debris from prepared soil; and to pull soil up into mounds, hills, or furrows.

> **Compost Pile** _____
>
> Any tool left lying on the ground unattended is potentially dangerous. This is especially true for rakes left tine-side up. It might be hilarious when one of the Three Stooges gets clocked by the rake handle when he steps on a rake head, but it's not a bit funny if it happens to you or an unsuspecting passerby. Always move your tools out of harm's way when you're not using them.

Getting Handy with Hand Tools

No gardener could survive without a few hand tools. The essentials include a trowel, a hand fork, a cultivator, and a pronged weeder. Most hand tools are made of the same materials as their larger relatives, described earlier in this chapter. Look for similar construction, too.

The key to a good hand tool is the feel of the handle. Get one with a smooth grip that won't splinter and isn't too big for your hand. Ash and beech are probably the top choices. It should also have a sturdy steel blade or tines. Cast-aluminum tools are a good choice if you have trouble with heavy tools, because they weigh less. And hand tools like Good Grips, with handles made of a soft, cushioned material, are great if you have arthritis or other conditions that make gripping difficult.

Indispensable Trowels

When it comes to trowels, I break my own rule about only buying the best-quality tools. I tend to lose at least one trowel a year and sometimes more. I can't tell you how frustrated I get when I search for my trowel and can't find it. A trowel is absolutely indispensable, especially for people like me who do a lot of container gardening.

Trowel blades should be pointed enough to pierce the soil and break up clumps, and wide enough to allow you to dig a hole pretty quickly. Transplanting trowels have long, narrow blades designed for making a deeper hole. I have one with depth markers that's handy for planting things like onion sets because I can see exactly how deep I'm going.

Handy Forks and Cultivators

The hand fork is a mini spading fork with wider tines. It's designed to turn over the top few inches of prepared planting beds or containers.

The hand cultivator has three bent prongs, usually with the center prong set higher than the other two. Use this handy tool to aerate surface soil and loosen soil around shallow-rooted weeds.

Food for Thought

Tools are one of a new gardener's largest expenses, and it usually pays to buy the best. Cheap tools tend to break easily. But those on a tight budget won't necessarily have to break the bank to have the tools they need. Yard and barn sales, Freecycle, and Craigslist are good sources for used tools. Also, look for end-of-season or off-season sales at hardware stores and farm supply vendors.

Wild About Weeders

Not an essential tool in everyone's garden, the hand weeder is indispensable where tap-rooted weeds like dandelions and thistle are a problem.

A hand weeder is a long, thin metal rod with a V-shape point on the end that lets you get down deep into the soil to root out weed menaces once and for all.

Grab Your Gloves

Some gardeners consider gloves a necessity, while others don't see the need for them. For the first 20 years of my gardening life, I refused to use gloves except for the most brutal tasks like pulling out bullthorn or poison ivy. I liked getting my hands dirty, and I didn't care much about the condition of my fingernails. On the flip side, a former neighbor, with impeccably manicured nails, would don a pair of flowered gardening gloves for *every* garden task, including watering potted plants and deadheading perennials. To each her own.

These are my favorite type of gardening glove—knit cotton with rubberized palms and fingers. They offer plenty of protection without compromising dexterity.

©iStockphoto.com/Richard Goerg

You can find almost as many garden glove designs as there are garden tasks to do. Here are a few types of gloves good for general gardening and for gardening where chemicals and water are involved, along with their pros and cons.

Cotton gloves and cotton/polyester blend gloves are inexpensive, but don't hold up to heavy use. They're often too bulky for delicate work, too. And they're not always available in varying sizes. *Knit cotton gloves with rubberized palms and fingers* offer good dexterity. They're sturdy and come in various sizes. All these gloves are washable.

Calfskin or goatskin gloves are comfortable and form-fitting and can offer good dexterity. The fingertips tend to rip with heavy use, and they can be pierced by sharp thorns or rocks. *Pigskin gloves* are comfortable, stronger than calf or goatskin, and offer good dexterity and better protection from thorns and sharp rocks. *Cowhide gloves* are strong and durable and are excellent protection from thorns and sharp rocks, but don't offer great dexterity. None of these animal skin gloves are washable, and they can become stiff after getting wet.

If you're gardening with chemicals and water, try these gloves:

Lightweight rubber gloves offer protection from water and noncaustic chemicals. Some brands come in different sizes. These gloves offer little dexterity, though, and rip easily. Similarly, *latex gloves* offer protection from water and noncaustic chemicals. Some brands come in different sizes. Latex gloves do offer good dexterity; however, they rip easily, and some people are allergic to latex.

Heavy rubber gloves are sturdy and offer good protection. Some brands come in different sizes. They're often bulky and offer little dexterity. *PVC gloves* offer good protection, and they're less bulky than heavy rubber gloves. Some brands come in different sizes, too. They cannot be used with gasoline because gasoline dissolves plastic, especially PVC.

Compost Pile _____

Always wear gloves when you handle chemicals like herbicides, insecticides, and fertilizers. Gloves are also useful when you're doing a lot of heavy digging or extensive planting, to help avoid painful blisters. Gloves are very handy for some gardening situations, particularly for the previously mentioned bullthorn and poison ivy removal.

Here are some other features to look for in a good gardening glove:

- Extra-long cuffs to protect your lower wrists and forearms from scratches, poison ivy, dirt, and so on.

- Small interior seams on cotton and leather gloves for comfort.

- Tight-fitting knit cuffs on cotton gloves to prevent soil from slipping inside.

- Rubberized "gripper" dots on palms and fingertips for good dexterity.

- Good range of sizes for best fit.

- Thermal lining for work in cold weather.

◆ Cotton lining for absorbency.

◆ Seamless lining for comfort.

◆ Nitrile exterior for resistance to caustic chemicals.

It's probably a good idea to get into the habit of wearing gloves whenever you work in the garden. It's just a little bit of protection. I try to use them, although I often forget and I do tend to lose a few pairs every year. But when I do remember and when I can find them, my fingernails are a lot more attractive.

A Little Help: Wheelbarrows and Carts

Only those who garden in tiny spaces can get away with not having a garden cart or wheelbarrow. There's always so much to haul around—bags of peat moss, mulch, or compost; flats of plants; ball-and-burlap fruit shrubs; tools; debris; or a big harvest of zucchini.

Get some wheels. They really help.

Workhorse Wheelbarrows

Wheelbarrows are an ancient device dating to not long after the invention of the wheel. Some wheelbarrows have two wheels, but most have one wheel in front and two handles with a tray or cargo box that together form a triangle.

Because the weight of the payload is carried on the wheel, the wheelbarrow enables you to move heavy things with relative ease. They are highly maneuverable, but they can be very tippy.

The old-fashioned heavy steel wheelbarrow with wooden handles is more or less a thing of the past for most home gardeners. Today, sturdy polyurethane trays on lightweight aluminum frames are a better choice.

Great Garden Carts

A slightly newer invention, garden carts are more popular with home gardeners because they tend to have larger payloads and are far more stable. Usually shaped like a large box with a wheel on either side and a U- or T-shape handle, garden carts are less maneuverable than wheelbarrows. But as mentioned, they are less tippy.

Carts range from the standard treated plywood with steel handles type to the rugged molded polyurethane varieties.

Here are some other things to look for when choosing a cart:

◆ Capacity from as small as 4 cubic feet to a whopping 12 cubic feet

◆ Flat bottom for carrying flats of plants or baskets of produce

◆ An opening at the front for easy dumping

◆ Coated or galvanized finishes on metal for rust prevention and durability

◆ Good balance

◆ Light weight

The Least You Need to Know

◆ Spades help you cut through sod and dig straight, deep holes.

◆ Use a shovel to dig in large areas of loose soil and to move large quantities of soil, manure, compost, and so on.

◆ Spading forks are good for digging into hard, compacted, or clay soils.

◆ Always buy the best-quality tools you can afford, and be sure to put them safely away when you aren't using them.

◆ The right gloves can offer the protection you need for any given garden task.

◆ A garden cart with a large enough cargo capacity for your needs can be a real time- and back-saver.

Chapter 5

Location Is Key

In This Chapter

- How much space does your garden need?
- Where's the water?
- Factor in your neighbors, animals, and kids
- Avoiding wet, dry, and toxic areas
- A look at USDA plant hardiness zones

Think of the garden you're planning as a piece of real estate. Then remember everything you've ever heard about buying real estate. It's all about location, location, location. You might have great ideas, lots of resources, and the skills to match, but if you put your garden in the wrong spot, don't expect good results. The better the location, the better the return. It's just like buying a house.

Finding the right location for a vegetable garden is even more critical than if you were growing an ornamental garden of flowers. If you're simply planting flowering plants and shrubs, you can adapt plant selections to the location—full shade, part shade, full sun, dry, soggy, hilly, rocky, etc. You can simply find the plants that like the situation you have. But if you want to grow tomatoes and cucumbers, you have to have good drainage and full sun. To get an abundant harvest of fresh herbs, you need to plant them in a place where the dog does not go. There's no getting around it.

In this chapter, we look at some important factors to consider as you contemplate the location of your vegetable patch.

Put It Where the Sun *Does* Shine

Sunlight is essential for most plants to grow. Nearly all vegetables and fruits and most herbs require at least 6 hours of full sun every day to photosynthesize and thus produce their produce. This is pretty much non-negotiable.

Prof. Price's Pointers

Most of the things we eat are part of a plant's reproductive or storage organs: leaves, fruits, seeds, tubers, and roots. All these represent a huge investment in carbohydrates (sugars and starch), which come directly or indirectly from photosynthesis, which requires light. Photosynthesis is the conversion of light energy into the energy that makes plants grow.

You have to know where the sun shines on your property so you can grow your plants in full sun. Sounds simple, right? But if you remember sixth-grade science, you know the sun's path changes over the course of the year.

To figure out the best spot for maximum sun exposure, spend the day watching the sun move across your yard. If you do this in early spring before the trees leaf out, be sure to allow for the shade produced by the tree canopies. I can't tell you how many novice gardeners are shocked to find that the garden they spent so much time preparing is in full shade by 2 P.M. after the leaves have grown.

Enough Room to Grow

How much space your garden needs depends entirely on what you want to grow in it. If you've always wanted to experiment with several varieties of corn, you'll need land, lots of land. If having a steady supply of fresh herbs is the full extent of your plans, you can get by with a few pots on the terrace.

Your garden style (see Chapter 3) determines the square footage, or acreage, you need to achieve your goals. To help you estimate how much room you need, consider the space requirements of a few favorite plants. The following table shows how much space some common plants need.

Plant	Space Between Plants	Space Between Rows
Asparagus	2 feet	5 feet
Beans	6 inches	3 feet
Cabbage	1 foot	24 to 30 inches
Collards	1½ feet	3 or 4 feet
Corn	4 to 6 inches	3 feet
Head lettuce	4 inches	1 foot
Jerusalem artichokes	15 to 18 inches	3 or 4 feet
Summer squash	3 or 4 feet	3 feet

Access to Water

In a perfect world, gardeners rely on rain to irrigate their gardens. But there's no such thing as a perfect world. Southeastern Pennsylvania, where I live, recently experienced 3 years of serious drought conditions. And we're not alone. Many parts of the country have on-going drought issues. Ornamental gardeners can add plant varieties that require less water, but vegetable growers have to resort to various methods of irrigation when Mother Nature is less than generous.

Unless you own stock in a company that makes garden hoses, you won't want to run miles of hose to get water to the garden beds. So it's important to locate the garden close enough to a reliable water source.

Food for Thought

If you'll be spending long hours working in your garden, you might need to use a bathroom from time to time. Be sure to factor that into your location equation.

What Will the Neighbors Think?

If you have acres of land with no neighbors in sight, the location of your garden in relation to property lines is probably irrelevant. But most folks do have neighbors, and it's important to consider the impact your garden will have on them.

First, if you spend all your waking hours raising vegetables and you're heavily into power equipment, be sure not to put your garden a few feet from your neighbor's patio. Think about your garden as an attractive diversion for neighborhood children, and protect your interests by making it inaccessible to them.

In a neighborhood where manicured lawns and well-tended beds are the norm, you might not want to locate your basic, utilitarian-style vegetable plot smack dab in the middle of the front lawn. (Some neighborhoods might have restrictions against this, too, so check with your neighborhood association, if you have one.)

Food for Thought

Remember that noise is a form of pollution. To keep it at a minimum, try to limit your use of power equipment, especially early in the morning, at dinnertime, or any time you see your neighbors enjoying their outdoor spaces. It's the right thing to do.

Also be considerate when it comes to smelly activities. Can you imagine your neighbor starting to greet guests to his daughter's engagement party in his backyard, and your load of fresh manure is delivered at the same time?

Consider the placement of your compost pile, too. Well-constructed, healthy compost bins and piles shouldn't have a bad smell, but they don't always function as they should. Try to place your compost well away from downwind neighbors.

Try to keep the unsightly aspects of your gardening efforts away from your neighbors' sightlines. No one wants a good view of dirt piles, a wheelbarrow full of weeds, or an overflowing compost bin.

©iStockphoto.com/Eira Fogelberg

It all boils down to using common sense and being considerate of others. If you play by those rules, you'll find the right location for your garden.

Out of Harm's Way

Plants don't do well in traffic, whether it's four-wheeled or four-legged, so when you're thinking of locations for your garden, you need to assess a number of important traffic factors, including vehicles, animals, and kids.

Most people don't intentionally drive cars through their gardens. Unfortunately, sometimes cars stray off the pavement. If you place your garden too near a driveway, it could be damaged by a not-quite-tight-enough turn or an overestimated back-up effort. Snowplows can overstep the pavement, too, resulting in compacted soil and crushed crowns on perennial plants. Bikes, trikes, and wagons also pose a threat to gardens.

To avoid death by vehicle in the garden, select a location well away from traffic patterns. This includes places where the kids have always thrown their bikes, the natural path you take from house to garage or shed, near a turn-around or back-up area of the driveway, or where the snowplows regularly push piles of snow.

Dealing With Four-Legged Friends

Fido might be your best friend, but dogs and gardens aren't great together. It's not that dogs mean harm, but let's face it, if your dog pees or poops on the asparagus, it becomes less than appetizing. In fact, the acids in dog urine can eat right through tree bark, so just think what a regular visit will do to plants with thinner skins. Not a pretty picture.

And animal excrement from meat-eaters like dogs and cats is not healthy stuff. All kinds of nasty microorganisms can live in it, so if, despite your precautions, your dog or the neighbor's cat has made deposits in your garden, remove it promptly to avoid the risk of contamination and illness.

If your dog has the run of the yard, you might have to fence the garden (see Chapter 6). Dog owners who use electronic invisible fences to contain their animals should put their gardens outside the electric perimeter if possible.

Garden Guru Says

Here's an easy, no-mess way to clean up after dogs or cats who have used your garden as a potty: put your hand inside a plastic bag, pick up the poop with your plastic-covered hand, and using your other hand, turn the bag inside out. Tie the top of the bag closed, and dispose of it in the trash.

Cats are another animal all together. The location of the garden has no impact on a cat's ability to use it for a litter box. (See Chapter 12 for some hints on cat control.)

Dealing With Four-Legged Foes

While many warm-blooded pests can wreak havoc in your garden (and some of these are addressed in Chapter 21), deer are the worst. Many farmers and gardeners in my neck of the woods have long-running battles with these "rats with hooves," as they call them. If you live in an area with a large deer population, just forget about having a successful garden without fencing. (Some more strategies for dealing with deer are discussed in Chapter 21.)

You would be wise not place your garden in a spot where you regularly see a large herd of deer grazing. But other than that, the garden location won't make much difference when it comes to these marauders.

Kids Rule

We love it when our children romp in the yard. It's wholesome and healthy, and it deters them from sitting inside watching TV, playing video games, or sitting in front of the computer. But although gardens are nice places, they're not always the safest place for a young child to be.

Chemical herbicides, pesticides, and fertilizers can be toxic to small ones. Just touching leaves or fruits that have been treated can cause allergic reactions. And because really little kids often put their hands in their mouths, the possibility of them ingesting toxic products is high. Even organic products like pyrethrins or iron phosphates can make a child sick if they are swallowed. Garden tools, especially pruners and knives, can also be extremely dangerous in the hands of youngsters. To avoid accidents, never leave very young children unattended in the garden. Teach them to respect tools and instruct even the tiniest ones always to wash fresh produce before eating it.

If you have small children, it's a good idea to place the garden in a spot where you have control over who comes and goes in it. So I can watch the kids and work in the garden simultaneously, I located my garden within sight of their play area.

Garden Guru Says

When your children have graduated from swing sets and sandboxes, you can reuse the space and recycle the equipment. The sandbox can become a raised bed planter or even a modified square-foot garden (see Chapter 12). Use the swing set legs and cross bars as a support system for climbing plants like beans and peas. You can also reuse an old dog pen as a garden space, with the fencing recycled as plant supports. You'll have to do some extra soil preparation in these spots, though. (See Chapters 8 and 9 for information on testing and preparing the soil.)

Environmental Factors

If your property is small, you may not have much choice in where to put the garden. It's either right here or nowhere. Larger lots, on the other hand, might have any number of sunny, childfree, dog-proof options.

The deciding factors might be environmental. Some issues could include the relative sogginess or dryness of the soil, previous uses of the land, wind patterns, proximity of tree roots, slopes, erosion, and lack of topsoil.

"Wet Feet"

Most of the plants we look at in this book prefer to grow in well-drained soil, so don't set up your garden in the swampy part of your yard or at the end of the sump pump drainpipe. Without elaborate modifications and drains, a wet yard will never support a successful vegetable garden.

Garden Guru Says

Watercress is one edible plant that likes to have what gardening types call "wet feet"—that is, soggy soil that retains moisture and rarely dries out completely. (In the wild, watercress grows in streams.)

Dry as a Bone

Some properties have sections that are dryer than others. Sandy soils that drain very quickly dry out fast and might not retain enough moisture to satisfy the plants' need for water. Chalky soils tend to be dry, too.

If the only land you have fits in this category, you'll need to do some heavy-duty soil amending. However, if there's another, less-desertlike location on your property, maybe use that instead.

Superfund Sites

Superfund sites are no laughing matter. Hundreds of sites around the country have seriously contaminated soil caused by toxic waste dumping. Some of that land has been cleaned and reclaimed. Other parts are still contaminated.

Not all contaminated sites have been placed on the Superfund list. Some have yet to be identified. If you don't know who previously owned your property or what it was used for, find out before you start a vegetable garden. Be especially vigilant if your property fits any of the following descriptions:

- Located near a gas station or a former gas station
- Adjacent to an active or former military base
- Near any existing or former manufacturing plant
- Near an existing or former dump or landfill
- Close to a junkyard or automobile salvage facility
- On a former farm

> **Compost Pile**
>
> Properties that border heavily traveled roads might have lead contamination in the soil. If your garden is near a highway or a congested traffic area, have the soil tested for lead before growing edible plants.

Although the chances of your property being contaminated are small, you don't want to find out about it *after* you've consumed a few years' worth of harvests. To find out if your property is near a Superfund site, log on to the Environmental Protection Agency's website at epa.gov/superfund/sites. Here you'll find a county-by-county guide to hazardous waste sites, the names and addresses of the sites (including aliases), and what action has been taken to clean them up.

Toxic Trees

In addition to making shade, some trees add other obstacles to successful vegetable gardening. Trees whose roots grow close to the surface and reach out in a wide circle (known as the drip line) are not good companions for your vegetable garden. The roots will interfere with cultivation and suck up moisture greedily. Most maple trees are in this category, with silver maples ranked as the worst culprit.

Black walnut trees are also bad neighbors for your garden. In fact, their roots produce a toxin that's deadly for a wide range of plants, including many vegetables. (The toxin can also have an allergic effect on humans and horses.) The Ohio State University, West Virginia University, and Purdue University's extension services have published fact sheets about black walnut toxicity. They include a list of plants that will not grow within a 50-foot radius—and in some cases, up to an 80-foot radius—of the trunk of a black walnut tree. Research shows that these plants will be injured or killed within 1 or 2 months of growth in proximity to this tree.

Some susceptible plants include the following:

Asparagus	Potatoes
Cabbage	Rhubarb
Eggplants	Tomatoes
Peppers	

These plants don't seem to mind the toxin:

Beets	Parsnips
Corn	Snap beans
Lima beans	Soybeans
Onions	Squash

If you remove a black walnut tree to plant a garden, pull out the roots and then wait about 2 months for the toxins to break down before you plant anything.

USDA Plant Hardiness Zones

If you've ever read a how-to gardening book or looked through a plant catalog, you've probably seen a USDA Plant Hardiness Zone map. The U.S. Department of Agriculture (USDA) created the map in 1960 based on more than 60 years of temperature data. It was revised in 1965 and again in 1990. In 2003, the U.S. National Arboretum created an online version, and in 2006 The National Arbor Day Foundation updated the zones. Some subtle differences exist in the various versions that have to do with environmental warming trends.

The map was designed to help gardeners and farmers determine what will grow where, when. The map is based on the average lowest winter temperatures throughout the country. Years ago, there were 10 zones, but the USDA expanded the number to 20 by adding "a" and "b" zones to zones 2 through 10, and also adding zone 11.

To find which hardiness zone your garden is in, go to usna.usda.gov/Hardzone, or arborday.org/media/zones.cfm.

> **Food for Thought** _____
>
> Within the USDA zones are microclimates—sort of zones within zones—where the range of temperatures are slightly higher or lower than indicated on the USDA map, due to environmental and geographic factors. These factors can change from year to year. For example, my home in southeastern Pennsylvania is in zone 6b. But because my garden sits below street level, faces south and east, and is protected on all four sides with fences and white plaster walls that reflect the sun, the garden behaves more as if it were in zone 7a. Other factors that might create a microclimate include prevailing winds and proximity to lakes, ponds, rivers, streams, mountains, hills, factories, and highways.

Knowing the hardiness of plants is particularly important when you buy them from websites or catalogs as opposed to your local garden center. Many companies ship plants based on a formula of your order date and your hardiness zone. For example, the Burpee website says that if you live in zone 7, your vegetable plants will arrive between April 20 and April 28. Perennials are shipped by March 16. It's a good system.

The Least You Need to Know

◆ Edible plants need at least 6 hours of sunlight a day, so locate your garden to allow them their due light.

◆ By calculating how much room each plant variety will require to grow, you can easily determine what you can plant in the space you have.

◆ Put your garden conveniently close to a water source so you won't have to haul water back and forth.

◆ Don't allow young, unattended children or pets access to your garden. It's just not safe for everyone involved.

◆ Determine prior uses of your property to protect against contamination.

◆ Know your zone. Your plants will thank you for it.

Chapter 6

Plotting and Planning

In This Chapter

◆ Ways to delineate your garden borders

◆ Plotting your garden with graph paper and a ruler

◆ Take it to the next level with stakes and string

◆ Where's the water?

◆ Good fences make good gardens

◆ A walk along the garden path

The plotting and planning stage of gardening is probably the least fun, especially for Type-A personalities who like to get things done, fast. This work can be time-consuming and—well, let's face it—dull. But it can make a big difference in the quality of your garden. Skip this phase, and you'll most likely make mistakes that will result in a garden that could have been better. The good news is, you really only have to do this stuff once.

In this chapter, you learn how to lay out the perimeter of your proposed garden *in situ* (right there on-site). Then you can use graph paper to make a scale drawing of the garden and a plot plan that will serve as your planting guide. After that, you stake out the garden, giving yourself (or your hired hands) a blueprint for digging and making paths. Then you can decide what kind of fences to use, the type of paths you want, and if and how to allow for an irrigation system.

Laying It All Out

Now that you have a general idea of how much space you'll need for the kind of garden you intend to have, you'll want to lay it out. This step is helpful because it allows you to see exactly how your garden fits in your overall landscape, how convenient (or inconvenient) it will be, and if, in fact, you've allowed enough space—or made it too big!

The easiest way to lay out the garden is with an old hose (or two or three, depending on how big your garden ideas are). Place the hose on the ground where you plan to situate the garden. You can create corners by sinking stakes and shaping the hose at right angles around the stakes.

When you have your garden shape outlined with the hose, make a semi-permanent outline. The best way to mark your space is with landscaper's spray paint. This neon orange paint is readily available at landscape supply stores or places like The Home Depot or Lowe's. Spray the paint right along your outline. (Be prepared if you get paint on the hose: it is permanent.) Remove the hose, and there you have it—the layout for your future garden. Use the orange line to keep the digging you'll do within the framework you've planned and as a guideline for setting up fencing.

Garden Guru Says

Most vegetable gardens are rectangles or squares, although no rule says you can't make it a parallelogram, a circle, or even a hexagon.

If you find that your first attempt at laying out the guidelines isn't going to work, simply mow the spray-painted grass and start over again.

Implementing Graph Paper and Ruler

Frankly, this next phase of the design is the part I don't particularly like. During the years I ran a landscape design business, my partner did most of the drawings, and that made me very happy. But unless you're very good at visualizing the garden you want to create, don't skip this basic groundwork.

You've already decided where the garden will go and how big it will be (see Chapters 2 and 5). And you've created a basic layout using the old garden hose trick. Using graph paper and ruler, now it's time to design the actual plot plan that describes where the entry will go, where paths and walkways will be placed, the location of any irrigation elements, and the placement of each plant variety.

To draw your garden plan, you need graph paper (any scale will do); a sharp pencil; sharp colored pencils or colored markers; a ruler or straight edge; and a flat surface like a desk, table, or kitchen counter.

Now just follow these steps to make a scale drawing of your proposed garden:

1. Determine your scale. The simplest way is to have one square on the graph paper represent a certain number of square feet in the garden.

2. Plot out the square footage by counting off the squares on the graph paper. For example, if you're planning a rectangular 20×50-foot garden, and your scale is 1 graph paper square per 1 square foot of garden, count off 20 squares across and 50 down. Mark the beginning and the ending points.

3. Use the pencil and ruler to draw lines connecting the marks.

4. Count off squares within your framework to determine the placement of fence posts, gates, arbors, paths, and any other *hardscape* elements you want to incorporate.

5. Count off more squares to measure specific planting areas. Use square footage needs based on seed packet information or the estimates you can find in Part 4.

6. Use the colored pencils or markers to indicate different planting areas. Make a key for yourself on the plot plan so you know what plant or group of plants each color represents.

7. Indicate where irrigation system elements will be positioned. (You might want to share your plot plan with the irrigation specialist if you hire one to install a system.)

8. If you're including an electric fence, note where the source of electricity should be.

Prof. Price's Pointers

The **hardscape** is the collection of structural elements in the landscape. Walls, fences, walkways and paths, gates, arbors, and buildings are all part of the hardscape.

Food for Thought

If the old paper-and-pencil style of design isn't your thing, look for garden design software. Many programs are devoted just for vegetable gardens, and a few are free to help you design your garden spaces.

When you've completed your scale drawing, you're ready to move on to the next step, staking out the garden.

Staking Out Your Garden

With your plot plan in hand, you can stake out your garden more precisely. If you have spray-painted the outline of the garden, you can go right to placing stakes at the corners and running string between the stakes. (If you have a garden with a curved outline, spray paint is your best option.) If you skipped the hose and spray paint option, you need to do some measuring before you put in your stakes. And if you're a complete fly-by-the-seat-of-your-pants type, just stick the stakes in any old place, or just start digging.

With your corner stakes in and the perimeter outline marked with string, you can stake and string the entry and any paths you plan to create. If you plan to have grass areas between growing rows, stake them out, too. Also use stakes to mark where irrigation system elements will be placed and where the electric current will enter the space in the case of an electric fence.

Be sure to refer to your plot plan as you stake, but be prepared to make alterations as you go along. Even the best garden designs can be changed for the better at this stage. And don't forget to make the changes on your plan as well as on the ground for future reference.

At this stage of the game, you might want to go ahead and do your heavy digging. This is the critical part of the job where you remove sod, turn the soil, and improve it. We look at this step in depth in Chapter 9. From this point on in this chapter, we assume that you've dug the garden.

Advance Planning for Irrigation

It would be wonderful if we could grow edibles without worrying about watering. It never works out that way, though. And because some vegetables and fruits require great quantities of water to produce, some form of irrigation might be the only option.

If you're going to install an underground irrigation system, or even just piping for a hose bib (the plumbing equipment that allows your hose to attach to the water source) in close proximity to the garden, this is the stage at which you lay the underground piping. It can be done later in the game, but it's best to do it now, after the garden is dug but before anything is planted. (If you want to skip ahead, turn to Chapter 19 to review the various irrigation options.)

A hose bib close to the garden saves you tiresome wrestling with hoses—or worse, hauling watering cans.

©iStockphoto.com/Pawel Hawrot

Do Fence Me In

Putting fences around your garden is a good idea for a couple reasons. The number one reason is to keep out marauding animals. A fence around the garden plot is also a safety measure to protect children and pets, whether they're yours or the neighbors'. And an attractive fence is the best way to keep the sometimes-untidy appearance of a productive garden out of sight, especially in a formal or otherwise well-manicured landscape.

To select the right kind of fence for your garden, first determine what you want the fence to do. If deer are a big problem, the height of the fence is an important factor. Digging

Compost Pile _____

Many municipalities and homeowners' associations have strict regulations about fencing, including height restrictions and materials allowed. Be sure to check with the appropriate governing bodies before installing fences on your property.

animals need another solution. To make the vegetable plot an integral part of the backyard, a well-designed decorative fence might be the right choice.

No matter what kind of fence you use, be sure to devise an entry to the garden. The entry point should be at least 3 feet wide, but you might want more room than that, depending on how you'll use and maintain the garden. If necessary, make your entry large enough for your garden tractor, cart or wheelbarrow, mower, and any other equipment you might want in the garden.

Simple Fencing Solutions

The most basic garden barrier is nothing more than a roll of wide wire fence material or plastic mesh strung between wooden or metal stakes. The stakes are set into the ground at intervals around the perimeter of the garden. You need to secure the fencing to the stakes somehow, either with twist ties or wire. Or if you're using wooden stakes, fasten the wire with heavy-duty staples.

These kinds of fencing aren't pretty, but if the look of the garden isn't an issue, go for it.

Food for Thought

To keep digging animals like rabbits, moles, voles, and dogs out of your garden, place wire fencing or plastic mesh below ground level. Dig a trench along the perimeter of the garden; you might have to go down as much as 1 foot. Then attach your fence material securely in the soil every couple inches with steel pins or use metal rods, flat metal bars, or strips of wood to hold the fencing in place. Curve the bottom of the fencing outward slightly to make it even more difficult for the pesky critters to tunnel under. Be sure to factor in the underground portion when you measure how much fence material you'll need to buy. You can add this underground insurance to any style of fence you install.

Another simple option is a chain-link fence. Also not pretty, and certainly not as inexpensive as wire or plastic mesh, chain link is usually less expensive than wood, PVC, or decorative metal fences. And it's very sturdy and durable.

Attractive Fencing Options

If the look of the garden is important to you, you might want to opt for a more decorative fence. You can choose from a broad range of styles and materials. You can find do-it-yourself fences with elements available at home and garden centers; component fences with mix and match elements; and custom-made fences.

The style of decorative fence you choose is all a matter of taste. If you only want the fence for decorative purposes, you won't need any modifications. If, however, you want an attractive fence that also serves as a barrier, you might have to modify it with wire fencing or plastic fence tacked on to the inside perimeter.

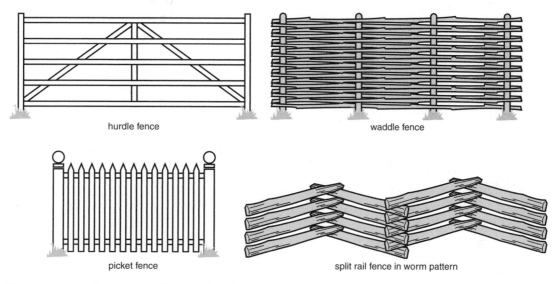

hurdle fence

waddle fence

picket fence

split rail fence in worm pattern

You can use one of a variety of fences to fence in your garden.

Here are a few decorative fence styles you might want to consider:

Hurdle fences, developed in England, were originally movable wood fences. They feature upright end posts, four or five thin rails, an upright center post, and two diagonal posts forming a triangle at the center.

Post and rail fences are generally made of wood but are also available in PVC. Each section consists of two upright posts with two, three, or four cross rails. Cross rails are usually round or squared. The crossbuck variation is similar to the hurdle fence but has two rails forming an X between the top and bottom rails. The rails either fit into notches in the posts or are attached with nails or screws.

Split rail fences are slightly more rustic than the post and rail style, with the split rails more roughly hewn. Generally there are two, three, or four rails, which are chamfered at the ends and fit into slots on the posts.

Stacked split rail fences come in many variations, including worm, snake, Virginia, Vermont, crooked rail, rick rack, and zigzag. All are made of rails stacked on top of each other. Some are supported by sunken posts, others by posts that form Xs. Still others have no posts at all.

A *picket fence* is the old-fashioned cottage fence. It comes in hundreds, if not thousands, of forms ranging from standard stock pointed pickets to hand-crafted styles. Usually picket fences are made of treated, stained, or painted wood. They're also available in PVC.

Food for Thought

In the eighteenth century, English landscape architects developed a landscaping style that turned its back on traditional formal gardens and focused on nature. This naturalistic approach included the creation of artificial lakes and woods and grand vistas. But because most English estates were also working farms, keeping animals out of planted areas, including kitchen gardens, became paramount. To avoid having fences ruin the views, the landscapers built ha-has to contain the sheep and cattle. Essentially a ha-ha is a deep ditch with a stone retaining wall or a wire fence set into the ditch. The device is still in use at many of Britain's great estates.

Stockade fences are narrow, picketlike, and are usually constructed of roughly hewn boards set flush one next to the other. These fences are secured across the back by horizontal boards attached to posts set in the ground. They're usually available in 4-, 5-, 6-, or 8-feet heights. Tall stockade fences cast shade, so these are best for large gardens where some shade won't matter.

Thatch fences hail from the days of thatched cottages in England. Thatch fences are made of bundles of twigs and small branches tied together with wire, rope, or vines and formed into panels. The panels are attached to twiggy posts and set in the ground. They're very decorative.

Wattle fences originated in England and were also used by early American farmers, including George Washington. The wattle fence was made of willow branches woven in a basket weave pattern between upright sticks. In Asia, some are also made of bamboo.

Fences made of *PVC* are long-lasting and durable. The PVC is made to look like picket, post, and rail fences.

The *powder-coated wire fence* is an inexpensive barrier fence that's better looking than plain wire or plastic mesh. It's also easy to install.

Wooden fences can last up to 20 years if they're made of treated wood. Cedar and redwood are the most durable, followed by Douglas fir, spruce, and pine.

An Electrifying Situation

When my parents had their large wooded property, an electric fence around the perimeter of the planted areas was essential. Until the fence was installed, the deer ate themselves silly. If deer are a problem in your area (that would be just about the entire Northeast, as well as other large areas of the country), you might want to consider an electric fence.

Be prepared: electric fences are not pretty, and they don't come cheap. But if you've devoted a lot of time and energy into growing vegetables, you don't want to be providing fancy feasts for Bambi and his friends.

Most homeowners will call specialists to install an electric fence on their properties. If you elect to do it yourself, be sure you know what you're doing.

> **Prof. Price's Pointers**
>
> There's a science to spacing and setting fence posts. For excellent step-by-step instructions, go to hometime.com/Howto/projects/fence/fnc.

Contact with an electric fence is, by design, uncomfortable. The recommended voltage is 4,000 or higher. If young children have access to your fenced area, this could be a dangerous situation. To protect them, and yourself, you might want to consider other fencing options or be sure to have an adult on hand when children are playing on property that has an electric fence installed on it.

Down the Garden Path

Unless your garden space is really tiny, you'll probably need to have some kind of paths or walkways in it, even if they're nothing more than the spaces between rows or planting beds. A path inside a garden should be at least 2 feet wide; 3 feet is even better.

People have written whole books about garden paths and walkways (including me!—*Paths and Walkways* [Friedman/Fairfax, 1997]), so if you're really interested in this topic, check out a couple. In the meantime, consider the options discussed in the following sections.

Packed-Earth Paths

The packed-earth path is the path of least resistance. After you've stripped the sod from your garden space (see Chapter 19), simply leave the spaces you've designated for paths as is. Over time, the soil will become compacted from being walked on, which helps keep weeds from sprouting.

Compost Pile

The growing and maintaining of grass lawns, including paths, is a big contributor to air, water, and noise pollution. So you might want to give very careful thought to how much grass you allow to grow in your vegetable garden.

Grass Paths

Very large gardens often have grass paths and walkways, just because it's a lot less work to leave some of the sod in place than to strip it all. Grass paths are an attractive foil to planting beds.

But grass paths do have to be mowed and watered. Be sure the path is wide enough to accommodate your mower. You don't want to wind up mowing vegetables by accident.

Mulch Paths

A thick layer of some form of mulch on top of a bare, packed-earth path is easy to maintain and has a neat, clean appearance. Use wood chips, pine bark, salt hay, seaweed, or even grass clippings.

This type of path does take some maintenance, though. Over time, as the mulch gets worn down, you have to replenish the mulch.

Fancier Path Solutions

If you're hoping to create a more formal garden space, you'll most likely want to design paths with a decorative touch. Grass paths work in a formal situation, but other materials such as these can be quite nice, too:

Bricks	Gravel
Cement pavers	Stones
Cement rounds	Wood planks
Crushed shells	Wood rounds

This well-organized garden features gravel paths that keep it neat and tidy.

©iStockphoto.com/James Camp

In the next chapter, we look more closely at how the garden path works in the overall design of a garden.

The Least You Need to Know

- To plot your garden space, you can use spray paint and a garden hose to determine the borders of your garden.

- Drawing a plot plan on graph paper before you start digging helps keep you on track.

- Use stakes and string to determine planting areas, entry points, and paths.

- Plan an irrigation system before planting.

- Select a fence style that meets the needs of your garden.

- If you want garden paths, build them with materials that suit your style of gardening.

7

Design Dilemma

In This Chapter

- ◆ Popular garden styles
- ◆ Different or unusual garden styles
- ◆ Dealing with utilities and unsightlies
- ◆ Minimalist gardens
- ◆ Incorporating decorative elements

At this point, you probably have a pretty good idea of how big your garden will be, what kinds of things you'll grow, where you'll locate the garden, and how to put some of your ideas into action.

This chapter is a little different because it's not about essential stuff. Instead, in the following pages, we'll go over some of the aesthetics of your garden. Not the nuts and bolts things, but how the garden will look. Do you want a basic vegetable garden, or do you want to re-create a mini version of a royal French *potager?* Do you want to add a little sitting area, a small terrace, a fountain, a potting shed, or another decorative feature to enhance the look of your garden? Do you want to follow feng shui principles? Read on and then decide.

A Sense of Style

We all have our own sense of style. Usually we express our style in the way we dress and how we furnish our homes. Sleek modernists often wear basic black and favor smooth granite countertops and unadorned floors. Traditionalists, in tailored sportswear, frequently have homes with lots of chintz and tabletops cluttered with frames and decorative mementos.

Your sense of style can also be reflected in your garden. Do you like cute vegetable-shape plant markers and lots of ornaments? Or do you prefer to take an unadorned approach? Whatever appeals to you most is what you ought to do. Some garden styles are more, well, stylized. In this chapter, we'll look at a few different approaches.

The Island Bed Garden

Think of your lawn as a body of water. Now create an island in that body of water. The island is the garden bed floating in the sea of lawn. Okay, I know that sounds kind of corny, but that's the best way to describe an island bed.

The island bed garden should be free form, with gently curving lines. Right away, because of the form, you know it's an informal space. And because it's free form with a curved outline, a wooden fence isn't going to work. If possible, leave an island bed unfenced.

A large island bed needs a path through it so you can tend all the plants. Make your path twist and turn gently from one end to the other.

And because the island bed is meant to be seen from all sides, plant taller things toward the center, then medium-size plants all the way around with the lower plants along the outer perimeter. Here are some suggestions for various-size plants:

Tall plants for center of island bed:

Beans on tepees or trellises	Large variety tomato plants
Broccoli	Okra
Brussels sprouts	Peas on tepees or trellises
Corn	Sunflowers

(Okay, sunflowers aren't really a vegetable, but they do have edible seeds.)

Medium-height plants:

Bush beans	Leeks
Cabbage	Peppers
Chard	Sage
Eggplants	Spinach
Kale	

Lower plants for perimeter of island beds:

Basil	Radishes
Carrots	Scallions
Oregano	Thyme
Parsley	

The Country Cottage Garden

The English cottage flower garden was all the rage a few years ago, and it's not hard to understand why. This is a very appealing garden style.

The cottage vegetable garden is equally appealing. It's easy on the eye, not too fussy, but not too bare. Each might have its own personality, but the best country cottage gardens have a few common elements, including a nice picket or split rail fence; an arbor over the gate; a little shed at one side; a bench; plenty of neat, straight paths in gravel, grass, or mulch; and a wide variety of well-tended plants.

Crisp edges aren't a priority in a country cottage garden. In fact, plants should appear to tumble out along the path. One of the lessons I learned from English gardeners is to design axial paths (straight intersecting perpendicular paths) bordered by thickly planted beds with plants that overstep the bounds of the beds on to the paths. It produces a controlled chaos that's enormously appealing.

The Feng Shui Garden

You've probably heard about the Chinese belief and practice called feng shui. The belief is that energy affects wealth, health, and relationships. In a house, feng shui dictates the placement of doors, windows, furniture, and other elements. The same principles can be applied to the garden.

Prof. Price's Pointers

Feng shui literally means "wind-water," and it refers to the flow of *chi*, or energy, in a space.

In a feng shui garden, the placement and shapes of beds are important. So is the use and location of certain materials and elements, including metal, wood, water, and color. You can even find feng shui experts to advise you on the best way to achieve proper feng shui in your home and garden.

To get started on your own, here are a few suggestions:

- Avoid having corners in the garden.
- Avoid straight lines or sharp angles.
- Use curving lines to encourage the flow of energy.
- Balance dark (yin) and light (yang) elements.
- Place water features and tool sheds to the north, never in the south.
- Use stone or earthen elements (brick, for example) in the northeast section of the garden.
- Use triangle shapes in the south.
- Use circular or arched shapes in the west.
- Avoid the use of metal to the east.
- Incorporate columns in the eastern part of the garden.
- Grow fruits and herbs in the eastern part of the garden.

Feng shui is much too complicated to cover completely here. For a few books on the subject, check out Appendix B, or consult an expert.

The Minimalist Garden

The minimalist design is a garden style that will appeal to people who don't like a lot of clutter. People who like these rarely have more than one thing on their coffee table and the kitchen counters are often bare. Clean lines. No fussy tchotchkes littering the scene.

A minimalist garden isn't necessarily simple. It just uses clean lines without excess ornament. Long, straight, well-manicured rows with neatly placed plantings is what's needed.

Children's Gardens

Many years ago, I attended a symposium on gardening for children hosted by a national gardening organization. In addition to all the speakers, forums, and booths, the event featured a dozen real gardens designed for children. They were really fantastic, with little places to sit or hide; wonderful colors, textures, and fragrances; amusing decorative details; and lots of opportunities for learning and pretending.

In Chapter 3, we looked at some of the things children enjoy growing and explored some ways to introduce kids to gardening. Here are a few design ideas that will make a child's vegetable garden an inviting and fun place to explore:

- Laminate seed packets and attach to Popsicle sticks to use as row markers.
- Make and install a scarecrow.
- Add a child-size bench or table and chairs so the garden becomes a living space.
- Construct a tepee with vines to use as a hideaway (see Chapter 3).
- Add fun decorative elements like a toad house, fountain, birdbath, bird feeder, or wind chimes.
- Install a child-size arbor.
- Plant flowers with the vegetables.

Formal Vegetable Gardens

Although all parterre gardens are more or less formal, not all formal gardens are constructed with parterre patterns. The formal feel of a garden is reinforced by the use of straight lines as opposed to curves, but they don't necessarily form patterns.

A simple formal garden might be a rectangle divided by two intersecting perpendicular paths. It might have a small, paved seating area covered by a pergola at one end and an open view at the far side.

This is a variation of a formal vegetable garden I designed several years ago. The original design had brick paths.

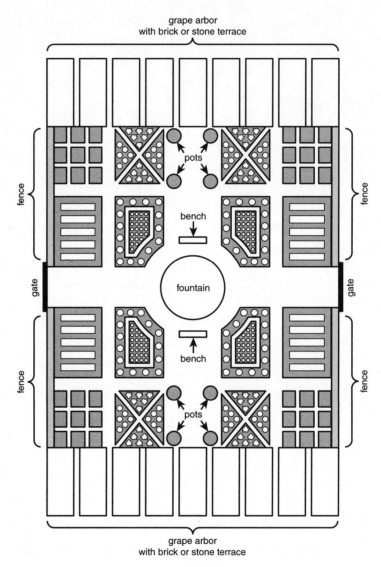

Neatness counts in a formal garden. Everything should be in its place. Planting beds are well defined with well-trimmed, edged borders.

Some of the most beautiful formal vegetable gardens are reproductions of historic gardens like Thomas Jefferson's kitchen garden at Monticello, George Washington's kitchen garden at Mount Vernon, and the great *potagers* in France.

Prof. Price's Pointers _____

Potager is the French word for "kitchen garden." These highly structured gardens were usually laid in perfectly manicured geometric beds intersected by axial paths. Several paths might intersect, forming a series of geometric planting beds. This patterned approach is called a *parterre*.

Parterre Gardens

Parterre is just a fancy word for describing the layout of paths and beds in a garden. The kitchen gardens at Monticello and Mount Vernon were done in a simple parterre style, while the seventeenth-century kitchen gardens at Versailles and Villandry in France were elaborate affairs that went on for acres and included great fountains and fancy trellising.

Although these gardens require an enormous amount of work to plant and maintain, it is possible to re-create your own. I would, however, recommend a smaller scale than Versailles!

Formal Herb Gardens

Herbs tend to be easy to grow and don't take up as much space as many vegetables do, so they make the perfect plants for creating a small formal garden.

Some of the most beautiful formal herb gardens are designed as knot gardens. Dating to medieval times, the knot garden features tiny hedges of evergreen herbs forming intersecting lines in simple patterns. Most often, herbs with contrasting colors are used so the intersecting little hedges stand out and the pattern is more vivid.

You can easily reproduce a typical eighteenth-century-style American herb garden. Typically a square space, the garden might have had a central space shaped as a diamond or as a square turned on its axis. Straight paths of brick or gravel might form an X at the center square and divide the other spaces into triangular planting beds. Most formal herb gardens are symmetrical.

A smaller parterre garden might not be as overwhelming a project for the home gardener as the Versailles parterre gardens.

1 — tepee for peas or beans
2 — cabbage
3 — lettuces
4 — tomato in cage
5 — onions
6 — kale or spinach or chard
× — various herbs
boxwood hedge
dwarf boxwood hedge

Architectural Garden Elements

Any kind of a wall or building in a landscaped area is known as an architectural element, and landscape designers love them. An architectural element creates a framework and a foil for plants.

If you already have an architectural element on your property and it's in an appropriate spot for the garden, give some serious thought to putting your garden nearby or even bordering it.

Consider some of these structures if you want to add architectural elements to your design. Any one of these would add architectural interest to your edible garden space:

Carriage house	Oversize cold frame
Chicken coop	Pool house
Garage	Potting shed
Garden shed	Smoke house
Greenhouse	Spring house
Lean-to	Tool shed
Old outhouse	

So let's imagine that you're fortunate enough to have one of these architectural elements in close proximity to your garden. How do you use it?

If you have a small building, use one wall, preferably not facing north, as one side of your garden. Enclose the other three sides with fence and your garden becomes a more important feature in the landscape. Add espaliered fruit, vining vegetables, hanging baskets, or window boxes along the wall, and it becomes even lovelier.

Out of Sight

If you're doing a down-and-dirty garden, you might as well skip this section. Here, we're going to look at ways to hide or disguise the less-attractive—but necessary—elements of the garden like compost piles, equipment, supplies, and other not so pretty but essential things.

Take Out the Garbage

Compost piles can be unsightly. I mean, let's face it. A compost pile is basically a pile of garbage! But that garbage eventually becomes compost, and there's nothing like it to make your soil rich. So in a garden where aesthetics are important, the compost pile is a liability.

There are a number of ways to hide or disguise the compost. You can put it on the other side of the garage or garden shed, if your yard is blessed with these structures. You can create a screen with panels of fence or trellis. Or you can grow a screen with bamboo, forsythia, evergreens, or another thick hedge.

> **Food for Thought** _____
>
> Be sure your compost pile is easily accessible from the house. You'll be far more inclined to take a pail of eggshells, coffee grounds, potato peelings, and the wilted remains of a head of lettuce to a compost pile when it's only a few feet from the kitchen door. If that's not possible, treat yourself to one of those cute little compost pails with a built-in odor filter. Then you only need to make a trip to the compost pile when it's full.

Another way to hide or disguise the compost pile is to keep it in nice tidy containers. You can either build your own, perhaps with recycled materials, or buy one of the many different styles available commercially. A large wooden compost bin can actually become an architectural element in your garden.

A clever and fruitful method of disguising your compost pile is to grow a vining vegetable or fruit like pumpkin, squash, or melons right on top of the pile. The vines grow rapidly, produce large leaves, and sprawl all over the pile. You can still add more scraps, clippings, and other stuff to the pile just by moving the vines around a little bit. Although this won't completely hide the pile of compost, it will cover it up a little. And when the pumpkins, squash, or melons start to grow and ripen, they'll take center stage.

Storage

Large gardens might require large quantities of mulch and fertilizer, a mower or tractor, lots of tools and hoses, and other equipment and products. Most of these things aren't all that decorative, so you might want to think about having some sort of structure for storage.

Custom-made or prefab tool and storage sheds are the ideal answer to garden storage problems. Some are more attractive than others, but even the ugliest prefab metal shed will look better than a big pile of peat moss and fertilizer bags, mower parts, mulch cloth, and any of the other stuff that seems to accumulate around the garden.

Garden Guru Says _____

An out-of-use outhouse can make a very attractive little tool shed. They might not be easy to find, but they're sometimes available when a developer takes over a country property. Old chicken coops also make great garden sheds.

To improve the look of a garden shed that's more practical than pretty, you can always attach a few sections of lattice along the walls and encourage vines to grow. The disguised wall then becomes a nice backdrop for other plantings, and voilà, the ugly old garden shed becomes an architectural element.

A Decorative Touch

If you like lots of stuff around your house, you might feel comfortable with decorative items in your garden as well. Here are some things you might add to your garden to give it that homey feel:

Arbors	Paths
Benches	*Pergolas*
Cloches	Pots
Edging	Scarecrows
Fences	Sundials
Fountains	Tepees
Ornaments	Trellises

Prof. Price's Pointers _____

Cloche is French for "bell jar," a bell-shape glass jar often placed over a delicate seedling to protect it from cold. A **pergola** is an arborlike structure with upright supports and cross pieces overhead that create a roomlike space underneath.

As your garden matures and your skills increase, you can incorporate new design ideas, omit those you find less appealing, and "grow" it into the perfect space for your needs and tastes, both visual and culinary.

The Least You Need to Know

◆ Let your personality help define your garden style.

◆ If feng shui's your thing, you can call on an expert to utilize feng shui in your garden.

◆ Look for an architectural element to enhance your garden's design.

◆ Try to disguise unsightly elements in your garden like compost piles or storage areas.

Part 3
Getting Ready to Plant

Now it's time to get your hands dirty. Part 3 is all about soil and digging. First, in Chapter 8, we look at what soil actually is, how it functions, and how to make it as good as it can be. We explore the mysteries of pH, and we also include a section on making compost, which many gardeners get nearly spiritual about.

Later in this part we offer rules for preparing garden beds, including the arduous double digging the English are so fond of. You'll find out why in Chapter 9, where we also go into quite a bit of detail on how to create raised beds and how to amend the soil. There's also a little bit in there about machine tilling for gardeners who like that kind of thing. And even if you're science phobic, you won't have any trouble understanding the plant biology lesson in Chapter 10.

8

The Science of Soil

In This Chapter

- ◆ The real dirt on soil
- ◆ Determining your soil's pH
- ◆ How does your soil drain?
- ◆ Testing … testing … your soil
- ◆ What's in—and what's not in—compost

For farmers, gardeners, and plant scientists, soil is a really big deal. So much so that some people get Ph.D.s in soil science. There are even entire departments at state universities devoted to the subject.

In this chapter, we look at the many properties and variables of soil, find out what pH is and why it's so important to gardeners (and plants!), and learn about the various nutrients that enhance the quality of soil. This is also where you find out everything you've ever wanted to know about compost.

Dirt Is a Dirty Word

If you want to call yourself a gardener, you must swear never again to use the word *dirt* when you mean *soil*. Just remove *dirt* from your vocabulary.

To provide plants with an environment in which they can thrive, gardeners need to know at least a little bit about the chemical and physical makeup of soil.

Prof. Price's Pointers

Soil provides the mechanical support, water, and nutrients plants need to grow.

Soil is made up of several layers of different materials. The top layer consists of leaves and organic debris. Just below that is what we think of as topsoil. It's also called surface soil, and it usually includes a fair amount of organic matter. Next comes the subsurface layer with decomposed organic matter and mineral compounds. Below that is the subsoil that can be a combination of enriched clay, minerals, organic compounds, and loose rocks. All these layers lie on top of bedrock. Different parts of the country have different thicknesses and even concentrations of materials at each layer, but the basic set of layers is more or less the same.

Typical soil contains several layers of materials, from the surface organic debris all the way down to bedrock.

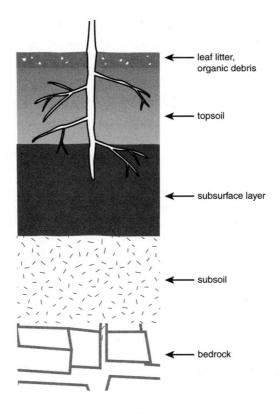

leaf litter, organic debris

topsoil

subsurface layer

subsoil

bedrock

Soil is also made up of mineral materials such as particles of gravel, sand, clay, silt, and organic matter, including broken-down plant and animal remains. Air and water are also soil ingredients.

Most soil components—such as clay particles, sand, and organic matter—are important for the soil's physical structure. They determine how well water and nutrients become available to plants. Soil also contains tiny amounts of minerals that actually are the nutrients. (We learn more about these nutrients and how they work in Chapter 20.)

The Feel of the Soil

Soil texture is an important factor because it affects how water passes through soil and how quickly the soil warms up and retains heat. Soil texture ranges from the finest silt to the densest clay. In between is loam, a rich soil containing clay, sand, and organic matter. Other soil types include silty clay loam, sandy loam, clay loam, sand, loamy sand, and sandy clay loam. Most vegetable plants like to grow in loamy soils.

You can improve the texture of your soil by adding peat moss, leaf mold, decomposed grass clippings, manure, and compost. Be cautious with peat moss, though, because it can become compacted and act like a moisture barrier, preventing moisture from descending to the plants' root zones.

Tip-Top Soil

Surface soil, or topsoil, is the best for growing plants. It's usually made up of 50 percent solid materials that are a combination of minerals and organic matter. The other 50 percent is open or pore space that is filled with either air or water.

Ideally, the pore space is half air and half water. After a rain or a period of irrigation, there will be more water than air. When it's been dry for any length of time, there's more air than water.

Organic Matter

Organic matter in soil refers to the remains of plant material. It can take the form of sawdust, wood chips, pine needles, kitchen scraps, dried leaves, straw, grass clippings, and manure. Over time and given the right conditions, organic matter decomposes.

The process of decomposition converts large chunks of organic material into much smaller particles, some even too small to see under a microscope. These particles act like miniscule sponges and soak up water. Then they loosely attach themselves to the minerals and nutrients in the soil. The result is a soil that's much more friable, or crumbly, a little like rich chocolate cake (that's the optimum soil texture), more moist, and more fertile.

In healthy soil, worms, insects, bacteria, and other microorganisms eat the organic matter and produce *humus* and soil nutrients.

Prof. Price's Pointers

Humus is the remaining part of organic matter in the soil after it's been completely decomposed. Gardeners love humus because their plants love humus. It's got the color and texture of chocolate cake, is easy to work with, and smells clean and woodsy.

Soil Structure

People who really know their soil usually classify soil structure as either weak or strong, with varying degrees of strength or weakness. This is a description of the shape of soil particles and how they group together. It's important to understand soil structure because it determines how air and water move through the soil and, therefore, what, if anything you need to do to amend it for your plants.

Soil particles cluster together in little groups called *aggregates*. The shape of these aggregates determines the structure of the soil. The aggregates range from microscopic grains of sand to what are called "massive" chunks. Some look like tiny pebbles; others look like slivers of mica. Some are porous; others are solid.

Granular soils, which have a texture like miniscule pebbles, allow water and air to pass through easily. This kind of soil has a strong structure. A weak soil has massive kinds of aggregates, making it more difficult for water and air to pass through and for roots to take hold.

You can improve the structure of the soil in your garden by adding things like course sand, vermiculate, perlite, peat moss, compost, manure, leaf mold, sawdust, seaweed, and straw. Be cautious with peat moss, though, as it can easily become compacted and prevent water from penetrating.

The pH Story

When we talk about *pH*, we're referring to how acidic or alkaline the soil is. Sometimes this is expressed as how "sweet" (alkaline) or "sour" (acid) the soil is. It's a logarithmic scale (which is way over my head—my high school math only went as far as a poor showing in algebra), but put simply, it means that a pH level of 6.5 is 10 times more alkaline than a reading of 5.5.

Prof. Price's Pointers _____

The **pH** of soil is actually a measure of the hydrogen ion activity in the soil. It's measured on a scale of 0 to 14, with 0 being the most acid and 14 the most alkaline. Neutral soil, which is ideal for many plants, has a pH of 7. The more hydrogen present, the more acidic, so a pH of 5.5 has 10 times the concentration of hydrogen ions as a pH of 6.5.

Why is pH so important? If the pH of the soil in your garden is out of whack with the requirements of the plants you're trying to grow, the plants will struggle to absorb the nutrients they need. For example, most vegetables like to grow in soil with a pH of about 6.5, which is just slightly acidic. If your soil measures 5.5, your tomatoes and peppers will grow slowly, won't produce as much fruit, and will be more prone to disease. But with 5.5, your corn, beans, kale, and garlic will manage just fine.

Soil That's Too Acidic

If your soil proves to be too acidic for the plants you plan to grow, you can raise the pH by adding ground limestone. Because relatively little lime is needed to raise the pH to the desired levels, you might want to consult with your local county extension or Farm Bureau office to help you determine the proper amounts for the soil in your area.

In regions like the Northwest and the Northeast, which tend to have acidic soils, an application of lime every 4 or 5 years using a formula of about 4 pounds for every 100 square feet of garden is usually enough for most vegetable gardens. It might take several months for the lime to affect the pH level throughout the beds. The best time to apply lime is at the end of the growing season so it has plenty of time to work.

If organic is your preference, look for organic products like aragonite or dolomitic limestone.

Soil That's Too Alkaline

If the pH is too high or alkaline, you'll want to add sulfur, gypsum, or aluminum sulfate. Aluminum sulfate is water-soluble so it will do the trick quite quickly. The other products take a bit more time. A good formula to follow is about 3 pounds sulfur or 5 pounds aluminum sulfate for every 100 square feet of garden.

Garden Guru Says

Used coffee grounds are an inexpensive and environmentally friendly way to add some acidity to a too-alkaline soil. Many coffee shops give away their coffee grounds for the asking. It takes a lot to make a big change in your soil, but if it only needs a little fix, coffee grounds might do the trick on the cheap. If you're striving for an organic garden, choose organic coffee when you make your purchases.

The Drain Game

The way water passes through soil is called drainage. Good drainage qualities help maintain a deep root zone, eliminate frost heave, bring warmth to soils earlier in the spring, improve soil aeration, and lower disease problems.

Soil with serious drainage issues is easy to spot. It's wet and squishy, puddles form easily in depressions and low spots when it rains, and the water stays there for a while. Moss growing on the soil is another pretty good indication that soil drainage is poor.

The more organic matter the soil contains, the better the soil is able to retain water. So if you have drainage problems, consider adding organic material to the soil—however, if your drainage problems are really serious, this won't be enough. You might have to consider cutting swails (ditches to divert water), installing drains, or bringing in a dump truck load of additional soil.

Testing Your Soil

Soil tests help gardeners determine the pH of the soil and the level of available nitrogen, phosphorous, and potassium. You'll also receive other information on the texture of the soil, the lime and salt content, and sometimes levels of toxic materials. This information helps you understand what adjustments you need to bring the soil to the fertility, texture, and pH you need to grow specific crops.

Unless you're growing particularly demanding crops or your land is flooded, you'll only need to test the soil every 3 or 4 years. It's best to test in the fall so you can add amendments and allow them to "percolate" through the soil over the winter.

Compost Pile _____

If your garden is near a heavily traveled road or in the vicinity of an older home that might have had lead-based paint scraped off and improperly discarded, or if there was any kind of industrial activity near where your garden is now, the soil might be contaminated with lead. You don't want to grow edibles in lead-contaminated soil. Be sure to have it tested.

Follow the directions on the soil test kit. Usually it will suggest 8 to 10 samples from various parts of the garden; if you have a tiny patch, 5 or 6 samples will do. However, if your gardens consists of a number of remote areas—the asparagus patch here, veggies over there, and ½ acre in corn—you'll need to perform several different tests. Most county extension offices sell soil test kits, as do some garden centers and garden supply stores.

DIY Compost

Compost is the decomposed plant material you collect from the kitchen, yard, garden, and barnyard for reuse as a soil enhancer. Just about any material that started out as part of a plant—including the manure of plant-eating animals—can be composted.

Compost piles need air circulation, moisture, and heat to do their magic, so place your pile accordingly. Avoid putting the pile in a spot that gets full sun all day unless you're prepared to water it regularly. A part-shade location is ideal.

Prof. Price's Pointers _____

Compost is plant material that microorganisms have decomposed. Compost microorganisms are those bacteria and fungi that can digest plant material. They occur naturally in soils.

Take the following steps to create a compost pile for your garden:

1. Establish a location for the pile. It should be close to the garden but also convenient to your kitchen.

2. Dig a pit about 4×4 or 4×5 feet and about 1 or 2 feet deep. (This step is optional; but having the pile start out in a pit helps keep in moisture.) Don't dig a pit if drainage in the area is poor.

3. Add an 8- to 10-inch layer of organic material like kitchen scraps, leaves, grass clippings, or seed-free weeds.

4. Cover the first layer with a thin layer of soil.

5. Water thoroughly, but not to the point of making it soggy.

6. Add more layers of organic material, alternating with thin layers of soil and watering between layers, until the pile is about 4 or 5 feet high.

7. Let it sit for a month or two.

Garden Guru Says

Microorganisms need to eat to multiply, but it can take them a long time to digest intact plant material. Give these bugs an energy boost with a big dose of sugar simply by emptying the dregs of soft-drink or beer bottles onto the compost pile after your next backyard picnic.

8. Keep the soil moist. If it's very hot or if there's no rain, water the pile occasionally, but be sure it never becomes soggy.

9. Cover the pile with a tarp if you get heavy rains for more than a day or two in a row.

10. After 2 months, and then once a month for 3 to 5 months, turn over the pile with a pitchfork or a special "compost screw."

11. With each turn, check to see that the pile is "cooking." It should feel warm to the touch.

12. When the material in the pile looks like soil, it's ready to use in the garden.

It's always a good idea to have a relatively even mix of green and brown materials, like grass clippings and dried leaves, for example, for good-quality and rapid compost. To accommodate all the organic material you might accumulate, you might want to have more than one pile going at a time. You also could consider a commercial compost bin or tumbler that works faster than a traditional pile.

Good composting material includes the following:

Certain manures	Newspaper
Cornstalks	Pine needles
Dryer lint	Straw
Grass clippings	Thin cardboard
Green plants	Weeds
Kitchen waste	Woodchips
Leaves	

Never, ever add grease, meat or fish scraps, dairy products, or bones to your compost heap. These attract vermin, and even worse, the bacteria that break down animal products can cause disease. Only use manure from horses, cows, sheep, goats, rabbits, and chickens. Cat and dog poop is a big no-no because these pets are meat eaters and because the excrement can contain harmful parasites and bacteria. And to prevent the spread of disease or invasive plants, avoid diseased plants and weeds with seeds.

Kitchen scraps make great additions to the compost pile. Keeping a container by the kitchen sink to collect the scraps means fewer trips to the pile outside; the more convenient it is to do, the more you'll do it.

©iStockphoto.com/Phill Danze

The Least You Need to Know

- The better your soil texture, structure, and pH, the better your plants will be.

- Organic matter makes a good all-purpose soil amendment.

- Adequate drainage is a must for vegetable-growing soil.

- Adjust and amend your soil based on the results of a soil test.

- Organic compost makes a rich amendment to your soil, and it's pretty easy to create your own compost pile.

Chapter 9

Tilling and Toiling

In This Chapter

- Preparing the soil for your garden
- Tips for removing grass
- A look at Rototillers
- The benefits of double-digging
- The pleasures of plastic mulch
- The advantages of raised beds

Up to this point, getting the garden ready has been a lot more thinking than doing. But now you have the opportunity to really get your hands dirty. Preparing the soil and getting it ready for planting is pretty important—some might even say it's more important than all the learning and planning you've done so far. The quality (and quantity) of the work you do at this point helps determine the quality of your garden and the quantity of the produce you grow in it.

In this chapter, we go over the steps to take for killing and removing sod where you want to start your garden. We also look at various methods of preparing the soil for maximum friability and fertility. And we explore some of the options to consider when it comes to creating planting beds.

Preparation Is Everything

It's impossible to overemphasize the importance of well-prepared garden beds. The health and fitness of the soil is as important to the future of the plants you grow as is the health and fitness of your body to the way you live. After all, the soil provides the support and the nutrients the plants need to survive and flourish. So be sure to give it your best shot. You'll have plenty of time to make improvements, but why not start out with the best you can create?

If you do it right, right from the start, you won't have to make up for mistakes later on. And the beauty of it is, if you do prepare quality beds from the get-go, you won't have to do all that really difficult work again. Any necessary improvements or adjustments will be comparatively easy.

Unsod It All

If your future garden space is nothing but bare soil, skip to the next section. But if you're creating a new garden space in an area that's currently lawn, you need to remove the grass.

Lawn, or sod, covers vast parts of America, and most homes, especially new ones, are surrounded by acres of green grass. But to grow a successful garden, you have to get rid of at least some of it. Lawns, after all, are responsible for all kinds of pollution: noise and air pollution from lawnmowers and water pollution from fertilizer runoff.

The Old Paper Trick

This is the low-energy, low-impact approach to grass killing, and it's a favorite of many organic gardeners. After you've finished all the plotting and planning tasks, and you've staked out your garden, you can begin.

You'll need lots of old newspapers and some big stones or several wood boards. The amount of newspapers and rocks and the length of board depend on how big your garden plot is.

Place sections of the paper, about $\frac{1}{8}$ to $\frac{1}{4}$ inch thick, opened at their midpoint, on the grass, and weight the paper with stones or boards. Cover every inch of the space with papers, and secure the paper thoroughly. Then walk away. For a long time. Eventually the grass will die. It can take many months, but if you're not in a hurry, nature will do most of the work for you.

Compost Pile

Common wisdom used to suggest that you remove the comics and advertising pages from newspapers prior to using them in the compost or for lawn killing. It was thought that the colored ink could leach out into the soil and might not be the healthiest additive. The U.S. Composting Council now suggests that most inks used in today's newspapers are nontoxic. If you still have your doubts, call your newspaper.

Alternatively, you can hold the newspapers in place with a thick layer of manure, rinsed seaweed, salt hay, grass clippings, compost, leaves, or soil. When the lawn is dead, you won't need to remove anything from the area and can simply move on to the next step, which is tilling. The newspapers and the organic material on top will be well on their way to decomposing.

The kill-your-lawn-with-paper trick is a good one to try in late summer or early fall. Leave the papers in place through the winter and by spring, the grass should be nice and dead.

This technique is best for small to medium-size gardens. If you're planning a very large garden, use another method.

Doing Some Heavy Lifting

As low energy as our first grass-killing option is, this next method is hard on the body. I've seen many a burly landscaper get weak in the knees at the thought of some heavy sod busting. Digging up the lawn is tough, physical labor, but if you're in decent shape and your garden space isn't overwhelmingly large, it's an inexpensive method, and one that will get the job done in a matter of hours, or at the most, days.

And speaking of burly landscapers, this is one of those times when a hired hand might make a lot of sense.

Here's how to dig up the lawn:

1. Use a spade with a sharp blade to cut through the grass, being sure you get down deep to where the roots are. Work across the space with an overlapping pattern so you don't miss any bits of sod.

2. After cutting through the sod, remove the clump and place it to one side.

3. Dig down one more spade depth, and place that soil back in the hole.

4. Return the clump of sod to the hole, roots side up, exposing the roots to the sun and air. You want the soil that clings to the roots to dry out a bit before the next step.

5. Finally, shake any excess soil from the clumps back onto the soil surface, and throw the clumps on the compost pile.

When you've finished digging the entire space, you should have an evenly distributed surface.

Compost Pile

The last time I dug a garden bed myself, I wound up with terrible blisters on the bottom of my right foot—the foot I used to push the spade into the sod. If you're trying this method, use a spade with a small lip at the top of the blade that spreads out the point of impact on the foot. And wear sturdy boots. Flimsy shoes just don't cut it.

Hand-digging a garden takes a lot of time. I spent the better part of an entire weekend (and I'm talking 8 hours or more each day) to dig a 6×30-foot bed in rich, loamy soil. And I was in pretty good shape back then. Plan on needing much more time if your soil is hard and rocky, and if your lawn is thick and healthy.

Cut It Out: Sod Cutters

Yet another method for removing unwanted sod is with a contraption called a sod cutter. There are two types of sod cutters: the gasoline-powered machine and the distinctly low-tech kick-type.

The heavy-duty machine looks a little like a power tiller but instead of having tines on rotary blades, it's fitted with sharp, flat blades. The machines are usually self-propelled. As they move across the sod, the blades penetrate the sod and cut through just below the roots. The grass is cut in long strips which you can roll up and use to make new lawn somewhere else.

A kick-type sod cutter looks like an old-fashioned plow handle with a flat metal blade attached where the plow blade would go. Just above the blade is a metal bar that you step on as you push the cutter forward. Your weight pushes the blade below the grass in a forward-cutting motion.

After you cut the sod, you must still turn the soil, either by hand digging or with a tiller.

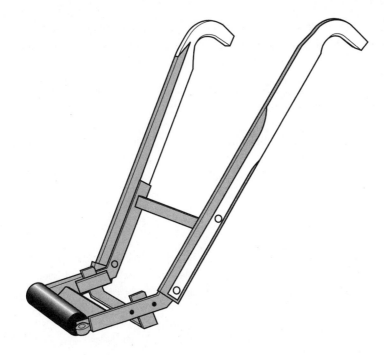

The kick-type sod cutter looks a lot like an old-fashioned plow without a plow blade. This method of sod busting requires heavy physical labor.

(Illustration courtesy of Quail Manufacturing)

Few home gardeners need to actually buy a sod cutter unless they plan on creating lots of new beds over a long period of time. These tools are usually available to rent from equipment rental businesses.

Taking Advantage of Tillers

There are times when machines make so much sense. The preparation of a large garden is one of those times. *Rotary tillers*, commonly known as *Rototillers*, are a wonderful invention, and you should definitely take advantage of one if your garden plans run to many hundreds of square feet or more. Even if your garden space is a small one, a Rototiller will cut your preparation time substantially.

Prof. Price's Pointers

The first **rotary tillers** were horse-drawn steam engines used by German, French, and Swiss farmers in the late 1850s. In 1910, Konrad von Meyenberg, a Swiss inventor, was granted the first patent for the kind of tiller we use today. In 1932, C. W. Kelsey, an American distributor of Swiss-made tillers, trademarked the name *Rototiller*.

Tillers are machines with a couple sets of rotary tines or blades attached. The engine turns the blades that dig through sod and deep into the soil, turning it over and breaking it up. Some of the large, gasoline-powered tillers are self-propelled and can be used for cutting through sod and tilling expansive areas of ground.

Some smaller tillers have electric engines and are much easier to handle than their larger counterparts. The Mantis Tiller, for example, advertises its ease of use with photos of a diminutive woman guiding the machine with one hand. These small versions are not meant for really heavy soil preparation. Instead, they're best used to turn cleared ground or to cultivate an already prepared bed, between rows, for example.

This small tiller is just the right size for turning over the soil in this good-size garden.

©iStockphoto. com/Baxternator

When using a large tiller, exercise caution. It can kick up and back when the blades hit a buried rock, root, or stump. And the blades are very sharp. My husband still has a scar on his leg from a run-in with a tiller more than 20 years ago.

Removing Obstacles

With all the sod cut, it's time for the next step: removing debris, rocks, roots, and clods of leftover grass. An efficient way to do this is to rake through the dug bed with a sturdy garden rake, pulling all the undesirable material to one spot. At that point you can go through the pile by hand, tossing out rocks and roots and shaking loose any soil that's clinging to the clumps of sod.

Food for Thought

Back in my obsessive bed-making days, I would sift the soil through a home-made screen made of rat wire attached to a frame of 2×4s. The rat wire was just the right size mesh to allow the soil to pass through without releasing the stones, roots, and so on that I hate to have in garden beds. Although a very time-consuming task, I think it was worth every minute. To this day, the texture and consistency of my soil is nearly perfect.

Double-Digging

This classic soil preparation technique all but guarantees great soil. But be prepared: it's time-consuming and really hard on the old back.

You'll need a sturdy, sharp spade; a spading fork; and a wheelbarrow or garden cart. In addition, depending on the quality of your soil, you might need quantities of compost, well-rotted manure, or peat moss.

Here's how to double-dig a garden:

1. Divide your garden space into sections about the width of your spade blade. Your work will be a bit easier if you make your sections across the shorter length of the garden.

2. Using the spade, dig a 6- to 8-inch-deep (or as deep as the layer of topsoil) trench the length of the first section.

3. Place the soil from the first section in the wheelbarrow.

4. Break up the subsoil with your spading fork, going down as far as you can. About 1 foot deep is ideal, but if your subsoil is very hard, just do the best you can. Remove any loose rock.

5. Add a 2- to 4-inch layer of compost, rotted manure, or peat moss to the bottom of the trench.

6. Repeat the process in the second section. But instead of placing the topsoil in the wheelbarrow, put it in the first trench on top of the peat or compost.

7. Repeat this process in each section, each time placing the topsoil from the current trench in the previous trench. In the last trench, use the topsoil from the wheelbarrow.

8. Finally, dress the top of the entire bed with a couple inches of compost or well-rotted manure.

9. Mix the top dressing with the top few inches of soil and rake smooth.

Double-digging is really hard work, but the payoff is a high-quality garden bed—one that will help plants thrive.

> **Garden Guru Says** _____
>
> When you've completed double-digging and your garden bed is ready for planting, avoid stepping on the soil. You want the soil to remain light and fluffy, and walking on it will compact it, undoing all that hard work you did. When planting seeds or seedlings, lay a wide board along the row you're working on, and stand or kneel on the board. This spreads out your weight over a wider area, keeping compaction to a minimum.

Using Sheet Mulch in the Garden

If weeding the garden makes you crazy, you might want to consider installing plastic mulch or mulch cloth after you've prepared your beds. Although not particularly pretty, this material greatly reduces the need for weeding. This is one of Prof. Price's favorite planting techniques.

Shiny black plastic sheeting was the standard many years ago. And although it works well enough, it does have its disadvantages. It rips easily, water and air don't penetrate so the soil underneath is compromised, and it's really ugly.

Mulch cloth is the next-generation material, and it's a big improvement. It's a finely woven mesh fabric, usually black, sold in large rolls. Because it's mesh, air and water can pass through to the soil beneath, but it's still dense enough to prevent sprouting weeds from penetrating. The weeds are also robbed of light so they don't grow.

To install mulch cloth, simply lay it out over your prepared beds. Overlap the edges by several inches to ensure that no soil is exposed. Secure the edges with rocks, boards, or metal U-shape pins. Or bury the edges in a shallow trench around the perimeter of the garden. (Planting in mulch cloth is discussed in Chapter 12.)

A large vegetable plot is easier to maintain with black mulch cloth covering the long planting rows and keeping out weeds.

©iStockphoto.com/Marty Heitner

If the idea of plastic anything in the garden rubs you the wrong way, take heart. Some clever Earth-friendly inventors have figured out a way to make a heavy paper film, manufactured from recycled materials, you can use instead.

Raised Beds (*Not* for Sleeping)

Raised bed gardening is a time-honored technique ideally suited for gardeners with serious soil problems, drainage issues, space limitations, time constraints, or physical disabilities. Plants grown in raised beds live in soil that's above the natural level of soil in the garden. Some raised beds are actually large containers, while others are simply beds of soil.

Railroad or landscape ties hold together a raised bed and give it a neat, tidy appearance.

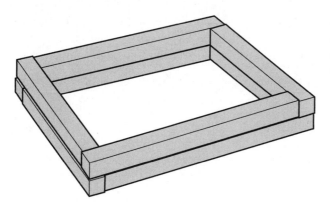

Sick Soil Solution

Your soil might be unacceptable for gardening for any number of reasons: contamination from pollutants, poor drainage, too much rock, too much sand, too compacted, or not enough soil.

Instead of doing a complete overhaul of the soil, which in the case of contamination might not actually be possible, consider installing a raised bed or even a collection of raised beds.

Space- and Time-Saver

If your garden space or the time you have to work in the garden is severely limited, growing vegetables in a raised bed could work for you because you can grow plants intensively (planted very close together) in high-quality soil.

Weed control is easier in the confined space, and watering takes less time than in large gardens.

This raised bed along a curb takes advantage of space that's usually relegated to grass.

©iStockphoto.com/Joe Klane

Easy Access

Raised garden beds built up to wheelchair or waist height enable the disabled or those with knee or back problems to enjoy the pleasures of gardening. These raised beds are generally constructed of wood like a table with sides. It should be high enough for a wheelchair to fit underneath and should be a bit narrower so reaching the center of the bed is not too much of a reach. For wheelchair access, be sure the surfaces surrounding the beds are smooth enough for the wheelchair to glide across.

Making Your Bed

To build your raised bed, follow the same steps for staking out the garden (see Chapter 6). The bed or beds should be narrow enough for you to reach all the way to the center from one side; 4 or 5 feet is about right. The length is up to you.

Kill any grass in the space. Loosen about 6 to 12 inches of the soil using a spade or spading fork. Then bring in enough soil to create a planting depth of 12 to 14 inches. You can buy good-quality topsoil by the truckload or in bags. Rake out the soil until it's a smooth, flat mound.

If you've determined that your soil is contaminated, dig out about 12 inches of soil and remove it. Replace that 12 inches of soil with new, clean soil and add another 12 to 14 inches worth to create the raised bed.

Enclosing a raised-bed garden with walls helps hold the soil in place and can give it a neat, even architectural appearance. Railroad ties or landscape ties, treated wood boards, or even cinder blocks are frequent choices for raised bed enclosures.

> **Garden Guru Says**
>
> The soil in a raised bed usually warms faster than ground level soil and tends to dry out faster. In the hottest part of the summer, plan on watering raised gardens more frequently than standard garden beds.

Amen to Amending the Soil

There is such a thing as perfect soil, and you have the opportunity to create it now. You've tested the soil, examined its texture, and determined the drainage situation. If you've discovered any problems, you can fix them. Do it at this stage of the game, after the soil has been tilled but before you've planted one seed, and you'll save yourself a world of trouble.

Now is the time to add the ingredients you need to raise or lower the pH, make the soil lighter, or improve drainage. Now is also when you can add compost, rotted manure, or fertilizer to boost the richness of the soil. Just dump it on top and mix it in thoroughly. For large quantities, you'll probably want to give it a quick once over with the tiller again to be sure everything is thoroughly combined. But if the amounts are small, spreading it all around evenly with a rake is fine.

Prof. Price's Pointers

Rotating the kinds of plants you grow each year in your garden beds helps avoid depletion and deterioration of the soil because different plants use more of certain nutrients than others. If you plant the same kind of plants year after year in the same spot, the nutrients are depleted.

The Least You Need to Know

- ◆ Before planting your garden, take the time to prepare your soil by removing the sod.

- ◆ A mechanical tiller can help you prepare the soil, but always exercise caution when operating a tiller.

- ◆ Taking the time to double-dig a garden bed can help create the optimum growing environment.

- ◆ Using mulch cloth in your garden helps reduce weeds.

- ◆ Raised beds can be a good solution to many gardening woes.

- ◆ Whether you plant a raised bed or not, always enrich your soil with compost or well-rotted manure.

Plant Biology 101

In This Chapter

- ◆ Identifying plant parts, inside and out
- ◆ Photosynthesis explained
- ◆ The drinking habits of plants
- ◆ The sex life of plants
- ◆ Annuals versus perennials

Before you can begin sowing seeds and tending plants, you probably should know a little about how plants grow. If you remember everything you learned in freshman biology, you can probably skip this chapter. If not, read on.

And be prepared, this stuff can get pretty technical.

Plant Parts

To understand how plants grow and reproduce, you need to be familiar with their various parts. It's actually pretty easy to understand, but to make it even easier, we look at this in terms of vegetables.

A Little About Leaves

Leaves are lateral outgrowths of a plant's stem. Most leaves are green (at least at some stage of their lives). Edible leaves include lettuce, cabbage, kale, mustard greens, bok choy, spinach, and parsley, among many others. The role of the leaf is to soak up the sun's energy.

Most leaves are green because they contain chlorophyll, the plant's green pigment. (*Chloro* means "green" in Greek.) The chlorophyll traps the energy from the sun. This is part of a process called *photosynthesis*, which we look at a little later in this chapter.

Garden Guru Says _____

Bulbs like onions and garlic are a collection of modified leaves that live underground. If you've ever peeled an onion, you can see how it's made of tightly wrapped layers. These modified leaves don't have the same role as green leaves that are exposed to sunlight. Instead, they store energy.

The Story of Stems

The stem is (usually) a slender growth of plant material that supports or connects one plant part to another. Stems function like arteries and veins, distributing water and nutrients throughout the plant. For example, a stem connects leaves to each other and supports a flower or fruit. Some of the stems we eat include celery, asparagus, and rhubarb.

The story of stems can get a little more complicated. Stems can also grow underground as stolons. The runners of strawberries are a good example of stolons. Some other underground stems are called tubers. Potatoes, yams, jicama, and Jerusalem artichokes fall into this category.

Get Back to Your Roots

The root is the part of the plant that usually lives below the soil. It serves as a sort of anchor for the plant and is the "machinery" the plant uses to absorb water and nutrients.

Roots also can enlarge and become a kind of storage tank of nutrients the plant will call on later in its life cycle. Usually, people eat these little warehouses before the plants get to use them. Among the edible roots we enjoy are carrots, radishes, beets, turnips, and parsnips.

Most plants have a primary root that goes more or less straight down into the soil with smaller lateral roots that reach out from the main root. At the ends of lateral roots, tiny root hairs are responsible for absorbing nutrients and water from the soil. Finally, at the very end of the root is a root cap, a little protective covering.

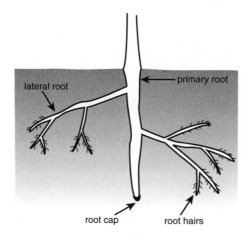

A plant's root system helps it stay stable in the soil and also soak up water and nutrients.

Some plants develop one very large main root with some lateral roots. This main root is called a tap root. Carrots, parsnips, and radishes are good examples. Other plants have fibrous roots, which are what you see with tomatoes, peppers, beans, and most other vegetable plants. The fibrous roots have a much smaller main root and lots of lateral roots.

Beautiful Buds

The bud is either a stem or a flower in the very earliest stages of its development. Some buds are vegetative and can become new stems and leaves. Others develop into flowers. Some flowers eventually become fruit.

> **Food for Thought**
>
> Vegetables like peppers, tomatoes, eggplant, squash, and cobs of corn are, botanically speaking, fruits, which, as you now know, are fully developed buds. Some other vegetables are actually flowers. Artichokes, for example, are flower buds. We eat the unopened petals one by one. The parts of broccoli and cauliflower that we eat are clusters of flower buds. Fruits including berries and watermelons are, well, fruits.

Inside Plants

The really interesting parts of plants are buried—but not hidden—inside the cells that make up plant organs. Most of these parts are very much like those in human and other animal cells, such as the nucleus, which contains a cell's DNA. But some of the tiny structures inside plants are very different from anything found in animals.

Chloroplasts

The one big exception where plants differ from animals is that plants have *chloroplasts*. These are little green engines that carry out photosynthesis (be patient, we'll get to it). Chloroplasts are green because they contain chlorophyll. (Remember, *chloro* means "green" in Greek.) Chloroplasts typically appear in leaves, which is why leaves are green, but they can also be found in other green organs like buds (broccoli), stems (celery), and fruits (bell peppers).

Several structures are closely related to chloroplasts. These other structures are not green and they don't carry out photosynthesis, but they have distinct functions critical to the life of plants.

Amyloplasts

One relative of chloroplasts is the *amyloplast*, which contains starch. (*Amylo* is Greek for "starch.") Amyloplasts are found in very large quantities in seeds and tubers. The starch they hold is where much of the energy we get from food originates.

The amyloplasts fuel the plant's reproduction. Developing seedlings harvest energy from the starch stored in amyloplasts as they grow until they are mature enough to soak up sunlight.

Chromoplasts

Chromoplasts are another relative of chloroplasts. (*Chromo* means "color" in Greek.) They accumulate large amounts of yellow, orange, and red pigments (called carotenoids), which are found in foods that are high in antioxidants like carrots and tomatoes, in nasturtium flowers, and in squash blossoms.

How Seeds Grow

Seeds, which plants make so they can reproduce themselves, are basically tiny undeveloped new plants with some extra things added on. Each seed contains an embryo (the undeveloped new plant) and some tissue that's packed with food that will feed the developing seedling until it's able to survive on its own.

The seed is enclosed in a tough jacket that protects it from the elements until the conditions for *germination* are just right. Usually this is when there's enough moisture and warmth in the seed's environment. When the seed senses that it's warm enough and that there's enough moisture, it breaks out of *dormancy* and begins to grow.

Prof. Price's Pointers

Dormancy is a rest period in a plant's life cycle. **Germination** is when a seed's dormancy ends and the seed begins to develop as a new plant. Plants also have an internal clock that's set by the length of the night. So when nights become shorter in the spring, the seeds of some plants, such as lettuce, say "Wake up! It's time to germinate." Other plants use this clock to decide when it's time to flower.

As the seed grows into a seedling, it uses its little storehouse of food. The stem of the seedling pushes up through the soil toward sunlight. When it finally "sees" the sun, it puts its energy into expanding its tiny leaves. At this point, the colorless leaves begin to turn green.

The Mystery of Photosynthesis

One of the great triumphs of plant science in the mid-twentieth century was unraveling the mystery of *photosynthesis*. Photosynthesis takes place inside the plant's chloroplasts in two separate processes called "the dark reaction" and "the light reaction."

Prof. Price's Pointers

Photosynthesis is the conversion of carbon dioxide and water into glucose and other sugars and starch using the energy of sunlight. Oxygen is produced as a waste product. Photosynthesis is how plants manufacture their own food.

The dark reaction converts carbon dioxide to sugar. This process can happen in the dark, but only for a few seconds. To keep on going, it needs a huge input of light energy. That's when the light reaction kicks in. This process starts when the chlorophyll in leaves soaks up the sun's energy, which is then converted through chemical processes to electrical energy. For all you chemistry buffs, this is when an electron is separated from a hydrogen atom, a lot like when you charge a battery.

The electrical charge is then converted to a complex chain of reactions that eventually fuels the dark reaction, which makes the sugar. Finally, the waste product of this process—oxygen—is released. Simple, right?

In a nutshell, photosynthesis …

◆ Produces food for plants.

◆ Occurs in cells that contain chloroplasts.

◆ Uses water and carbon dioxide.

◆ Requires the energy of the sun.

How Plants Drink

Do you remember the science "experiment" you did in third grade when you put a stalk of celery in a glass of water mixed with red food coloring? After a few hours, the celery had magically turned red!

Even if you didn't realize it at the time, that was a lesson on how plants drink. You might even remember that the process was called *osmosis*. That elementary school lesson gave you part of the story about how plants drink, but it's a little more complicated than that.

Why Plants Wilt or Don't Wilt

Plant cells are filled with *solutes*—these are salts, sugars, organic acids, and so on. The solutes create what's called an *osmotic potential*, which decreases the energy of the water being absorbed. As a consequence, plants absorb water until the pressure inside the plant cells matches the *osmotic pressure*.

The balance of osmotic pressure and internal water pressure is what makes plant stems get stiff when they have enough water and makes them wilt when there's not enough. The firmness of the plant's tissues is called *turgor*.

More Drinking Stories

Osmotic potential pulls water into a plant only so far, so plants have another trick: evaporation. The leaves of plants have thousands of tiny openings called *stomata* that allow water vapor to diffuse out. (They also permit carbon dioxide, needed for photo-synthesis, to diffuse into the leaves.)

The loss of water by evaporation through the stomata creates a negative pressure that literally sucks water up through the stems. This process is called *transpiration*.

Food for Thought

Because leaves don't photosynthesize at night, the stomata in the leaves close down and save water. When the sun comes out, they open again for business. If the water pressure in the plant drops too low, the stomata close again to save water. So if you forget to water the tomatoes, the plants themselves will bail you out. But don't do it again; there's only so much a plant can do on its own.

How Plants Reproduce

When it comes to reproduction, plants are a bit more flexible than animals. Plants can reproduce using sexual reproduction or asexual, or vegetative, reproduction.

It's All About Sex

Sexual reproduction in plants happens when the ovules (egg) and pollen (sperm) from flowers are combined and form an embryo. Most plants produce "perfect" flowers that contain both pollen and ovules, but in some plants, the sexes are separated. In members of the squash family, for example, the first flowers to appear on the stem are strictly male, producing only pollen. Later flowers are strictly female, with the baby fruit looking like a slight swelling behind the petals.

Birds, bees, other insects, the wind, and sometimes even humans all help plants with sexual reproduction. This occurs when pollen, which is usually carried on the *stamen* (the little yellow bundle inside the flower), is mixed with the *ovule*, which is usually at the center of the bloom inside the ovary. Bees and other insects and some birds visit flowers to drink the nectar in the petals. As they pass by the stamen, a little of the pollen rubs off on their wings or feet and then lands at the *stigma*, where it can enter the ovule.

When bees are scarce, pollination might not happen as often as it should, and plants produce less fruit. Sometimes gardeners can help with the process by hand-pollinating their plants.

A Vegetative State

Some plants are sterile (they cannot reproduce on their own) so the only way to make new plants is by vegetative reproduction. This is usually done with stem or root cuttings.

Most vegetative reproduction is done with woody plants or houseplants and rarely with vegetables. Fruit shrubs and grape vines can be reproduced with root or stem cuttings, as can some herbs. Vegetative reproduction is considered asexual reproduction.

Growing Seasons

So far in this chapter we've looked at the parts of plants and what makes them tick. Now it's time to talk about how they actually grow. Instead of thinking of growing seasons in terms of simply summer, spring, fall, and winter, gardeners look at seasons of development, growth, fruit production, and death or dormancy.

Plants have a growth cycle that basically goes like this:

1. The seed germinates.

2. It becomes a seedling.

3. It becomes a full-grown plant.

4. The plant grows.

5. It produces food (photosynthesis).

6. It reproduces itself by growing a fruit that produces a seed.

7. The plant dies.

8. The seed grows into a new plant.

Some plants, notably woody plants like trees and shrubs, go as far as producing the seed and then go into a dormancy period that is usually related to temperature and daylight. At the end of the dormant stage, they wake up and start over again. And of course, trees such as maples or redwoods will go on for years, even centuries, with this cycle.

But herbaceous plants—that is, plants with a soft, nonwoody stem, like tomatoes or oregano—have a different life cycle. They are usually classified as either annual or perennial plants.

Annuals

Just about all the common garden fruits and vegetables we grow from seeds or seedlings (tomatoes, peppers, squash, watermelons, and so on) are annual plants. This means their entire life cycle is spent in one growing season. They sprout, grow into a plant, produce fruit, make seeds, and then die.

Perennials

Perennial herbaceous plants, on the other hand, have a longer life cycle. They sprout, grow into a plant, produce fruit, make seeds, and then die back to the ground. Their roots or stems, especially underground stems, remain in a dormant state. At the start of the next growing season, new growth forms and they start over again.

Perennial edible plants include asparagus, artichokes, rhubarb, and many herbs.

The Least You Need to Know

◆ Most plants have the same basic parts: leaves, stems, roots, buds, and flowers.

◆ Plants use photosynthesis to harness sunlight in the process of manufacturing food.

◆ Plants pull water into themselves using osmosis.

◆ Bees, other insects, birds, the wind, and humans help plants reproduce by distributing pollen to the stigma where it might eventually reach the ovule of a plant.

◆ Most vegetable plants are either perennial and live through several life cycles or annual and have one life cycle.

Seeds and Seedlings

In This Chapter

- ◆ Jump-start the growing season indoors
- ◆ A look at cold frames
- ◆ Starting seeds outside
- ◆ Selecting seedlings
- ◆ Establish seedling time frames and support systems

In this chapter, we finally arrive at what many consider the best part of gardening—planting seeds. Here we focus on starting seeds indoors and the steps to follow to take them from seed to healthy young plants.

We learn about starting plants from sets, crowns, and plant divisions, and we also talk about what you should look for when you buy young vegetable seedlings. We also look at cold frames that help extend the growing season. This chapter finishes with information on when to plant your seedlings outdoors and how to create support systems for your new plants.

Sowing Seeds Indoors

Gardeners who live in Florida, Southern California, and other warm spots won't need to spend much time with this part of the chapter. But if you live where it gets cold, pay attention.

One of the reasons gardeners start seeds indoors is to get a jump on the growing season. It's also a great way to save money because seeds are a lot less expensive than plants, even young seedlings.

Some seeds take many weeks to germinate and then many more weeks to produce ripe fruit. Consider, for example, a growing season (that is, when it's warm enough to plant tender plants without risk of frost) that doesn't start until May 15. So if the seeds require 10 days to germinate and about 80 growing days until the fruit is ready to harvest, you'll be waiting until the middle of August before you get those juicy Beefsteak tomatoes. But if you start the seeds indoors and have nice, hearty seedlings ready for that set-out date of May 15, you might have tomatoes for your salad by the end of July.

Here are a few other good reasons to start seeds indoors:

◆ You can ensure the quality of the plants you grow.

◆ You know exactly what your plants have been exposed to. This is especially important if you plan to garden organically, or just take a more chemical-free approach.

◆ Seed catalogs and specialty vendors offer far more variety than garden centers' and nurseries' seedlings.

◆ There's less chance of introducing disease to your garden than when you bring in seedlings or plants from other places.

◆ Starting seeds indoors has a very low cost.

Where to Start Seeds

Finding containers to start seeds in is an area where ingenuity counts. You can start seeds indoors in all kinds of containers. I've seen it done in cardboard milk cartons, wooden fruit crates, aluminum pie plates, and olive oil cans. More traditional methods are plastic cell packs and trays, peat pots, fiber packs, and flowerpots. And in more than one catalog I've seen a clever device that forms cute little pots from old newspapers.

The key things that a container must do are hold soil and allow for drainage. If you use unconventional containers like pie plates and milk cartons, be sure to punch holes in the bottom so water can drain out. The peat pots, fiber packs, and little newspaper pots are all biodegradable, so you can plant the container and the seedling together directly in the soil, without the risk of disturbing tender new roots. Keep in mind that some newspaper ink is made with toxic chemicals. You may want to call your newspaper to find out if it's printed with soy-based or other nontoxic inks.

If you reuse old containers, be sure they're scrupulously clean. Wash them with disinfectant or a diluted bleach solution. Or if your approach is nonchemical, use an Earth-friendly soap.

Garden Guru Says

Some of the easiest and most Earth-friendly seed-starter containers are eggshells. Collect carefully opened eggshells, with about ¾ of the shell intact. Clean them thoroughly, fill them ½ full of potting mix, place one or a few seeds in each shell, and water. Place each shell back in the egg carton, and put cardboard cartons on a tray to avoid a wet mess. (Styrofoam cartons don't tend to leak.) When it's time to transplant the seedlings outdoors, plant them shell and all. The little roots won't be disturbed, and eventually the shell will break down.

When you're ready to start seeds indoors, fill the container with potting soil or seed-starting mix, plant the seeds the recommended distance apart, and water.

Mixed Media

The quality of the planting mixture you use to start your seeds indoors is a crucial element to the ultimate success of your plants. After all, it's the first home to the tiny, emerging plant, so it has to be a safe and nutritious environment.

Any number of potting media work well for starting seeds, including the following:

◆ Commercial potting mixes

◆ Commercial seed-starting mixes

Prof. Price's Pointers

Vermiculite is a micalike mineral that's added to soils, especially in container gardening, to increase the soil's water-holding capacity. Perlite is a volcanic lava that's been crushed and heated at very high temperatures to create a lightweight material used in potting mixes.

- Horticultural *vermiculite*

- Half *perlite* and half horticultural vermiculite

- One part each vermiculite, perlite, and peat moss

- One part each peat moss, compost, coarse sand, and vermiculite

- One part each commercial potting soil, compost, and vermiculite

- One part worm castings, coarse sand, and vermiculite

The key to a good-quality planting medium is that it be light and fluffy so the tiny roots and shoots have an easy time pushing their way through the mix. It also should drain easily.

It's also very important that the mix be disease and pest free. To ensure this, you can sterilize your previously used potting mix. Heat it on a baking sheet in a 250 degrees Fahrenheit oven for about 30 minutes, being careful to not overheat or overcook it. Although it won't smell very good, the process will kill off bacteria and fungus that could damage or kill young plants. You won't have to go through this process if it's a new, commercial mix.

Perlite and vermiculite are natural mineral products available at home, farm, and garden centers. The easiest way to measure these products and the peat and compost is with a coffee can, children's sand pail, or large measuring cup. Mix your potting soil in a large bucket or trash can for handy access.

How to Plant Seeds

When you plant your seeds indoors depends on when you want to set out your seedlings. And that date depends on the weather. (You'll learn a little more about that later in this chapter.)

When you've established your set-out date, you simply consult the information on the seed packet. It should tell you how many days before the set-out date to plant the seeds. This ranges from a couple weeks to as many as 12 weeks.

To plant the seeds, follow these steps:

1. Fill your containers to about $\frac{1}{2}$ inch or so from the top with your chosen planting medium.

2. Sprinkle the mix gently with water. A mister is helpful for this task.

3. Press the planting mix gently with your palm or with a flat surface. You don't want to create any dips or impressions.

4. Sow the seeds according to the directions on the seed packet. (We'll talk more about this in later chapters.)

5. Mist with a fine spray of water.

6. Place the container in a warm spot, preferably about 70 degrees Fahrenheit.

Off to a Good Start

Keep your germinating seeds warm and moist until they pop through the surface of the soil. After they appear, the tiny seedlings need a little less warmth but a lot more sun.

The best temperature for most seedlings is about 65 degrees Fahrenheit during the day and 5 or 10 degrees cooler at night. Some plants might have different requirements, so consult the seed packet.

Ideally, you should place the seedlings in a southern window where they'll get as much sunlight as possible. Turn the pots or trays every day so all the seedlings get an equal exposure to the sun.

If you don't have adequate window space, you can install a special grow light for the plants. You can even rig one up in the basement. When the seedlings are very small, put the plants about 6 to 8 inches from the light. As they grow, move the lighting fixture up so it doesn't burn them. Keep the light on at least 12 hours a day and up to 16 hours. Install a timer for convenience.

The Next Step

When the plants have grown their first set of true leaves, you can begin transplanting them to larger containers. Don't do this if you've planted individual seeds in peat pots, eggshells, or cell packs. If they're in their own containers, you can allow the seedlings to mature.

At this stage, you should also start a feeding regimen. Use a liquid fertilizer about every 2 weeks according to the directions on the package. Or use a nice, light manure tea (visit gardengrapevine.com/ManureTea.html for a recipe) or fish or kelp emulsion (recipe at faq. gardenweb.com/faq/lists/organic/2002080041031). If in doubt, err on the side of a weaker solution.

Compost Pile _____

Many seedlings succumb to a condition known as *damping off*, in which the seedlings die from excessive moisture. But it's a fungus that comes with the overwatering that actually causes the plants to die.

Keep the seedlings moist but not wet. A fine mist is better than direct watering. Overfertilizing and overwatering young seedlings are two mistakes people make most frequently when starting seeds indoors.

Hardening Off

About 2 weeks before your set-out date, you need to get the seedlings ready for transplantation. Specifically, they need to be *hardened off.*

Prof. Price's Pointers _____

Hardening off is the process of slowly acclimating plants to a new environment, usually from indoors to outdoors.

To do this, you can start by lowering the temperature in the room where the seedlings are growing and reducing the amount of light. After a couple days, you can move the plants outside to a protected, shady spot during the day. Don't do this if it's windy, raining, or below 45 degrees Fahrenheit outside. Try the garage, near a window, or an unheated sunroom instead. Bring the plants back inside at night. During this process, water regularly but sparingly.

In about 2 weeks, your seedlings should be acclimated enough to make the big move to full-time life in the great outdoors. But don't push it. Keep a close eye on weather forecasts, and be prepared to rush outside with protective coverings for your newly planted babies should a cold front come through.

Starting Early with Cold Frames

A cold frame is essentially a greenhouse device, usually made of glass or transparent plastic and set directly on the ground. Cold frames give you the opportunity to start the spring planting season early and extend fall growing time past frost dates.

You can use a cold frame for hardening off young seedlings without the nuisance of moving pots in and out of the house. Or plant seeds of cool-tolerant plants (like peas, lettuce, or spinach) directly in a cold frame laid on prepared soil. The sun will warm the soil inside the cold frame well before it does the exposed garden soil.

Cold frames should have the slanted, glazed top facing south for maximum sun exposure. It helps to place them up against the southern wall of the house, garage, barn, or garden shed because the wall helps capture warmth. Painting the interior white and sinking the foundation a few inches also makes it warmer.

Food for Thought

Make a cold frame using old storm windows and some scrap lumber or metal, cinder blocks, or bricks. Ask contractors you know to save old windows and lumber from renovations, or put a "wanted" post on Freecycle. You can find precise instructions from a number of sites on the Internet. Just type "make a cold frame" into Google or another search engine.

Cold frames can become too warm inside, which can encourage disease and fungus. Keep a thermometer inside the frame; if the temperature goes above 70 degrees Fahrenheit, open the frame to vent it. Most commercial cold frames have optional automatic vents like a greenhouse.

Planting Seeds Outdoors

Planting seeds outdoors is a far less complicated undertaking than doing it indoors. All you really have to do is prepare the soil properly and plant the seeds according to the directions on the seed packet.

Although just about all plants can be grown from seeds (there are a few exceptions, but we'll get into that later), it's not always the most practical approach. The seeds of some plants can be difficult to germinate or might take an inconveniently long time to sprout. Home gardeners typically grow some plants from sets, tubers, crowns, divisions, and offshoots.

Set Out the Onions

Onions, garlic, and shallots are all members of the same plant family. And as you learned in Chapter 10, the bulb part you eat is actually a collection of leaves that

Garden Guru Says

Most onions are grown from sets, but there's one exception: scallions. These small green onions with edible stems are typically grown from seed.

grow underground. Almost no one except commercial growers attempts to grow these plants from seed. Instead, we use sets.

Usually the sets are sold in bunches of 50 or 100 and look like tiny flower bulbs. Some might have sprouted a little stem by the time you buy them in the spring, but that's okay. Each individual set grows into one large plant.

One Potato, Two Potato ...

Potatoes (*Solanum tuberosum*) and sweet potatoes (*Ipomoea batatas*) are usually grown in the home garden from little tubers. These are basically tiny potatoes that are grown commercially as seed stock.

Prof. Price's Pointers

The **crown** is the part of the plant where the roots and stem meet.

Other plants that home gardeners don't generally grow from seed are asparagus, which are usually started with dormant *crowns*, and rhubarb, which are grown from rooted offshoots or divisions of existing plants. These are available from garden centers, nurseries, and specialty mail-order houses.

Seed potatoes are available from garden centers, farm supply stores, and online. If you have old potatoes in the pantry that have grown some "eyes," you can plant those, too.

©iStockphoto.com/Peter Garbet

Starting With Seedlings

Gardeners who want more immediate gratification can start their gardens using seed-lings. It's really a much easier way to go and is also helpful if you get a late start in the spring or early summer.

Vegetable seedlings are readily available at garden centers, nurseries, farm markets, and even grocery stores and places like Kmart and The Home Depot.

When you pick out seedlings, look for plants with strong, thick stems and plenty of healthy-looking leaves. Avoid any wilted plants. Stay away from yellowed leaves, those with brown or curling edges, and any with signs of insect damage. Look under the leaves to be sure there aren't any nasty bugs lurking there either. Plants with some tiny flowers might set fruit earlier, but that's not guaranteed.

When you take home your new plants, water them thoroughly and put them in the shade until you have time to plant them. They've probably had a rough life up to this point, so pamper them a bit.

Planting Time Frames

Most plants have a preference as to what time of year they're planted, especially in places where the climate ranges from very hot to very cold. In parts of the country where the temperatures stay within a much smaller range, planting seasons are less meaningful.

Most plants fall into one of three categories: cold weather, cool weather, and warm weather. This refers to the time frame in which to plant them whether as seeds or as seedlings, sets, crowns, or divisions.

Cold-weather plants should be planted in the early spring, as soon as the soil can be worked, in places like the Northeast, Midwest, and Northwest. In the South and the Pacific Southwest, many of these plants are planted in the late summer or early fall for late fall harvest.

Some plants to start in cold weather include the following:

Chives	Peas
Garlic	Radicchio
Leeks	Shallots
Onions	

Garden Guru Says

Rhubarb divisions prefer an early spring planting.

Cool-weather plants are usually planted just before the last expected frost of the year. They don't like frost, but they'll survive a mild hit. These plants generally don't do as well in very hot weather. In places where it never frosts, plant these so they'll grow during the coolest part of your year.

Some plants to start in cool weather include the following:

Arugula	Lettuce
Broccoli	Parsley
Cabbage	Radishes
Chervil	Spinach
Coriander	Swiss chard
Kale	Turnips

The majority of vegetables and annual herbs are warm-weather plants in colder zones. These plants won't tolerate cold weather and shouldn't be put out until all danger of frost is past. Many of them like the soil to be nice and warm, too. They might not die if you plant them too early, but their performance might suffer.

Some plants to start in warm weather include the following:

Basil	Peppers
Beans	Sorrel
Dill	Tomatoes
Eggplants	

If in doubt about what to plant when in your area, call on your local county extension office or Farm Bureau for advice.

Setting Up Support Systems

Most plants can grow with little help beyond regular watering, feeding, and weeding. But some plants want to climb, sprawl, or otherwise spread out and need a support system to keep their foliage and fruits from winding up on the garden floor.

To keep plants tidy, to support their climbing habits, and to protect ripening fruits, gardeners use a variety of support systems, including stakes, trellises, netting, and old-fashioned string.

String It Along

Lightweight twining plants like peas and beans will happily climb up trellises, fencing, or other structures, but you can also meet their needs by preparing a grid of twine strung between a few bamboo poles.

This is a one-year-at-a-time technique because the twine will probably rot after one season. You can use plastic twine for a long-lived grid.

Tomato Cages

Tomato plants, especially the larger varieties, generally want to sprawl. This can become very untidy and often results in too many fruits lying on the ground where they'll rot or pick up insects.

To support the tomatoes, place a wire tomato cage over the plant when it's still small. The tomato will grow up inside the cage and rest its stems on the wire, making it easy for you to harvest the tomatoes. Cages also hold the plant so more of it is exposed to sunlight, which encourages growth.

You can buy tomato cages at home and garden centers. Or you can fashion your own using fence wire or concrete reinforcing wire and heavy-duty metal stakes. Be sure the openings between the wires are large enough for a big tomato to grow through.

Stake Your Claim

Stakes made of bamboo, metal, or plastic are indispensable in the garden. You'll need them to support pepper or eggplant plants that are heavy with fruit. You can also stake smaller varieties of tomatoes, especially the grape and cherry types. And you'll want to stake up any plant that seems to need a little bit of help standing up straight.

Use twist ties, twine, plastic plant ties, or foam-covered wire ties to attach the plant to

Compost Pile

To avoid choking or breaking delicate stems, tie your ties gently around the stem. The ties should be tight enough not to cut into the stem, but not so loose that they'll slip down. Also be sure to place enough ties on long stems so they won't bend over and break off above the tie.

the stake. Or place three stakes around the plant and wrap twine around the stakes to make a support all the way around.

The Least You Need to Know

- ◆ You can ensure an earlier, more diverse harvest by starting seeds indoors.

- ◆ Use a light, airy potting mix to give your seedlings their best possible start.

- ◆ Harden off young seedlings before planting them in the garden.

- ◆ Use a cold frame to extend the growing season in the spring and fall.

- ◆ When purchasing seedlings, select healthy ones with no signs of yellow, browning, or curling leaves or insect damage.

- ◆ Use stakes, cages, netting, or twine to support your plants.

Chapter 12

How to Plant

In This Chapter

- Making neat planting rows
- Garden hills and mounds
- Learn how to make furrows
- Tips for sowing seeds and transplanting seedlings
- Get into square-foot gardening

Now we get to the really fun part: planting outside! If you're like me, you can't wait to get your hands in the dirt—whoops, I mean *soil*.

In this chapter, we dig in and get our hands dirty. We look at various planting methods, including creating rows, hills, mounds, and furrows. I tell you how to plant seeds and transplant seedlings. And you learn all about square-foot and intensive gardening.

Planting All in a Row

My favorite vision of a vegetable garden is a tidy rectangle divided into neat rows of plants. Rows are orderly. They keep everything in place. They make sense. When your plants are set up in rows, you know what's a weed and what's supposed to be growing there.

It's not hard to make garden rows, but it helps if you go back to your original garden plan. How many rows are you going to have? Will they run the length or the width of the garden? Or both ways? How wide will each row be? And how much space will you put between each row?

The answers to these questions depend on what plants you intend to grow. When you've made your selections, you'll figure out how much space each plant needs and create rows to accommodate that amount of space.

Now with a little sketch plan, you can lay out the rows. Measure the length of each row, and use stakes and string to mark them. You could also use spray paint, but it doesn't stick as well to soil as it does to grass. Chalk string that you snap against the soil so it leaves a mark is another approach.

Leave the stake and string in place until you've finished planting each row. This helps you keep your rows straight and your spacing the way you want it.

Planting in Hills and Mounds

In addition to planting seeds and seedlings in little holes in nice straight rows, you'll probably plant some things in hills and mounds.

Hill Country

Crops like beans, sunflowers, and any other large seed can be planted in small hills spaced evenly along a row. A hill might be as small as 6 inches or as high as about 1 foot.

To create a hill, just scoop up a handful of soil in each hand, pull the handfuls together in one pile, and smooth it down. Then it's ready for planting one big seed right in the center.

When scooping the soil, be sure you pull it evenly from all around the hill. You can even make a tiny moat around the base of the hill to trap water during dry weather.

Mounds and Mounds

A planting mound is a large hill of soil pulled up from the surrounding area to create a raised planting environment. Traditionally, mounds are used for growing big and sprawling vegetable plants like zucchini, cucumber, summer and winter squash, pumpkins, and melons. A mound might be anywhere from about 18 to 24 inches high.

A group of mounds with big vegetables like pumpkins and watermelons can take up a lot of space in a garden. If your space is limited, stagger the mounds in a zigzag pattern so you can fit more in.

To form the mounds, start with a well-prepared garden bed. Determine the spacing for your mounds based on the distances for the plant you're putting in the mounds. Mark a midpoint for each mound. Then using a garden rake or a hoe, pull soil from the surrounding ground until it forms a pile. Be sure you take soil away evenly so there are no big dips around the mound, although a shallow moat at the base of each mound does help retain water in dry weather.

Prof. Price's Pointers

An advantage of growing on mounds is that the loose soil they're formed of allows for very good drainage. Planting on mounds also helps deter insects and protects against disease to some extent.

Flatten the pile a little on top and smooth the sides so the soil is evenly spread all the way around. Then follow the planting directions for each type of vegetable. Seeds or seedlings are generally planted in a circle or a triangle on a mound.

Planting in Furrows

A furrow is a shallow trench—a long, narrow hole with a flat bottom. Using furrows makes sense when you're planting a lot of one kind of plant that requires a little more depth, like asparagus, rhubarb, turnips, and potatoes.

Make a furrow using a hoe. Mound the soil up on one side of the furrow to make it easier to push back in on top of the seeds or roots you put in the furrow.

Irrigation furrows are another story. These are trenches that are used to move water through the garden.

Planting Seeds One by One

Planting seeds one at a time can either be very satisfying or unbelievably tedious. I guess it has to do with your frame of mind. There's something really basic and reassuring about making a little hole, dropping in a seed, filling the hole back up with soil, and firming it down with your hand.

Bean seeds are usually planted one by one.

©iStockphoto.com/Fred Didier

Some seeds—beans, corn, cucumbers, melons, and squash most notably—are quite large so handling them one at a time is easy to do.

When you plant one seed at a time, you have a lot of control over your spacing. But if many of the seeds don't germinate or fail to grow well, you'll need to replant in those spaces. This isn't necessarily a bad thing. It's just a kind of forced succession planting. (Succession planting is discussed later in this chapter.)

Food for Thought

Some seed sellers prepare seed tapes to make the job of planting easier than it already is. These tapes are long strips of biodegradable material with little seed packets strung out along the tape. To plant, just dig a tiny trench, gently bury the tape, water, and wait. This is a great way for kids to plant.

The Scatter Method

You've probably seen old paintings or prints of a charming rural scene with a farmer scattering seed across a field. This is a perfectly good method of sowing or broadcasting seed if you have lots of space and want large quantities of one kind of plant.

Keep in mind that broadcasted seed won't necessarily space itself evenly in the garden, but you can thin out young seedlings that are too close together.

You can also scatter seeds in very confined spaces like a large pot or planting box. This is a great way to grow mixed lettuce varieties. Just fill your planting box, tray, or pot with soil and scatter a handful of seeds as evenly as possible across the surface of the soil. That's it. You can thin any plants that are poorly spaced as you harvest young seedlings for your salad bowl.

The scatter method won't work for seeds that need a soil cover. Be sure to check the information on individual seed packets before you start throwing seeds around your garden.

> **Garden Guru Says**
>
> You can sow some very tiny seeds like carrots and radishes by the scatter method. But because the seeds are so small, it's difficult to get an even coverage. If you mix the seed with a little bit of dry sand and then scatter the seed, you'll probably have more success.

Transplanting Seedlings

When transplanting seedlings, give them a little more care than you would seeds or already-established plants you buy in the store, ready to plant.

First, to ensure the health of your plants, transplant seedlings on an overcast day if possible. If you live near Prof. Price in San Diego, where there never seems to be a cloudy day, do your transplanting in the late afternoon or early evening when the sun is low in the sky. The point is to protect tender, new plants from a heavy dose of sunlight when they're at a very vulnerable stage.

Dig a hole that's about twice the width of the container you are transplanting, and the same depth. Be sure the sides of the hole are roughed up a bit. (Tender young roots will find it easier to push into than soil that has been made smooth by the blade of a spade or trowel.)

After you've placed the seedling in the hole, fill the hole with soil, gently pressing down all the way around. You want to be sure you haven't left any voids that could fill with water and drown your seedling, and that the soil is evenly distributed around the roots.

Food for Thought _____

My dear friend Pat McKearn (who is also my former partner in our landscaping business) used to have a nifty way of avoiding working in the garden during the heat of the day. She wore a miner's helmet that had a battery-powered headlight so she could work anywhere in the garden well into the night without having to set up floodlights. Gardeners may prefer one of the headband-mounted lights sold by L.L. Bean or in hardware stores.

Water all the seedlings well before and after transplanting. Some gardeners dunk the plant, pot and all, in a big bucket of cool water. Just don't leave them there for too long or the roots won't have access to air.

While you're planting seedlings, pick off dead or damaged leaves, flowers, and any tiny fruits. This allows the plants to put all their energy into producing thick, healthy foliage that will, in turn, help the plant make plenty of its own food for later fruit production.

Some for Now Some for Later

Before the advent of railroads and interstate highways, consumers didn't have access to fresh fruits and vegetables all year long. They could buy what was grown locally and had to accept the fact that strawberries were only available for a couple weeks in June or that once the beets were harvested, that was it. Everything is different now. We can have anything we want just about anytime of year, thanks to the global marketplace.

Compost Pile _____

The issue of food traveling around the world to wind up on our tables—and the resulting carbon imprint that transportation makes—is one of the reasons so many Americans are turning to growing their own food.

If you want to grow your own food, you're still limited to the nuances of the growing season where you live and garden. But with some ingenuity, you can stretch the harvest time. With repetitive or relay planting of the same vegetable over the course of several weeks, you can have a staggered and drawn-out harvest.

For example, in early spring, you might plant a row of lettuces. A week later, plant another row, and plant another row a week after that. As one row matures and is harvested, the other two continue to grow. So instead of all your lettuce maturing at once, it's stretched over many weeks. Some plants, like lettuce and spinach, can also be planted in the spring and then again in the fall.

Some of the plants that work well with repetitive planting include the following:

Basil	Lettuce
Beans	Parsley
Corn	Peas
Dill	Spinach

Plants with a long growing season, such as tomatoes, melons, and pumpkins, aren't good candidates for repetitive planting. To extend your harvest period, plant several varieties of these plants with different growing times, and you'll be able to pick for weeks instead of days.

Success with Succession Planting

Even with lots of effort and many repetitive plantings, some plants just peter out and are finished early in the growing season, leaving you with empty space in the garden. It's a shame to waste that space. That's where *succession planting* comes into play.

Native Americans were the first to practice this method of planting. They planted "the three sisters"—corn, beans, and squash—together on the same hill. The corn grows up at about the same rate as the beans, and the beans use the corn as a kind of living trellis. The squash grows at the base of both the beans and corn, keeping the soil cool and shading out weeds. The beans mature quickly and the plant dies back as the corn begins to ripen. The squash continues to grow happily below. It's a beautiful relationship!

Another good example is planting beans with peas. The peas go in very early in the spring. While they're growing, you can plant beans among them. By the time the beans begin to grow, the peas are finished for the season and the beans climb up over the poles or netting.

Prof. Price's Pointers

Succession planting is planting different crops with differing rates of maturation in the same spaces at the same time; or the same crop, but different varieties with different maturation rates, at the same time; or two or more types of crops with different maturation rates planted at the same time; or the same crop but planted at timed intervals for successive harvests.

Planting onion sets among larger, slower-growing plants to be harvested young as scallions before they start to interfere with their larger neighbors is a good example of interplanting, which is very similar to succession planting.

For successful succession planting, be sure the plants you use have the same nutrients, pH, and moisture requirements.

Square-Foot Gardening

We looked at square-foot gardening briefly in Chapter 2, so let's take a closer look now.

Square-foot gardening is frequently done as a raised bed, although that's not a requirement. The garden is laid out in 4×4-foot sections (or squares of similar dimensions). Each of these sections is then further divided into 1-foot squares. The sections are best marked with string and little stakes. (Popsicle sticks work well.)

Each square is designated for a plant or type of plant. For example, lettuce might go in one square with a mixture of radishes and carrots in another. A third square would provide space for a few onion sets, and the fourth one could be planted with three or four basil plants. Or you could devote four squares for one tomato plant.

Square-foot gardening …

- Provides efficient use of space.
- Requires careful planning.
- Requires loose, fluffy, rich soil.
- Requires regular fertilizing.
- Results in cooler soil due to intensive planting.
- Requires less watering than gardens with exposed soils.
- Has fewer weeds.

This approach to gardening is ideal for gardeners with limited space and time.

Planting in Mulch Cloth

Mulch cloth is a layer of plastic fiber material used to create a planting environment that warms the soil, retains moisture, and deters weeds. The cloth creates a barrier that plants can't break through, which is how it keeps weeds from growing. But if weeds can't grow there, how will your vegetable plants?

Here's how:

1. Using a measuring tape, or your own good estimation, measure your spacing.

2. With stakes, spray paint, chalk, or stones, mark the spots where each planting hole will go.

3. Using a utility knife, cut an X in the cloth, fold back the cloth, dig a planting hole with a trowel or your hand, insert the seedling, and tamp down the soil.

4. Fold the flaps of mulch cloth back down around the seedling, but just away from the stem.

Garden Guru Says

It's easiest to plant seedlings, as opposed to seeds, in mulch cloth. Small mounds with a couple seeds, like zucchini or melons, work well with mulch cloth, too. But rows of seeds would require a long slit in the cloth, which is not ideal.

Later in the season, when the weather has warmed up considerably, spread mulch on top of the mulch cloth to help keep the soil temperature from rising too high and "cooking" your plants.

The Least You Need to Know

♦ Neat garden rows help you keep track of what's a vegetable and what's a weed.

♦ Vining and sprawling plants grow well in mounds.

♦ Make furrows for rows of plants that require a deeper planting hole.

♦ Transplant seedlings after the sun goes down to help them get a good start.

♦ You can use square-foot gardening in small spaces to get the most bang for your gardening buck.

♦ Maximize garden efficiency with succession planting.

♦ Planting in mulch cloth helps keep down weeds.

Part 4

What to Plant

In Part 4, you learn about the different kinds of plants you might want to consider growing in your garden. The hardest part of putting together this information was having to leave out so many interesting and wonderful vegetables. There just wasn't room to include them all.

(If you go to some of the websites or books listed in the Appendixes, you'll find additional suggestions for interesting plants you can include in your garden.)

Planting the Basics

In This Chapter

- ◆ Growing salad greens
- ◆ Tomatoes straight from your garden
- ◆ The skinny on cucumbers
- ◆ All about squash and pumpkins
- ◆ Bountiful bean info
- ◆ Getting corn-y

Your idea of "basic" vegetables might differ from mine. It all has to do with what you grew up on and what you've become used to. So in this chapter, I'm going to make some generalizations. I think salad fixings are about as basic as you can get. And quite frankly, I can't imagine a garden without at least one tomato plant. Corn and beans are also right up there as first-tier basic foods, as are squash varieties. In this chapter, we look at the art and science of growing these vegetables.

We also talk about soil requirements, planting techniques, and some of the idiosyncrasies that make growing these edibles so much fun.

Salad Stuff

We take our salads very seriously today. Think about it: many grocery stores and restaurants feature salad bars. And even McDonald's offers a variety of salads on their menu.

Salad expert Karan Davis Cutler, a guest editor for the Brooklyn Botanic Garden's publication *Salad Gardens*, discovered that salads have been around for a long time. She found a reference to an English salad recipe dating to 1390 that called for herbs, greens, onions, and leeks dressed with oil, vinegar, and salt. That sounds pretty familiar. Other recipes include even more raw ingredients like lettuce, sorrel, purslane, mustard, flower petals, and turnip greens.

In this section, we look at basic salad ingredients like lettuce, tomatoes, cucumbers, and radishes.

Let Us Grow Lettuce!

Food historians have found that the Babylonians grew lettuce more than 3,000 years ago. It might have been big with the pharaohs, and it was certainly a popular vegetable with the ancient Greeks. It's even more popular today. On average, Americans eat more than 30 pounds of lettuce per person each year. If you grow it yourself, you might wind up eating even more than that.

Lettuce, whose Latin name is *Lactuca sativa*, falls into four general categories:

- Leaf or loose-leaf
- Semi-heading or soft-heading
- Heading or crisp-head
- Cos

Leaf lettuces are the easiest to grow. They're quick to germinate and fast to mature. Some varieties can go from seed to salad bowl in as little as 3 weeks. Diverse varieties range from pale green to dark red and can be frilly, crinkly, knubbly, or smooth.

The most common varieties of soft-heading lettuces are Bibb, Boston, and Buttercrunch, which have small, loosely formed heads. Soft-heading lettuces are almost as easy to grow as loose-leaf varieties.

You can harvest semi-heading lettuce a few leaves at a time or by cutting the entire head at the base with a sharp knife.

©iStockphoto.com/Visionsurf

Iceberg lettuce is the best-known crisp-head lettuce. It's the one you see most in the grocery store and in plain-Jane salads. Cos lettuces include romaine and endive.

Dozens of varieties of lettuce fall into these four categories, including the following:

Bibb	Iceberg
Black-seeded Simpson	Italian chicory
Blush Batavia	Mache (a.k.a. corn salad)
Boston	Mesclun
Butterhead or Buttercrunch	Oak leaf
Chicory	Purslane
Curly endive or escarole	Romaine
Deer tongue	Speckled troutback
Four seasons	Winter red
French or Belgian endive (a.k.a. witloof chicory)	

Grow a few different ones, or sow a mix of varieties together. You'll want to grow like varieties together so that planting, maintenance, and harvesting are easier.

Garden Guru Says

To harvest loose-leaf lettuce, simply pick the largest leaves, breaking them off right at the base. You can also harvest individual leaves from soft-heading lettuces, taking just a few outer leaves at a time. Or pick the entire head by slicing it off at the base of the stem. Use the same procedure for harvesting crisp-heading varieties.

Large head lettuces like iceberg and romaine should be grown about 12 inches apart in rows that are 2 or 3 feet apart. Smaller head lettuces such as Bibb, Boston, and Butterhead and loose-leaf lettuces should also have about 1 foot between each plant. But the rows can be closer together, perhaps 1 or 2 feet. Loose-leaf lettuces can also be planted intensively with little or no spacing. Harvesting young, tender leaves provides room for the remaining leaves to grow.

Seedlings are readily available at nurseries and garden centers, but growing lettuce from seed is really easy. It also gives you the opportunity to experiment with many different varieties, especially the ones you'd never find at the grocery store.

Lettuce seeds require light to germinate, so sow them on the surface of a prepared bed of loose, rich soil with plenty of organic matter. Gently pat down the seeds, and water with a fine mist. Don't allow the soil to dry out, but avoid letting it become soggy.

Sow new lettuce seeds every week or so until the weather gets very hot, and again when it starts to cool off. That way you'll have a nearly continuous supply.

You Say *Tomato*, I Say *Tomahto*

Tomatoes (*Lycopersicon lypersicum*) might very well be the favorite vegetable of American gardeners. Yet as late as 1820, many people believed tomatoes were poisonous. Thomas Jefferson was one of the first people to grow tomatoes as an edible rather than an ornamental. If I could grow only one vegetable in my garden it would be a tomato plant. There's nothing like picking a ripe tomato on a hot day and eating it right there in the garden.

Plant breeders have been messing around with tomatoes for years. They've managed to make faster-growing, uniformly shaped, and pest-resistant varieties, but the resulting tomatoes have also become less and less tasty. This is particularly true of commercially grown tomatoes. Fortunately, many of the tomatoes available for home gardeners still retain the flavors we like so much, including some of the rediscovered heirloom varieties.

Tomatoes fall into a number of categories, described more or less by use (slicing, plum or paste, and cherry or grape), by season (early, mid, and late), and by vine type (determinate or indeterminate). The characteristics for determinate and indeterminate varieties are as follows:

Determinate Tomatoes	Indeterminate Tomatoes
Vine ends in fruit	Keeps forming new vine
No new fruit after first fruit ripens	Keeps forming new fruit
Smaller plants	Bigger plants
Grows in smaller spaces	Needs lots of space
Doesn't always need staking	Needs staking or caging
Produces early in season	Produces later in season

Tomatoes are also differentiated by color, ranging from yellow to orange, and pink to burgundy. When selecting tomatoes to grow in your garden, you'll want to consider all these factors.

To start tomatoes indoors, sow seeds about 8 to 10 weeks before the last predicted frost date in your area. Then harden off for about 2 weeks. (Remember hardening off from Chapter 11?)

Plant seedlings, whether your own or store-bought plants, with 2 or 3 inches of stem under the soil. The stem will soon sprout roots that help stabilize the plant and make it stronger. Place the plants from 1¹/₂ to 3 feet apart, depending on the variety.

The number of days from planting to maturity can range from a short 59 days (Early Girl) to as long as 95 (Aunt Ruby's Green). Maturation times for other popular varieties include 78 (Big Boy), 70 (Super Sweet 100), and 80 days (Viva Italia).

Tomatoes are heavy feeders and need fertilizer every 2 or 3 weeks. Use the formula suggested on the fertilizer packaging.

Cool as a Cucumber

Cucumbers are members of the cucurbit family, whose relatives include melons, squash, chayote, and gourds. A native of India, cucumbers arrived in the New World with Christopher Columbus and are now, of course, a salad staple. In fact, according to a report by the U.S. Department of Agriculture, Americans eat more than 3 billion pounds of cucumbers a year!

Prof. Price's Pointers

Cucumber vines produce both male and female flowers. The first flowers are staminate, or male, and simply fall from the plant without becoming fruit. The second flowers are both staminate and pistillate, or female, allowing pollination to occur. Some newer varieties are gynoecious or only female. These plants need some staminate plants planted nearby for pollination to occur.

Although popular with backyard gardeners, cukes aren't the easiest veggie to grow. They're a bit fussy about soil, need a lot of water, and are susceptible to pests and disease problems. But even with those few negatives, growing cucumbers can be very satisfying.

There are three basic types of cucumbers: slicing, pickling (both *Cucumis sativus*), and gherkin (*Cucumis anguria*). Slicing and pickling varieties are available in bush and vining form, although vines are far more common. Slicing varieties tend to have thicker skins than the pickling types and are generally larger.

Garden Guru Says

Thicker skins contribute to cucumbers' "burp" factor. Some gardeners favor the "burpless" varieties, which are usually longer and thinner than standard cukes and have a thinner skin.

Plant cucumber seeds or seedlings outdoors after all danger of frost has passed. They like very rich, well-cultivated soil with a pH in the 6.0 to 7.0 range. Cucumbers don't take kindly to transplanting. If you start seeds indoors, use biodegradable planting pots so you don't disturb the tiny roots when it's time to set them out.

Sow cucumbers in hills with about 4 or 5 seeds or plants per hill. Seeds should be planted about $1/2$ to $3/4$ inch deep. Allow 4 to 6 feet between hills. If you prefer row planting, allow the same distance between rows with about 2 or 3 feet between each plant. Cukes can also be trained to grow up a trellis or netting. Or you can use tomato cages; in that case, make smaller hills with just 1 plant per hill.

Expect cucumbers to take about 40 to 60 days from seed to maturity, depending on the variety.

Plan on a fertilizing program beginning with an application about 1 week after the first flowers appear and continuing every 3 or 4 weeks. Keep your cucumbers well irrigated, and never let them dry out. A thick mulch around the roots helps hold moisture in and keeps the soil a little cooler when the weather gets steamy.

Be sure to harvest your cucumbers as they mature. If you leave ripe fruit on the vine, the plants will stop producing.

Rows and Rows of Radishes

One of the fastest-growing vegetables, and great for introducing kids to the joys of gardening, radishes are also among the easiest vegetables to grow.

Radishes are almost always grown from seed. They prefer cool weather, so it's best to plant them as soon as you can work the soil in the spring. The soil should have a pH of 5.8 to 6.8 and it should be well cultivated and well drained. If you plan to grow the long varieties like daikon, white icicle, salad rose, or Chinese white, be sure to cultivate the soil down at least 8 to 10 inches.

Plant seeds in shallow furrows, about $^1/_4$ to $^1/_2$ inch deep. If you plant more than 1 row, make the rows about 1 or 2 feet apart. Radish seeds are very small and are usually sold in large quantities (Burpee packs about 300 to 400 seeds per packet, for example), so you can sow them in a slow dribble along the furrow. Then when the seeds begin to sprout (it usually takes less than a week), you can thin the seedlings to about 8 to 10 inches apart.

Sow additional radish seeds every week until the weather gets hot. Then start again in the late summer or early fall for fall harvesting. Harvest them before they become woody and overly hot.

The Three Sisters

In Chapter 12, we talked a little about the three sisters, the Native American concept of growing squash, beans, and corn together. In this section, we take a closer look at these three plants.

Squish, Squash

Pumpkins and all kinds of squash are members of the cucurbit family and relatives of melons and cucumbers. They're generally vining plants and tend to grow very large.

Just about all squash (and we use that term to include pumpkins for our purposes here) require a fair amount of growing room.

In American gardens, the most commonly grown squash types include summer and winter varieties. The summer types mature earlier in the season and tend to have thinner skins than the winter varieties. Many of the winter varieties, including pumpkins, can be stored for several weeks or even months, which is one of the reasons they were an essential staple of Native Americans and early settlers in America. The following list should help you understand the summer and winter types:

Summer Squash	Winter Squash
Crooked neck	Acorn
Straight neck	Buttercup
Zucchini	Butternut
	Lakota
	Spaghetti
	Patty pan
	Pumpkin

Squash are relatively easy plants to grow; many varieties are downright prolific. The vines grow from 6 to 15 feet long, depending on the variety. Although many of the summer varieties grow in bush form, they still need a lot of space.

Squash are generally grown on large hills with 2 or 3 seeds or seedlings per hill. Give each hill about 6 to 8 feet of space all the way around the hill. Summer squash needs about 40 to 50 days from seed to maturity. The winter varieties take much longer, with maturation times of 70 to 100 days, depending on the variety. The soil must be nice and warm when seeds or plants are first planted.

All types of squash require regular watering and should never be allowed to dry out. About a month after planting, feed the plants with a low-nitrogen fertilizer. Then follow up with a feeding every 2 or 3 weeks.

Bushels of Beans

Beans are another one of those really easy vegetables to grow. No garden should be without a crop of them. There are three types of beans: snap beans, shell beans, and dry beans.

Beans probably originated in South America and have become a staple all over the world. The dry beans—like kidney, pinto, great northern, navy, and black eye—are fully mature bean seeds that are harvested and dried for future use. They're not generally grown in home gardens but rather as crops on farms. Snap beans are young beans harvested before their seeds mature, whereas shell beans are harvested when the seeds are almost mature but still tender. We limit our discussion here to snap and shell beans.

Prof. Price's Pointers

Snap bean is the newer name for what we used to call string beans. Plant breeders have bred beans without the strings that used to run along the "seam" between the two halves of the beans, so now they are more or less stringless and have a new name.

Both shell and snap beans are available in bush or pole (climbing) varieties. They aren't particularly fussy about soil, as long as the drainage is good. The pH should be in the 5.8 to 6.3 range. Sow the bean seeds in shallow furrows about 1 inch deep and 2 or 3 inches apart. Water gently. Don't worry about fertilizing unless the leaves begin to yellow or if the plants don't seem to prosper.

Snap beans include green or string beans, wax beans, Italian snap beans, filet beans, and scarlet runner beans. You could start them indoors, but there's really no need to. Snap beans are incredibly quick to germinate, emerging 7 to 10 days after planting. Just be sure to wait a week or two after your last predicted frost to plant. These beans take about 40 to 50 days from seed to harvest.

The most commonly grown shell beans are limas and favas. They are grown the same way snap beans are, although their maturation time is considerably longer—about 70 to 85 days, depending on the variety.

Beans produce more if you harvest them diligently. The more you pick, the more prolific they become. And beans have a tendency to mature all at once, so it's a good idea to plant several varieties with varying maturation rates, or to sow new seeds every week for a month or so. This prolongs the harvest.

Everybody Loves Edamame

Edamame is growing in popularity as a home garden crop. Edamame is a soybean that's harvested while still green and is often served in Japanese restaurants. It's delicious as a snack food (boil them in the pod in salted water and then pop out the seeds) or can be used like a lima bean in soups or stews or as a side dish.

Planting edamame is similar to planting bush beans. Edamame likes rich soil with lots of organic matter. Because the plants' roots are able to fix nitrogen, which means they can take nitrogen from the atmosphere and convert it to a more usable form like nitrates, you won't have to feed them much during the growing season. The key is in inoculating the seeds—that is, treating the seeds with a bacteria that allows the roots to fix nitrogen. You can buy the seeds already inoculated or do it yourself.

Edamame is ready for harvest when the pods are slightly rounded with seed.

©iStockphoto.com/Brian Wathen

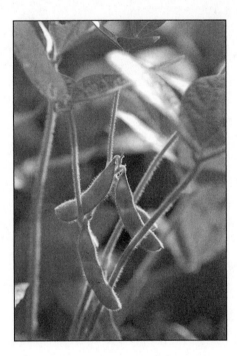

For more information on growing edamame, go the National Soybean Research Laboratory's website at www.nsrl.uiuc.edu/aboutsoy/edamame.html.

Can-Do Corn

An all-American meal isn't complete without corn on the cob. And I don't mean just modern America. Corn, which is, by the way, a member of the grass family, was the main staple for Native Americans going back centuries. It's thought to have originated in Central America some 80,000 years ago and was one of the first crops to be cultivated in the New World.

Today's corn is very different from that early native corn. Plant breeders have developed new varieties that are sweeter, bigger, more prolific, and more resistant to pests and diseases than ever before.

Corn is grown as three types that are genetically different: normal sugary, sugary enhancer, and supersweet. They each contain genes that control the sugar content and texture, tenderness, and color of the kernels. Many varieties must be isolated from each other so that cross-pollination doesn't cause the plants to revert to undesirable characteristics. Generally speaking, home gardeners prefer the sugary enhancer hybrids because of their high sugar content and the pleasing texture and tenderness of the kernels—and because they don't need to be isolated from other types of corn.

Garden Guru Says

Most corn is wind pollinated. To be sure the pollen blows onto all the tassels of your corn crop, make short rows in a block rather than just a few long rows.

Corn is a relatively heavy feeder so be sure to amend your soil with manure or a nitrogen-supplying cover crop. Because of its need for nitrogen, corn is not the most eco-friendly crop you can grow. If you plan to have corn, think about planting a green manure, otherwise known as a cover crop, in that part of your garden to help reduce the amount of nitrogen you'd otherwise need to add to the soil.

Good drainage is important, too. Plant seed corn in furrows about 1 inch deep when the soil has reached at least 60 degrees Fahrenheit. Corn is one plant that doesn't mind really hot weather, so you can keep planting every week or so well into the summer. Just keep in mind that you'll need 60 to 90 days until the corn is ready to harvest.

Although corn will survive dryer weather than many vegetables, it must have regular irrigation. Weed control is also important, but use care when cultivating around corn plants, as the roots damage easily.

The Least You Need to Know

- Leaf lettuces are easy to grow. Sow new seeds every week or so as long as the weather isn't hot for a long harvest season.

- By providing tomato plants with a soil rich in organic matter, you'll have a healthy crop to harvest.

◆ Keep cucumbers well watered for the best cuke results.

◆ Radishes are easy to grow.

◆ Give squash plenty of room to spread out, and they'll be happy plants.

◆ Keep up with bean harvesting to encourage the plants to continue production.

◆ Early Americans grew corn, and so can you—with some care and tending.

Chapter 14

More Great Veggies

In This Chapter

- ◆ Meet the cabbage family
- ◆ Go green with leafy greens
- ◆ Perfect peppers and peas
- ◆ Expand your eggplant expertise

In this chapter, we look at a few more great vegetables. These could easily have been in the previous chapter on basic vegetables because they're not that far from "basic," but there just wasn't enough room to put them there and do them justice.

In the next few pages, we look at members of the cabbage family, including broccoli, cauliflower, and brussels sprouts, and peas, peppers, eggplants, and leafy greens.

The Cole Family Album

Let me introduce you to the cole family, also known as *Brassica oleracea*—and just to confuse things, also sometimes known as the *Cruciferae* family or *Crucifers* for short. Members of the cole family include cabbage, broccoli, cauliflower, kale, brussels sprouts, Chinese cabbage, and kohlrabi.

Garden Guru Says

Cabbage family plants are prone to quite a few ailments and are a big target for destructive insects, many of which linger in the soil. To avoid using harsh chemicals to control pests and diseases, try to change your cabbage patch location in the garden every couple years. This is called *crop rotation*.

The *Brassicas*, which are sometimes referred to generically as the cabbage family, originated as Old World plants, with some, like cabbage, beloved by ancient Egyptians and Romans, Russians, and many others for the past 2,000 years. In this section we talk about all these family members except kale, which is discussed later in this chapter, and Chinese cabbage and kohlrabi, which are covered in the next chapter.

All the *Brassicas* prefer rich, well-drained soil with lots of organic matter like compost or well-rotted manure worked in thoroughly. With the exception of cauliflower, they're all cool-weather plants and are pretty tolerant of a fairly broad pH range of 5.5 to 7.0.

You can start most *Brassicas* from seed indoors about 4 to 6 weeks before setting out, or plant them directly in the garden about 1 inch deep … but why bother? Unless you're planning on growing heirloom or specialty varieties, young plants are readily available.

Give the plants a good feeding when you set them out and then again every 3 weeks or so after that.

Colorful Cabbage

Cabbage (*Brassica oleracea capitata*) is sort of the mother of all *Brassicas*. It's very easy to grow, and I think the big, fat heads look beautiful in rows in the garden, especially if you plant a variety of green, red, Chinese, and Savoy varieties. Be prepared though: if you have a large crop, you might find that cabbage has a certain, well, stink.

Cabbage seedlings should have four complete sets of leaves before they're transplanted. Set them out, or plant seeds, as early as you can work the soil for a summer harvest, or in early summer for fall harvest. Plant them deep, with the stem buried right up to the first set of leaves to encourage root development along the stem. Plant cabbages $1^1/_2$ to 2 feet apart, or more if you're growing any of the giant varieties.

To harvest, use a sharp knife to slice straight across the base of the stem.

Cabbage and kale grow among peppers and fennel in this diverse and densely planted garden.

©iStockphoto.com/Adrian Assalve

Compost Pile

Insects love cabbages, so it's difficult to grow them without using some kind of insect intervention. *Mother Jones* magazine suggests planting dill and chamomile around cabbages (as well as leeks and onions) to deter pests. And the Kentucky State University Organic Agriculture Working Group has had success spraying cabbage plants with the bacterium *Bacillus thuringiensis* (Bt). It kills cabbage worms and seems to discourage flea beetles.

Blooming Cauliflower

Cauliflower (*Brassica oleracea botrytis*) used to be the wimp of the cole family. It didn't like cold weather and couldn't take the heat either. Plant breeders have taken cauliflower to new levels with weather-tolerant early and late varieties and some that are bred to overwinter in the ground for spring harvest. Cauliflower produces old-fashioned white "curds" (heads) as well as purple and green ones.

Even with the newer varieties, cauliflower isn't the easiest plant to grow. It prefers a pH of 6.5 to 7 and requires lots of rich organic matter in the soil. Cauliflower has trouble setting its curds if irrigation is irregular.

Set out cauliflower plants about $1^1/2$ to $2^1/2$ feet apart in rows about $2^1/2$ feet apart. Feed them with a high-nitrogen fertilizer when you plant and then again every couple weeks. With overwintering varieties, stop the feeding program at first frost and pick up again when the weather warms.

To harvest, use a sharp knife to slice through the stem at the base.

Bunches of Broccoli

When my older daughter was little, she would eat an entire head of broccoli for dinner. It's one of our family's favorite vegetables. (Apparently that's not the case for former president George H. W. Bush, though!) Broccoli has a delicious flavor to begin with, and the homegrown stuff is fabulous. Although not as fussy as cauliflower, it's still not the easiest vegetable in the world to grow.

Set out plants with at least one full set of leaves after the last frost, allowing about $1^1/2$ feet between plants. If you start from seed, plant them about 1 inch deep. Feed transplants with a high-nitrogen liquid fertilizer and then repeat every 3 weeks or so.

We eat the unopened flower buds of the broccoli plants, so harvest when the buds are still tightly closed. If they start to open or produce little yellow flowers, you've waited too long. Cut the buds with a bit of stem using a sharp knife. The broccoli plants will send out new bonus stems with buds a little later.

Brussels Sprouts

How brussels sprouts got their name is a little murky. It seems they were popular in Belgium in the 1700s. There's surely more to it than that, but no one seems to be able to come up with the final answer. There is pretty good documentation, however, that Thomas Jefferson imported some seeds from Europe to grow at Monticello in 1812. Today, American vegetable farmers produce about 70 million pounds of brussels sprouts each year.

You can add to that poundage by growing them in your garden. It's not very difficult. Give them a soil pH of about 6.5; lots of organic matter; and a long, cool growing season. Plant seeds indoors about 4 or 5 weeks before setting them out in late spring or early summer. Or plant them directly in the garden.

Brussels sprouts require 70 to 110 days to mature and are best when harvested in cool or even cold weather. Some varieties overwinter for a spring harvest. When the sprouts look like little cabbages, cut the long stems off at the bottom with a sharp knife. You can let the brussels sprouts grow longer and larger if you want. The smaller they are, however, the sweeter.

Leafy Greens

Health experts tell us to eat plenty of leafy green vegetables. If you grow your own, eating them will be easy, not to mention a pleasure.

We discussed salad greens in Chapter 13, so here we look at kale, spinach, and chard.

Cold-Hardy Kale

As mentioned earlier, kale is a member of the *Brassica* family (*Brassica oleracea sabellica*). It's one of the most cold-hardy leafy vegetables grown in North America.

Kale does best when grown in very rich, well-drained soil with lots of organic matter and a pH of 7.5 to 8.0. Plant seeds individually about ¹/₂ inch deep or broadcast them for intensive planting. Do this as soon as you can work the soil for spring harvest and in early fall for a late fall harvest. In warm areas, kale is a winter crop.

Kale requires regular, thorough irrigation and feeding every 2 weeks or so with a high-nitrogen fertilizer.

Food for Thought

Years ago in my New Jersey garden, I harvested some incredibly delicious kale in February from under at least 6 inches of snow! Kale's flavor actually improves when it's harvested after a frost.

This super-nutritious crop is one of those plants that keeps on giving. You can harvest individual leaves as soon as they are 6 or 7 inches long, or allow them to grow larger. The plants will continue to produce leaves for months.

Popeye's Favorite: Spinach

Popeye scarfed down a can of spinach when he needed to supersize his muscles. I don't think canned spinach has much of a market share these days, but the popularity of fresh spinach is on the rise because of its amazing nutritional benefits.

Spinach (*Spinacea oleracea*) is a relatively easy vegetable to grow as long as you keep it cool and well fed and provide it with a rich soil with plenty of organic matter and a pH of 6.4 to 7.0. Sow seeds about $^1/_2$ inch deep and 2 inches apart as soon as you can work the soil. You can also broadcast seed in a small area for intensive planting, covering them with a light layer of soil. Some gardeners even broadcast spinach seed over frozen ground, leaving the seeds to germinate when the snow thaws.

Prof. Price's Pointers

Spinach has a tendency to bolt. This is an undesirable early maturity of leafy plants whereby they rush through their life cycle to the flowering and seed-producing stage. This is typical of spinach, lettuce, and radishes and usually happens when the weather gets too warm for them. When the plants have bolted, they are inedible.

Water spinach regularly and thoroughly, and feed it every couple weeks with a high-nitrogen fertilizer. Harvest by thinning the plants to about 4 to 6 inches apart and picking individual leaves of larger plants. You can also harvest whole plants by pulling them, roots and all, from the row.

Spinach is one of the few vegetables that will tolerate some shade.

If you plan to grow spinach to enjoy mostly in salads and as "baby spinach," choose one of the smooth leaf varieties. The kind of spinach Popeye preferred (boiled and canned) is a curly leaf type. Both can be grown in the home garden.

Chard

One of the prettiest of all vegetables, chard is often overlooked for anything more than a garnish. What a mistake! When picked nice and young, chard leaves are a delicious addition to a salad, and more mature leaves are a tasty alternative to spinach.

Chard has thick, celerylike stems and large, thick leaves. Some varieties, like so-called rainbow chard, are very colorful with red, yellow, burgundy, white, or green stems and veins. Chard, whose Latin name is *Beta vulgaris var. cicla*, is a relative of the beet. It's easy to see the resemblance in the red-veined varieties.

Chard prefers a high pH, in the 6.5 to 7.0 range, and rich soil with plenty of organic matter. This is a cool-weather plant, so you can sow seeds outdoors 2 to 4 weeks before the last predicted frost date. Plant the seeds $^1/_2$ to $^3/_4$ inch deep and just a couple inches apart.

As new chard plants appear, you can harvest them for salads by thinning the plants to about 6 to 8 inches apart. Later, harvest outer leaves as they grow. As with kale, chard will continue to produce new leaves as you harvest the older ones.

Chard wilts in really hot summer weather but does well in cool fall temperatures. If you baby it along during the dog days, it will reward you later.

Pick a Peck of Peppers

Christopher Columbus, bless his exploring ways, gave peppers their name when he first bit into a hot chile pepper on arrival in the New World. (Remember, he thought he had found a new route to the Spice Islands, and he believed he had discovered a brand new kind of spice pepper.) Peppers, hot and sweet, originated in South or Central America, found their way to Europe via Columbus, and eventually were exported to Asia, where they caught on big time.

Peppers fall into two general categories: sweet and hot. Dozens of varieties are available, including the following:

Anaheim	Jalapeño
Cayenne	Pepperoncini
Cherry	Poblano
Chiltepin	Serrano
Green sweet bell	Sweet banana
Habanero	Thai dragon
Huasteco	Yellow, orange, or red sweet bell
Hungarian wax	

Peppers prefer well-drained and well-cultivated soil that ideally has a pH of 6.0 to 6.8, although you won't see much difference with more acidic soil. Space pepper plants from 1^1/$_2$ to 2 feet apart. Peppers should be well irrigated but do poorly in soggy conditions.

You can also plant pepper seeds indoors 8 to 10 weeks before the last predicted frost date, but that's a long time to tend seeds indoors. Most people prefer using seedlings.

Prof. Price's Pointers

Capsaicin is a substance peculiar to peppers that we taste as pungent (hot). Several genetic factors control the level of capsaicin, which determines the level of hotness of specific pepper varieties.

As soon as the pepper plants begin to set tiny fruits, apply a high-nitrogen fertilizer according to the package directions and then feed every 2 or 3 weeks. Mulching around pepper plants is also a good idea, as it keeps moisture in and weeds out. Peppers take 60 to 80 days from the set-out date to first harvest. Pick the peppers as soon as the fruits are ripe to encourage more production. Do it gently, using garden snips. Most peppers keep producing until frost.

Sweet pepper varieties include green, red, orange, and yellow varieties. The green types stay green even as they mature. The colored varieties, which have high levels of carotenoids (the same ingredient that makes carrots orange), are green in their immature form and then take on the bright color at maturity.

Exotic Eggplants

Eggplants (*Solanum melongena*) used to be considered a fairly exotic plant, but they've become much more commonplace in the last 25 years or so. Old World natives, eggplants are members of the nightshade family (*Solanaceae*) whose relatives include New World plants like tomatoes, potatoes, and peppers.

Food for Thought

Black plastic mulch isn't my favorite product, but eggplants seem to do really well with it. The black plastic absorbs the sun's heat and keeps the soil temperature high, which is right up an eggplant's alley. The plastic also keeps moisture in and weeds out.

Eggplants are very tender plants and have no tolerance for cold weather, which isn't surprising, considering they probably originated in India. Eggplants need lots of long, hot days to thrive. They also like a soil with a pH of 6.0 to 6.8.

Most gardeners start with seedlings, setting them out a week or 2 after the last predicted frost. If you have the patience, you can start seeds indoors about 8 to 10 weeks before the set-out date. Be sure to use biodegradable planting pots to avoid disrupting the roots during transplantation. Give eggplants 1 or 2 feet of space between plants.

Eggplants require regular irrigation, particularly when the weather gets very hot. Give them a dose of high-nitrogen fertilizer at planting time, follow up with another feeding when the first fruits appear, and then feed again every 2 or 3 weeks. Use the formula on the packaging.

Begin harvesting your eggplants when they're at least $1/3$ their mature size (these are baby eggplants which cost a fortune in gourmet stores) up to fully ripe. If you leave them on the vine too long, they'll become bitter. Keep up with harvesting to encourage production, and use garden snips to avoid breaking the stems. Eggplants have sharp, thorny growths on their stems and calyx (the little green "cap" at the top of the fruit) that can prick your fingers, so wear gloves when you harvest.

If you like eggplant, you might want to experiment with several different varieties, such as those in the following table.

Variety	Shape	Color	Skin
American	globular and/or elongated	dark purple	thick
Chinese	long, thin	pale purple	thin
Filipino	elongated	green to purple	thin
Green	elongated	green	thin
Heirloom	various shapes	green, white, or shades of purple	thin
Indian	small, round	purple	thick
Italian	short, wide, or elongated	dark purple	thick
Japanese	thin, elongated	light to dark purple	thin
Mini	small, elongated	shades of purple	thin
Thai	tiny, round	green, yellow, or white	thin
White	egg shape or round	white	thin

Peas, Please

Natives of China (or maybe the Middle East), peas have been an important staple for thousands of years. But for most of that time, peas have been dried after harvest for later use. It wasn't until sometime in the 1600s that a clever European snacked on some raw peas and started a whole new culinary trend.

Peas fall into three categories:

- ◆ Snow peas
- ◆ Snap or edible-podded peas
- ◆ Garden, shelling, or English peas

Each of these types is relatively easy to grow and makes few demands on the home gardener. Peas prefer a well-cultivated, neutral to slightly acidic soil, ideally with a pH of 6.0 to 6.7. If your soil is more acidic than that, the peas won't mind too much. What's far more important is that the soil be well drained. Although they must be watered well and regularly, peas hate to have wet feet.

Sow pea seeds outdoors in the early spring. St. Patrick's Day is the traditional pea-planting time in northern zones. In zones 9, 10, and 11, peas are a winter crop. The seeds, which are tiny, should go in a shallow furrow about 1 inch deep and about 2 or 3 inches apart.

Snow Peas

Snow peas are the delicious edible pods so familiar in Asian stir-fry dishes. They require anywhere from 55 to 70 days from seed to harvest and should be picked when they're still young, small, and flat.

Snow peas will climb pea netting or a small trellis about 2 to 4 feet tall, depending on the variety. Look for one of the newer stringless varieties when you buy seed.

It's a Snap

Snap peas are more or less a cross between snow peas and garden peas and are grown for their edible pods. But the big difference between snap peas and snow peas is that the snap peas develop little peas in the pod. They're usually eaten raw in salads or cooked in stir-fries. Some snap pea varieties are bushy and don't require a support, whereas others climb a bit up netting or a trellis.

Pick snap peas just as the little peas develop. If the harvesting gets ahead of you, you can shell the snap peas just like garden peas, but they won't have that sweet, delicate flavor.

A Garden of Pea Delights

There are dozens of varieties of garden peas from which to choose. These peas are also called English or shelling peas. They've been bred for early or late season harvest, so you might want to mix several varieties to stretch out the picking time.

Most garden peas grow from 1$\frac{1}{2}$ to 3 feet tall and need some support. Most prefer cool weather and rapidly die back when the weather gets hot. Some newer varieties have been bred to be more heat tolerant.

Pea Shoots, Pea Scores

Also called pea greens, pea shoots are delicate little tendrils that are becoming increasingly popular with high-end chefs and in-the-know gourmet cooks. They're very hard to come by in regular grocery stores, and they're very expensive in the specialty shops that do carry them. Their delicate flavor is a fresh and welcome addition to salads, and they make a very tasty garnish. Although their season is relatively short, and they won't thrive in hot climates, you'll be happy you made the effort to grow some extra peas just for their shoots.

To encourage pea plants to send out lots of shoots, start pinching back leaf buds on the plants when they get about 1 foot tall. Also pinch off the flower buds—but remember, no flowers, no peas.

> **Food for Thought**
>
> Oregon State University Extension (extension. oregonstate.edu—look at Gardening Hints in the Gardening section) sells a publication devoted to growing pea shoots and also offers lots of helpful information in an online article.

The Least You Need to Know

- The cabbage family includes cabbages, cauliflower, broccoli, brussels sprouts, kale, and kohlrabi.

- Good-for-you kale can be harvested very late, even after a snowfall.

- Spinach bolts when the weather gets hot, so plant a second crop for fall harvest.

- Add some of the more unusual eggplant varieties to your garden repertoire.

- Grow peas for their delicate shoots as well as for the tasty pods.

Chapter 15

Back to Your Roots

In This Chapter

◆ Growing spuds

◆ Digging in to sweet potatoes and yams

◆ The real dirt on rutabagas, turnips, beets, and parsnips

◆ The original rabbit food: carrots

◆ Introducing onions and their relatives

In this chapter, it's time to get back to our roots and learn all about root vegetables. These are, for the most part, the solid, basic starch vegetables that play such a big part in our images of old-fashioned holiday dinners. Think Thanksgiving and potatoes, turnips, rutabagas, parsnips, beets, carrots, sweet potatoes, and onions. They're all here. All that's missing is the turkey.

Super Spuds

Potatoes (*Solanum tuberosum*) are an ancient food, dating back thousands of years to their *roots*, if you will, with the Incas in Peru around 200 B.C.E. From there they traveled with the Spanish conquistadors back to Europe in the fifteenth century.

Potatoes have become the world's largest food crop, beating out rice and corn (at least according to a potato trade association). The United States produces 35 billion pounds of potatoes every year, and we eat them in prodigious quantities.

Potatoes are classified in a number of ways based on their size, skin color, flesh color, harvest time, starch level, use, and shape. Some of the descriptions include the following:

- Early, second-early, and main crop
- Round, long, oval, and oblong
- Yellow and white flesh
- Thin and thick skin
- White, red, russet, brown, pink, yellow, blue, and purple skin
- High, medium, and low starch
- Baking, chip, french fry, mashing, and all-purpose

You might want to grow several different kinds, especially the unusual varieties that are so expensive to buy in stores.

Compost Pile

Planting your potato patch in the same part of the garden each year can introduce or spread diseases or pests. If you can, move it around from year to year.

Home gardeners generally start their spuds from seed potatoes, which are very small tubers with several eyes on each one. Be sure to buy only certified seed potatoes. You can use potatoes from your pantry that have grown some eyes, but if it's sickly looking, toss it.

Get seed potatoes ready to sprout by warming them up a bit and exposing them to sunlight for a few days. A bright window in a warm part of the house will do.

Plant potatoes in the spring when the soil has warmed to about 45 degrees Fahrenheit or just before the last predicted frost. But if tender young plants have appeared and a heavy frost is predicted, be prepared to run out with newspapers, blankets, row covers, or straw to protect them. Otherwise, they won't stand up to a heavy frost.

Give your potatoes a well-drained, well-cultivated bed with loamy soil, rich with organic matter. Potatoes like a pH of 5.8 to 6.5, but they'll tolerate anywhere from 4.7 to 7.0.

You can grow potatoes in mounds or in rows. If you choose rows, make a furrow about 4 inches wide and 6 inches deep. Cut the seed potatoes into 1½-inch chunks with at least one eye per chunk, and plant them spaced according to the size of the potato you plan to harvest. For example, if you want full-size potatoes, plant the seeds 10 to 15 inches apart. If you're planning on harvesting a lot of baby potatoes, place them every 4 inches.

You can easily harvest potatoes grown in mounds or furrows with a garden fork.

©iStockphoto.com/Arkady Slavsky

Put the seed potatoes cut side down in the hole and fill it ½ full with soil. When you see little plants push through the soil, add more soil. Keep doing this as the plant grows, but don't cover the foliage after it develops. Just keep adding soil to cover the stem. Potatoes grow just under the soil, but they should never be exposed to the sun. (Young potatoes exposed to too much sunlight will turn green. A toxic substance, causes the color change and makes them inedible, so toss them on the compost pile.) The continual soil additions as the spuds grow help avoid sun exposure.

Give the potatoes a regular, thorough watering, but never allow the soil to become soggy or you'll wind up with rotten potatoes.

Food for Thought

Grow potatoes in old tires? Sure! Simply add a tire on top of the first potato as you mound the soil over the stem. Or you can grow potatoes in double-thick, black plastic garbage bags. Just punch a few holes for drainage.

They'll manage better with too little water than with too much. As for feeding, give them a low-nitrogen fertilizer so they don't put too much energy into their leaves.

You can harvest your potatoes by hand, a few at a time, beginning about 2 or 3 weeks after the flowers have fallen off. The remaining potatoes will continue to grow, and by picking the larger ones from each plant, you can encourage the plants to produce more tubers. Do this gently, by hand, feeling around in the soil, without pulling up the plants. Or wait until all the leaves have died back and then carefully pull the spuds out of the soil. But take care because they damage easily.

For really comprehensive information on growing potatoes organically, read the article from the University of California, Davis at www.vric.ucdavis.edu/veginfo/commodity/potato/organic_potatoes.pdf.

Sweet Potatoes and Yams

Sweet potatoes aren't really potatoes, and yams aren't really yams. Confused? Let me explain.

Although sweet potatoes (*Ipomoea batatas*) look a lot like potatoes, they belong to the morning glory family and are native to Central and South America. Yams are another species all together, hail from Africa, and aren't grown in the United States. The confusion came when sweet potato growers introduced the orange-fleshed varieties and began calling them yams to distinguish them from the more familiar pale-yellow-fleshed earlier varieties.

Sweet potatoes are a warm-weather crop that requires a long, hot growing period. They like well-drained loamy or sandy soil that has been well tilled. Many sweet potato growers create raised hills to grow them in.

Start with seedlings (called slips) that have been certified as disease free. After all danger of frost has passed, plant the slips about 4 inches deep and 8 to 12 inches apart in raised rows. Feed with a liquid fertilizer, and water regularly. Sweet potatoes take from 100 to 150 days to mature, so if you live in a cooler climate, you might want to hurry things along a bit by using black plastic mulch. It raises the soil temperature substantially and also keeps the weeds down. Weeding is important in the early stages of the sweet potato's life, but eventually the vines will sprawl all over the place and crowd out any interlopers.

Garden Guru Says

Rotate your sweet potato crop to another part of the garden every 2 years to avoid introducing or spreading diseases and pests.

Harvest the sweet potatoes before the first frost. First cut back the stems and leaves and then gently sift through the soil with a garden fork. Sweet potatoes are fragile, so if you have a small crop, do this task by hand.

Turnips and Rutabagas

Turnips and rutabagas are members of the *Brassica* clan, cousins of cabbages and kale. The Latin name for the turnip plant is *Brassica rapa*. Rutabagas go by *Brassica napus*. They are very similar plants, with many of the same growing requirements and preferences.

They both prefer a loose, well-prepared soil with a pH of about 5.5 to 6.8. Raised beds provide an excellent environment for turnips and rutabagas because they do best when the soil is prepared to a depth of at least 1 foot. You might also consider working in some superphosphate a few months before planting to promote strong root growth.

From the Turnip Truck

Plant turnip seeds indoors 3 or 4 weeks before the last predicted frost date. Outdoors, seeds can go in 4 to 6 weeks before that date. Place them in holes $1/2$ inch deep and a couple inches apart. Thin to about 4 inches apart when the seedlings are a few inches tall. You can use the thinnings as greens. Successive sowings 2 weeks apart will give you a longer harvest season for both the tops and the roots.

A second planting in late summer provides a fall crop as long as you can allow about 80 days for them to grow. A late crop might actually have an improved taste, although the flavor will not get better with exposure to frost.

Turnips appreciate a layer of mulch to keep weeds down and moisture in.

You can harvest individual turnip leaves without jeopardizing the root as long as you don't injure the crown. Harvest the roots any time after they mature. There aren't too many varieties, but each one has a slightly different maturity time so you'll want to consult the seed packet. Remember that smaller roots have a better flavor and more pleasing texture.

Food for Thought

According to Irish folklore, the first jack-o'-lantern wasn't carved out of a pumpkin. Some fellow named Jack put a candle in a hollowed-out turnip. Or maybe it was a Swedish turnip, a.k.a. rutabaga.

If you're more interested in the turnip greens than the roots, add a bit more nitrogen to the soil to promote leaf growth.

Rutabagas (a.k.a. Swedish Turnips)

If you've read many English novels, you might have seen a mention or two of people eating *swedes* for dinner. These aren't stories about cannibals! Europeans refer to what we in the United States call rutabagas as swedes, which is a shortened version of the full name, swedish turnips. Rutabagas are actually a cross between a cabbage and a turnip.

Turnips have a small, round or elongated root; rough, hairy leaves; white flesh; and a tinge of purple at the neck. Rutabagas have a large, round root; smooth, blue-green leaves; and yellow flesh.

Rutabagas are cool-weather plants with a very long growing period. They require 80 to 100 days from seed to harvest, depending on the variety and the growing conditions. Generally, rutabagas are planted in early summer for a fall harvest. They are grown from seed planted $^1/_4$ to $^1/_2$ inches deep about 6 inches apart.

The flavor of rutabagas is improved when the plants have been exposed to a light frost or two. And you can leave them in the ground well into the winter if you give them a light blanket of mulch.

Better Beets

Cultivated since prehistoric times, *Beta vulgares*, better known as beets, were originally grown for their green tops. It was the Romans who began eating the round, red roots.

Today, there are many types of beets, including these:

Baby	Round
Cylindrical	Striped red and white
Gold	White

Beets like well-drained, well-cultivated soil with plenty of organic matter and a neutral pH (6.0 to 6.8 is best). To help with root development, mix in some superphosphate well before planting. Beets prefer cooler weather and tend to bolt quickly if temperatures get too hot for their tastes. If you live in the South, try to find some of the heat-tolerant varieties for your garden.

Start beets from seeds right in the garden as soon as the soil can be worked in the spring. You can plant again in the late summer for a fall harvest. Plant the seeds evenly in a shallow furrow about $1/2$ inch deep. When the new plants have a few leaves, thin the seedlings to about 2 or 4 inches apart and use the thinnings as greens for salad.

Sow beet seeds successively to extend the harvest period. Beets are ready to harvest whenever you think they're large enough. But don't let them get oversized, even the larger varieties, because they'll be woody and tough.

Pokey Parsnips

Pastinaca sativa, parsnips to you non-Latin speakers, is part of the *Umbelliferae* family whose relatives include carrots, celery, fennel, parsley, and chervil. No one seems to be exactly sure where parsnips came from, but they were around for the ancient Romans to enjoy way back when. And in the Middle Ages, parsnips were used as a meat substitute during Lent. Although they don't taste a bit like meat, they do have a heavy, satisfying quality that might have felt like meat to serfs. (After all, who knows what kind of meat they were used to!)

Parsnips look a little like thick, white carrots. They are another cool-weather crop that takes a long time—16 to 20 weeks—to mature.

As with all the root vegetables, parsnips prefer their growing environment to be well drained and deeply cultivated. Many gardeners grow parsnips in an area of the garden with soil that was improved the previous year. Parsnips do best with a pH of 6.5 to 7.0.

Parsnips have an aversion to too much nitrogen, so don't add any to the soil where you plan to plant parsnips. If the soil is too rich, parsnips will produce poor-quality roots that might split, fork, or grow unappetizing hairs.

Plant seeds in the garden in early spring to early summer, and be prepared to wait a long time for the new seedlings to appear—it might take a couple weeks. In fact, parsnips are notoriously slow to germinate. Many gardeners grow radishes in among the parsnips so they know where the parsnips are. Radishes germinate quickly and are harvested well before the parsnips need the space. Plant the parsnip seeds about $1/4$ inch deep, 2 to 4 inches apart in rows that are from $1^1/2$ to 2 feet apart.

Prof. Price's Pointers

Parsnips and turnips have a sweeter flavor after they've been through a heavy frost or two because the plants respond to the cold by storing more sugar in their roots.

Parsnips are ready to harvest when the foliage has died back. Let them stand through a few hard frosts to improve the flavor. You can also keep them in the ground over the winter if you cover them with a layer of mulch. Because parsnips are biannual plants (see Chapter 16 for an explanation), they push out new growth in the spring. If you overwinter your parsnips, harvest them before any new growth appears or they'll lose all their flavor.

Uh, What's Up Doc?: Carrots

Bugs Bunny's penchant for carrots (*Daucus carota*) is a latter-day thing in the history of food. Carrots have been around for 5,000 years, although in colors and forms we might not recognize today. The orange thing Bugs loves was developed, legend has it, in the sixteenth century by Dutch horticulturists who wanted to honor the royal House of Orange.

After potatoes and onions, carrots are probably the most popular root vegetable in the United States, grown in gardens everywhere. As with all the root veggies, carrots like well-drained, deeply cultivated soil.

Carrot seeds are tiny, so they're a bit of a challenge to grow. Try mixing the seed with some sand to help with the sowing. Carrots are usually planted in the spring, and sometimes again for a fall crop. Scatter the seeds over a prepared bed and cover with a light layer of soil. You'll have to thin them, so plant far more than you think you'll need.

Keep carrots well watered. Harvest when they're the size you want.

The Allium Family Album

Onions, leeks, garlic, chives, and shallots are all members of the Allium family and are also distant relatives of lilies. We've already learned (in Chapter 10) that the bulb part of the onion and its cousins are not actually bulbs at all but are in fact a collection of modified leaves that live underground in the form of a bulb. But for our purposes here, we'll just call them bulbs.

A parterre-type garden with raised beds requires an investment of time and resources, but pays off with low maintenance and a high yield.

©iStockphoto.com/James Camp

You don't need acres of ground or even a backyard to raise vegetables. Here, a clever gardener has reclaimed the strip between street and sidewalk to grow veggies.

©iStockphoto.com/Joe Klune

Perfectly prepared soil—made light and fluffy with rich organic matter—almost guarantees that your vegetable plants will grow and thrive.

©iStockphoto.com/Don Nichols

Cultivating the soil carefully by hand around tender young plants helps avoid damage. Even a tiny nick on a stem can make the plant vulnerable to diseases and pests.

©iStockphoto.com/Denis Pogostin

A backyard vegetable garden needn't be limited to rows of plants. Many gardeners easily mix flowers and edibles in unruly groupings, with beautiful results.

©iStockphoto.com/Peter Eckhardt

Good garden hygiene, including careful weeding, is key to keeping your garden healthy.

©iStockphoto.com/Jure Porenta

A vegetable garden is a great place for new adventures. Try growing something new like these elegant Japanese eggplants.

©iStockphoto.com/Alison Stieglitz

We all have different motivations for growing vegetables, but in the end, it's all about freshness.

©iStockphoto.com/Tobias Helbig

The long stems of hardneck garlic are often braided so the garlic can be hung to dry.

©iStockphoto.com/Chris Fertnig

If you grow your own zucchini, you can harvest these beautiful squash blossoms to serve sautéed, lightly breaded, or stuffed.

©iStockphoto.com

Think about adding heirloom vegetables to your garden. By preserving old varieties, you can help strengthen the plant world's gene pool and promote biodiversity.

©iStockphoto.com/Liza McCorkle

Rhubarb stalks look like beautiful red celery. The raw stems are tart when they're young and thin, but as they mature, they turn remarkably bitter.

©iStockphoto.com/Stefan Fierros

©iStockphoto.com/Darren Wise

Mulch is a must in an organic or earth-friendly garden. It keeps down weeds and retains moisture, and when it breaks down, it adds nutrients to the soil.

©iStockphoto.com/Gaffera

Basil and other herbs grow happily in containers. Just be sure to grow plenty—there's nothing like the taste of fresh herbs.

If you only do one earth-friendly activity in your garden, let it be composting.

©iStockphoto.com/Phill Danze

Bees are essential to successful gardening because they are the chief pollinators. Keeping your own bees is one way to ensure a healthy bee population

©iStockphoto.com/Brendan Hunter

Crying Over Onions

Humans have been eating onions for thousands of years. And every year they seem to want more. According to the National Onion Association, 105 billion pounds of onions are produced worldwide each year. Americans, on average, eat 18.8 pounds per person annually. But that's nothing compared to Libyans, who consume a whopping 66.8 pounds per capita each year!

Onions prefer a soil pH of 6.5 to 6.8 but tolerate a pH level as low as 5.5. As with most of the plants we've been looking at, onions like the soil to be well drained with plenty of organic matter to help with moisture retention and boost fertility. Onions are also heavy feeders requiring fertilizing when the young plants are a few weeks old and then again in a month or so.

The common, everyday onion (*Allium cepa*) is white, yellow, or red in color and varies from sweet to strong flavored. The bunches are small, with green stems, and the shape of the onion is either a round or flat globe. You can grow some such as Egyptians as annuals or perennials and use them fresh or store them for later.

Onions are grown from seeds, sets, or seedlings, generally in the early spring as soon as the soil can be worked. Scallions, which are also called green onions, can also be planted in the late summer or early fall for additional harvests.

Prof. Price's Pointers

Plant scientists and agriculture experts call the length of the day or the number of daylight hours in the day the **photoperiod**. Knowing the photoperiod requirements of the plants you want to grow helps you determine when and what to plant.

Scallions or green onions can be grown as simply immature white onions or from seeds or seedlings specifically designated as scallions. Burpee, for example, offers a variety called Evergreen Long White Bunching Scallion that takes 60 to 120 days to mature from seed sown in spring or summer for harvest in fall through the winter.

Plant onion seeds about $1/2$ inch deep, or place sets about 2 inches below the soil. Allow 3 to 5 inches between plants, depending on the variety you're planting.

You can harvest onions at almost any time after the bulb has formed to use fresh. Onions to be harvested for storage should be left in the ground until the leaves have dried up. Then they must be "cured" or dried. Get instructions for curing onions from your county extension office.

Great Garlic

If you have any experience with Italian, French, Mexican, or Chinese cooking, you've worked with garlic. It originated somewhere in Asia, but people from all over the world claim it as their own.

The biggest difference between garlic and its onion cousins is that the bulb (which, as we know isn't really a bulb) is actually a grouping of cloves that fit together forming the shape we recognize so easily. The other difference is in the leaves. The leaves of onions, leeks, scallions, chives, and shallots are hollow, like straws. But the garlic leaf is flat.

There are three basic kinds of garlic:

- Common or softneck (*Allium sativum*)

- Stiffneck or hardneck (*Allium sativum ophioscorodon*)

- Elephant (*Allium ampeloprasum*)

As with onions, garlic is a heavy feeder and appreciates a rich soil enhanced with organic matter and fertilizer. Plant seed cloves in early spring in northern zones or as a fall or winter crop where the weather is warmer. Plant the small cloves $1/2$ to 1 inch deep and 3 to 5 inches apart.

Softneck garlic will grow in many climates, but the hardneck varieties are fussier. They don't like hot weather and do best where it is cool.

Elephant garlic is an extra large type. An individual clove can be as large as an entire head of it's relatives, although the flavor is mild and almost sweet.

Harvest softneck garlic when the green tops have dried up and fallen off. Hardneck garlic, which is often preferred by chefs and gourmet cooks, produces a curly green stem that should be cut before it straightens and forms a flower at the end. This helps divert the plant's energy from flower formation to bulb growth. The stems, called scapes, are an ephemeral treat—add them raw to salads or use them in stir-fries. Some people even make a garlic scape relish.

Sowing Shallots

These elegant little members of the onion clan are *de rigueur* in French cuisine and add a delicate flavor to all kinds of dishes. They aren't grown all that often in the home garden, but they should be—they aren't particularly difficult and don't take up much space.

The long stems of hardneck garlic are often braided so the garlic can be hung to dry. Store fresh garlic that hasn't yet dried in the refrigerator.

©iStockphoto.com/Chris Fertnig

Shallots (*Allium ascalonicum*) have the same basic requirements as other onions. New plants are grown from sets and planted as early as the soil can be worked in cool zones or as a fall or winter crop in warm parts of the country. Plant the sets pointy end up about ¹/₂ to 1 inch deep and 3 to 5 inches apart.

Harvest shallots when the foliage begins to die back.

Leeks (a.k.a. Poor Man's Asparagus)

The leek (*Allium porrum*) is the national symbol of Wales, but in France, it's known as the poor man's asparagus. Although still not an everyday vegetable in the United States, leeks' popularity is growing as Americans become more adventuresome in their cooking and eating.

Leeks look like scallions on steroids. They have thick stems that are white at the bulb end and become increasingly green toward the leaf part. The bulb never actually develops but stays about the same width as the rest of the stem. The stem must be blanched before it will turn white.

Leeks are generally grown from seed, which can be planted indoors about 10 to 14 weeks before they're set out in early spring.

To plant the seedlings, dig a narrow trench about 6 inches wide and 1 foot deep. Place each leek transplant upright in the trench, spacing them about 4 inches apart, and add just enough soil to hold them upright. Water thoroughly, but don't fill in the trench. As the leeks grow, add more soil so the stem is nearly covered. Keep on filling the trench as the plants grow, eventually hilling the soil up so just a couple inches of green stem show.

Allow anywhere from 12 to 15 weeks for leeks to mature for harvest. Try growing a few extra plants to harvest early as baby leeks.

The Least You Need to Know

- ◆ Don't allow young potato tubers to be exposed to the sun. If they are, and they turn green, throw them out.

- ◆ Harvest rutabagas after they've experienced a light frost or two for enhanced flavor.

- ◆ Don't give parsnips a very rich soil.

Chapter 16

Growing Herbs

In This Chapter

- ◆ Easy-to-grow culinary herbs
- ◆ Annual herbs to grow from seeds or seedlings
- ◆ Perennial favorites
- ◆ Exotic and esoteric herbs
- ◆ Growing herbs with medicinal powers

It didn't take long for our ancestors to figure out that certain plants taste good or satisfy hunger, some plants improve the taste of food, others make folks feel sick, and still others make them feel better when they're under the weather. Obviously this sequence of discovery didn't happen overnight, but took only several thousand years. Eventually, someone developed the bright idea of growing all those feel-better and taste-better plants, and the concept of the herb garden was born.

Today, herb gardening is one of the most popular forms of gardening— and one of the easiest. Herbs will grow in poor soils, thrive with a minimum of care, and generally take up far less space than most vegetables. In this chapter, we explore growing a wide variety of herbs, from the culinary basics to exotic specialty types, as well as those known for their curative powers.

Easy and Essential Herbs

There are a few herbs no good cook can do without. Can you imagine a world without basil or parsley? And what's a baked potato without a few snips of fresh chives? I can't bear the thought of iced tea without a few sprigs of fresh mint to liven it up. These four essential herbs are among the easiest of all herbs to grow.

Partial to Parsley

Parsley (*petroselinum crispum*) is the number one essential herb. Cooks of every persuasion use both the curly variety and the flat-leaf Italian type to enhance just about any food you can imagine.

Food for Thought

Grow your herbs in a spot that's convenient to the kitchen for easy harvesting.

This biannual plant is easy to start from seed especially if you soak the seeds overnight. In cooler zones, start the seeds inside about 7 weeks before the last predicted frost.

In warm areas, sow outside directly in the garden. When the seedlings are a couple inches tall, you can thin them to about 3 inches apart. If you're pressed for time (or just lazy!), buy young plants.

With its 2-year life span, parsley can survive in cold conditions. I actually picked parsley in the snow in my zone 5 vegetable garden, although it can become a little bitter and tough in its second season.

Because parsley is so easy to grow from seeds or seedlings, most gardeners treat it as an annual.

Basil Is Best

Known officially as sweet basil or *Ocimum basillicum*, this easy-to-grow annual herb is essential in Italian cooking. Several varieties are available, including a very pretty purple type. But the medium-green classic variety is the one to grow for making pesto and spaghetti sauce and to serve with fresh tomatoes and mozzarella cheese. I begin to drool just thinking about it.

In cold climates, sow basil seeds thinly (about 8 or 10 seeds per inch) indoors in mid-spring. Plant seeds directly in the garden as soon as temperatures are reliably over 50 degrees Fahrenheit.

Set out seedlings when they have four leaves and after all danger of frost. As the plants grow, pinch back the tops to make them bushier. Also pinch back any flower buds as they form to encourage the basil to keep producing leaves. And always grow lots of it. You'll need handfuls to make fresh pesto.

Much Ado About Mint

I'm including mint in this selection of easy and essential herbs mostly because mint is easier to grow than just about any plant I can think of. Mint is a perennial herb. In fact, we can include mint in the "invasive plant" category, meaning you can't get rid of it even if you want to. But a little bit of mint is, as Martha would say, "a good thing."

The two most common varieties of mint are spearmint and peppermint. You might also find apple, pineapple, and orange flavored mints. All are available as seedlings.

Garden Guru Says

To prevent mint from taking over the entire garden, place plants in plastic or terra-cotta pots and plant the pots. Leave a bit—about an inch or two—of pot rim above the surface of the soil. Every few years, dig it up and replace the pot with a larger one, adding more soil. Or unpot the mint, trim back the roots, and repot with fresh soil.

Another method for growing mint is from a root cutting. (Ask someone with mint growing in his or her yard for a handful of roots.) Just stick a bit of the root with some stem and leaves attached into a pot with some soil, water it, and stand back.

Crazy About Chives

Think of chives as itty, bitty onions, because that's exactly what they are. Chives are especially easy to grow, unless you insist on starting them from seed. But why bother? Chive plants are easy to find. And once you have a mature clump or two growing in your herb garden, you can divide them to produce more (see Chapter 22). You'll need to divide them every 3 or 4 years to keep the clumps healthy anyway.

When planting, place chives about 1 foot apart as soon as the soil can be worked. To harvest, snip the hollow stems at their base.

Chives produce pretty, papery, pink blooms, which are very decorative in the herb garden, in pots, or among other perennials. They're also edible. This is one herb plant you can allow to bloom without sacrificing flavor.

One at a Time

As you've most likely figured out by now, some herbs are annual plants, or go through their entire life cycle from germination to flowering and seed production in a single year. The following annual herbs are among gardeners' favorites.

Delightful Dill

One of the tallest herbs we'll look at in this chapter, dill can reach 4 feet, though there are dwarf varieties. Feathery dill leaves are used to flavor pickles and fatty fish like salmon. The seeds are also used as a flavoring. I love cucumber and onion salad with sour cream and lots of dill.

Growing dill from seed is a bit of a pain in cold zones. The seeds can't be planted outside until the last frost, but they need about 3 weeks to germinate, so you wind up waiting well into the summer season to harvest.

And because dill doesn't transplant very well, starting the seeds indoors is iffy unless you start the seeds in peat pots, eggshells, or homemade paper starting cups. The seeds need light to germinate, so lay them directly on top of the soil. Be sure to do successive plantings every couple weeks until the weather gets too hot. Dill hates hot weather.

I prefer to buy dill as seedlings so I can start harvesting it early. I also like to use it as a decorative addition to pots of flowers on my terrace.

Garden Guru Says _____

Some herbs are known for their insect repellant qualities and can be helpful in the garden as well as in the house. Dill, chives, oregano, sage, borage, coriander, rosemary, hyssop, and mint are among the most effective. Plant the herbs among the most susceptible vegetables for a little natural assistance. For a comprehensive list of which plant repels what insect, visit www.rexresearch.com/agro/comp1.htm.

Cilantro (a.k.a. Chinese Parsley or Coriander)

Unless you've been living in a cave for the last 10 years, you probably already know about cilantro. It's an essential ingredient for Mexican and Chinese cooking and another relatively easy-to-grow annual herb. I say *relatively easy* because it does have one little quirk—cilantro hates hot weather.

The seeds germinate in about 10 days, so there's no need to start them indoors. Instead, plant them outdoors after the last frost and then start a new crop every couple weeks. The plants will grow quickly until the heat gets to them. Then they'll either stop growing and look awful, bolt to flower, or die.

Not to worry. As soon as the weather cools a little in the early fall, start another crop. In places like Arizona, Florida, or South Texas where summer temperatures soar, consider cilantro a winter herb.

Food writers, by the way, almost always refer to the leaves of this plant as cilantro and the seeds as coriander.

Summer Savory

More gardeners should grow this great herb. It's easy to start from seed indoors (about 2 months before the last frost), although it takes up to a month to sprout. The seeds need light to germinate, so place them on top of the soil. You can also grow this herb from cuttings. The easiest way to add summer savory to your herb garden is to buy small plants, although you aren't likely to find them everywhere.

Plant seeds and plants in a good potting soil with some compost added because this is one herb that likes a richer soil than most.

Summer savory is very versatile in the kitchen. It tastes a little like thyme but a bit spicier. Use it to add flavor to meat, fish, poultry, beans, eggs, and potatoes.

Summer savory grows to almost 2 feet and might need to be supported (see Chapter 11).

Fabulous Fennel

The herb fennel is a totally different plant from the Florence fennel grown for its bulb, though both share that delightful anise flavor. In fact, fennel is sometimes referred to as anise.

The herb fennel grows easily from seed in ordinary or even sandy garden soil. Plant it after the last frost, and it germinates in about 2 weeks. To keep the leaves looking their best, pinch out flower buds regularly. A few weeks before the first frost of fall, you can allow the flowers to bloom and then collect the seeds to use for winter cooking, to flavor fish, chicken, and pasta dishes and to add an anise flavor to baked goods.

In warmer zones (although not where it's really hot), fennel behaves like a perennial.

Chic as Chervil

No French chef could survive without a source of fresh chervil to use in salads and as a flavoring for meat, poultry, fish, vegetables, eggs, and vinegar. It's also an essential ingredient for the herb blend *herbes fines.*

But it's still not a household herb in the United States, even though it's so easy to grow.

Start the seeds outdoors in spring as soon as the soil is workable. Like dill seeds, chervil seeds need light to germinate. New sprouts appear in about 2 weeks. If you find you like using chervil in your cooking, plan on making successive plantings so you have a steady supply.

Like cilantro and dill, chervil hates the heat, so avoid new plantings in very hot weather. Unlike most herbs, chervil tolerates shade. In fact, it prefers a shady location, and it doesn't like to dry out.

> **Garden Guru Says** _____
>
> To help herb plants produce the tastiest and most aromatic leaves, use fertilizer sparingly. It's better to underfertilize than to use too much. Follow mixing directions on the product label, but don't use it as often as prescribed. Or mix the fertilizer at half-strength and use it according to the suggested schedule. If you're making your own fertilizer, water it down to a weak solution.

Perennial Favorites

One of the most beautiful herb gardens I've ever seen is at Sissinghurst Castle in southern England. It's a huge square intersected by flagstone paths and surrounded by a tall hedge. And it's *full* of perennial herbs—including such culinary varieties as thyme, rosemary, and sage—that form a gorgeous tapestry of colors, shapes, and textures.

Perennial herbs are the aristocrats of the herb world. As important as parsley and basil are, somehow the perennials described in this section are a step above.

They're also a boon for thrifty souls. Buy a few of these plants (or start them from seed), and you can enjoy the harvest for years.

Oh, Oregano!

You can't make spaghetti sauce, pizza, or an Italian hoagie without this pungent perennial herb. Oregano (*Origanum onites*) is easy to grow from seed, germinating in just 8 to 10 days. But it needs a pretty long growing season before the leaves are ready to harvest. So in cold areas, start seeds indoors 6 to 8 weeks before the soil can be worked. In warmer zones, they can go directly in the garden. Plants are also easy to find.

Oregano is a low-growing herb, never reaching more than about 18 inches tall. It spreads rapidly but doesn't become invasive like mint. Divide oregano plants every 3 or 4 years to keep them full. Frequent harvesting also encourages lots of new growth.

Oregano might need a little bit of protective mulch in very cold climates, unless there's continuous snow cover.

Food for Thought

You can find several varieties of oregano available in seed catalogs and nurseries, including Spanish, Mexican, and Cuban. But when cooking Italian, use the Greek type (go figure!).

Sage Savvy

For years I neglected a large sage plant that just refused to die. Originally I planted it so its silvery color would complement the bright annuals in a large container. The savory, mint-flavored leaves were just a bonus for flavoring poultry and fish dishes. After 3 years in the pot, I pulled it out because it had become too large. It then sat in a corner of the garden, where I had dumped it without any sort of proper planting. After about a year of this abuse, it finally succumbed. I don't recommend this kind of treatment. But it does prove just how tough sage is.

Sage, whose Latin name is *Salvia officinalis,* prefers dry conditions with a slightly alkaline soil, but don't go out of your way to meet these needs. You can sow sage seeds outside as soon as the soil is workable or start them indoors about a month earlier. The seeds sprout in a week or 2. Young plants are readily available, too.

Sage produces spikes of pretty purplish-pink blooms that are very attractive to bees. Pinching out buds forces the plant to put more energy into its leaves. Or you can look for one of the bloomless varieties such as Dalmatian or Berggarten, although they might not be easy to find.

Time for Thyme

Sissinghurst Castle (which is sort of a mecca for gardeners), has another herbal wonder—a large walkway completely carpeted with thyme plants. The concept is that when you walk on the springy, low-growing lawn of thyme plants, the fabulous scent is released. It's quite a romantic, although impractical, design.

Thyme (*Thymus vulgaris*) is an important herb for French cuisine. And although it's usually used sparingly because of its strong flavor, no herb garden should be without at least one plant. Look for English or French thyme for the basic flavor.

Garden Guru Says

Specialty nurseries sell orange-, lemon-, caraway-, and even coconut-flavor thymes for the gardener who has everything.

Grow thyme from cuttings, or buy small plants. They like dry conditions and require a light soil. Pinch a few sprigs regularly to encourage healthy new growth, and be prepared to replace tired plants after 3 or 4 years.

King Tarragon

The French call tarragon the king of herbs, and we should be paying attention. It is used to flavor poultry, fish, and cheeses and is essential for creating béarnaise sauce.

Creative cooks also make flavored mayonnaise, butter, vinegar, oils, and mustard with tarragon, which is called *Artemisia dracuinculus* in Latin. But it's important to use only French tarragon for these things. The very common Russian form of the herb is all but flavorless.

Tarragon is a bushy herb that grows to 2 or 3 feet in height and width. It doesn't mind very poor soil and likes dry conditions. It's hardy even in very cold climates as long as it has excellent drainage. Be prepared to divide or replace tarragon every few years.

Tender and Tasty

Among the most-often used culinary herbs are a few that are part of a class of plants known as tender perennials. This means that they live for several years as long as they're protected from cold weather. Some are more tender than others.

Fragrant Rosemary

If tarragon is the king of herbs, rosemary is the queen. If they could choose only one herb to grow, more than a few cooks would select this exquisitely aromatic herb used to flavor poultry and meats, especially lamb and pork, and vegetables.

Don't even attempt to grow rosemary from seed. It's too hard. You can buy young plants at any good garden center. You can start new plants from cuttings, but it's still easier to buy young plants. Rosemary isn't too fussy about soil as long as it's well drained. Be diligent about not overwatering, and give your rosemary plants plenty of room and good air circulation—they're prone to mildew.

What's really important to remember is that this plant won't survive winters in any-place cooler than zone 8. But if you live where it's warm, you can have rosemary shrubs up to 6 feet tall.

Garden Guru Says

To grow rosemary in cool places, keep it in pots so you can bring it inside easily. Put the pot in your sunniest window, or even consider using a grow light during the short winter days. Water your rosemary sparingly, letting it dry out between waterings, and never let the pot sit in standing water. Use a mister to keep humidity levels high.

The Noble Bay

Another of the herb world's aristocrats, bay leaf (a.k.a. sweet bay or bay laurel) has a long history, going back to ancient Rome and Greece. (Think of the laurel wreath around Caesar's head.)

In warm areas (zones 8 to 10), bay grows as an evergreen tree that can reach 10 feet or so. Everywhere else, it's grown as a potted plant. Bay grows slowly and can be kept to a manageable size with root pruning.

Don't bother trying to start a bay plant on your own. Buy an established one and be prepared to baby it for a long time. This means a slightly acidic soil (a pH of 6.2 or so), full sun indoors, afternoon shade outdoors, careful attention to watering (don't let it dry out but don't let roots become water logged), and moderate amounts of fertilizer.

Bay leaf is used to flavor soups, stews, shellfish dishes, and a variety of sauces.

Sweet as Marjoram

A close relative of oregano, sweet marjoram has a slightly stronger flavor and is less hardy (except for another cousin, pot marjoram). It grows in nice, neat clumps to about a foot or two high and is evergreen in zones 8 to 10.

Marjoram can be grown indoors from seeds started about 6 weeks before the last hard frost or from cuttings. Plants are easy to find, too. This herb prefers a more alkaline soil in the pH range of 7 to 8.

For the best flavor, pinch back flower buds as they form. And to keep the plant nice and bushy, harvest small sprigs of leaves frequently.

Not Your Everyday Herb

Dedicated foodies as well as ambitious gardeners might enjoy experimenting with some other herbs that might not be as well known or as often grown as the traditional parsley, sage, rosemary, and thyme.

Thai One On with Lemongrass

If you like to cook Thai or Southeast Asian food, lemongrass is a must. A tropical perennial, lemongrass is grown as an annual everywhere except in the hottest climates. Start new plants by dividing existing ones, or look for young plants to buy.

Lemongrass plants tend to need a richer soil than most herbs, and they like slightly more moist conditions. You can bring these plants indoors before the weather gets cold and they'll do pretty well. A grow light and regular misting helps.

Food for Thought

Cats like to chew on lemongrass leaves—which could be a plus or a minus, depending on your point of view.

High on Hyssop

Hyssop is a really old-fashioned herb, one that was grown by the ancient Hebrews and perhaps even earlier. Known mostly for its medicinal properties, the fresh leaves of the hyssop plant are also used to flavor salads and soups and to make tea.

Hyssop is a very hardy perennial that can stay evergreen even in severe cold climates. Where winter temperatures regularly drop below 0 degrees Fahrenheit, you might need to use a thick layer of mulch. It grows to about 3 feet high and about half as wide.

Start seeds indoors about 2 months or so before the last predicted frost. Hyssop can also be grown from cuttings or by dividing existing plants.

Expect to replace hyssop plants every 4 years or when they become very woody and rangy.

Borage Is Not Boring

Borage is an annual herb with cucumber-flavored leaves that are used in salads or to flavor meats and vegetables. The crunchy stems and the beautiful blue flowers are also edible.

Plant seeds or seedlings outdoors after the last predicted frost. New sprouts appear in a week or so. Do successive sowings every 2 or 3 weeks for a steady supply until it gets very hot.

Other Exotic or Esoteric Herbs

If the preceding sections weren't enough to get you interested in growing your own herbs, the following table might be all you need to make the decision.

Herb	Usages	Annual or Perennial
Anise	Licorice-flavored leaves, seed, and flower	Annual
Curry plant	Curry flavor	Tender perennial
Horehound	Used for teas and candy	Tender perennial
Lovage	Celery-flavored seeds and leaves	Perennial
Mexican mint marigold	Substitute for tarragon	Tender perennial

continues

continued

Herb	Usages	Annual or Perennial
Mitsuba	Japanese wild parsley	Perennial
Shiso	Tastes like mix of cilantro, cumin, and parsley	Annual
Winter savory	Spicy seasoning for meat, fish, and poultry	Perennial

A Taste of Your Own Medicine

Before herbs were stirred into the cook pot to flavor foods, they were used to cure every kind of illness from headache to insomnia. Some medicinal uses were nothing more than quackery, but many continue to be reliable alternatives to what we now consider traditional medical practice.

A word of caution: some herbs can cause allergic reactions or can become toxic in combination with certain foods or substances. If you plan to use herbs as alternative remedies, you'll want to do some more reading so that you'll have as much information as possible.

The following table contains just a few of the many herbs used for medicinal purposes.

Herb	Medicinal Use
Calendula	Heals wounds
Chamomile	Encourages sleep; cures upset stomach
Chervil	Skin freshener
Chicory	Diuretic; laxative
Clary sage	Treats eye ailments
Comfrey	Skin care
Feverfew	Stops migraine; helps with digestion
Horehound	Cures sore throat; helps with digestion
Hyssop	Expectorant; cough suppressant
Italian parsley	Diuretic
Lemon verbena	Encourages sleep

Herb	Medicinal Use
Lovage	Eases intestinal gas
Rosemary	Headache cure
Sage	Reduces fever
Tansy	Treats worms
Tarragon	Antibacterial
Thyme	Helps with digestion; antiseptic
Valerian	Sedative; pain relief

Windowsill Herb Gardens

Fresh herbs are an essential ingredient of fine cooking year round, but I hate to pay grocery store prices for a bunch of rosemary, basil, or tarragon in the winter. And even more annoying, I have to buy a whole bunch even when I only need a few sprigs. The rest winds up rotting in the vegetable drawer of the fridge—an expensive mess.

Instead of overpaying and wasting, grow a few frequently used herbs on a sunny windowsill right in the kitchen. This is also an option for those would-be herb-growers who don't have land outside to plant in.

Herbs are among the easiest plants to grow in containers. You can have a full assortment of culinary herbs in one planter on the front step or on the windowsill.

©iStockphoto.com/Gaffera

You might have to replace indoor plants more often than the ones you have outside because they might not like the conditions in the house. But your chances of success will improve with plenty of sun and a relatively cool temperature.

The Least You Need to Know

◆ Herbs are annual, perennial, and biannual plants with culinary, medicinal, or aromatic qualities.

◆ Provide herb plants with well-drained soil and at least 6 hours of sunlight a day.

◆ Avoid overfertilizing herb plants to ensure the best flavor.

◆ Pay close attention to the cultural requirements of each herb you plan to grow so you can adequately meet their needs.

◆ Many herbs have medicinal properties.

Exotic and Unusual Edibles

In This Chapter

◆ A taste of Asian vegetables

◆ Planting specialty vegetables

◆ Growing heirloom vegetables

◆ A look at some more esoteric vegetables

In some parts of the country, some plants are everyday fare. In other parts of the country, those same plants are considered exotic.

For example, okra is almost ubiquitous in Deep South gardens, but might be rarely seen in Maine or Michigan. Artichokes are common along the central coast of California but an uncommon sight almost everywhere else. Bok choy, mitsuba, and mizuna are staples in gardens tended by Koreans, Chinese, Vietnamese, and others of Asian descent, but are still far from standard in mainstream backyard gardens. And specialty roots like kohlrabi, horseradish, and fennel have devoted followings, but aren't in everyone's garden vocabulary.

In this chapter, we broaden our gardening horizons and perhaps help bring a little more diversity to our dinner tables.

Asian Specialties

As the number of Asian Americans increases, so does our awareness of the specialty vegetables many people of that community consider everyday fare. Most grocery stores now carry bok choy and Chinese cabbage.

In the following sections, we look at some of these basics. We also suggest a few more you might want to try.

Get to Know Bok Choy

An essential for stir-fried vegetable dishes, bok choy has become more or less a mainstream vegetable in many markets. Bok choy is a cool-weather green that grows in rich, well-cultivated soil, and bolts when the temperature rises. It's becoming an important fall and winter farm crop in parts of the Southwest where winters are warm.

Garden Guru Says

Bok choy, whose Latin name is *Brassica rapa sp. Chinensia,* goes by many names, depending on the heritage of the person who is growing or buying it. You might see baak choi, pai tsa, chongee, pak choy, joi choy, or tak tsai.

Sow bok choy seeds about 1 foot apart in well-prepared beds as soon as the soil can be worked, and keep them well watered. The seeds germinate in a week or so, especially if the soil is nice and warm.

You can begin harvesting individual leaves when they're a few inches long. Small heads of bok choy can be cut at the soil line when they're as little as 6 inches high—then it's baby bok choy, which is really expensive to buy. You can continue to harvest individual leaves or wait to pick nice big heads later in the season.

Mitsuba (a.k.a. Japanese Parsley)

Cryptotaenia japonica, or mitsuba, looks a lot like cilantro but with slightly larger leaves. It is a hardy perennial that grows in zones 4 through 9. In colder places it's grown as an annual.

Sow seeds in late spring and again in late summer for an abundant harvest. You can make additional sowings every month or so throughout the summer. Mitsuba grows in the shade and prefers rich soil with plenty of organic matter worked into it. Harvest about 50 days from seed planting by cutting individual stems.

Mizuna (a.k.a. Kyoto Greens)

Mizuna is a loose-heading lettuce-type green with curly leaves that look a little like endive but are very dark green. Mizuna tolerates more heat than most lettuces and is grown much the same way.

Prepare the soil so it's rich and light with lots of organic matter. Sow the seeds on top of the soil (they need light to germinate), and pat them gently into the soil. Keep the seeds well watered using a fine mist.

The seeds germinate quickly, and you might actually begin to harvest tiny, baby greens just a couple weeks after sowing.

Hybrid Senposai

A new Japanese hybrid, Senposai is a cross between cabbage and Komatsune mustard greens. The rounded, fan-shape leaves somewhat resemble collards and have a texture similar to lettuce. You can add the tiny leaves to salads or use the more mature leaves in soups or stir-fries as you might kale or chard.

Sow seeds indoors in regular potting mix or outdoors after all danger of frost has passed. Space seedlings 9 to 12 inches apart. You can begin to harvest small leaves in 30 to 40 days after germination.

Other Asian Favorites

If the preceding sections didn't give you enough flavor of Asian vegetables, the following table lists some other Asian favorites you might want to check out.

Vegetable	Description
Choy sum	Chinese flowering cabbage
Dau gok	Chinese long bean, like a snap bean
Een choi	Amaranth spinach
Gai choy	Chinese mustard green
Gai lum	Chinese broccoli
Hon-tsai-tai	Leafy green
Kailaan	Chinese kale
Kintsai	Asian celery

continues

continued

Vegetable	Description
Kobu takana	Horned mustard
Komatsuna	Chinese mustard spinach grown for leaves, stalks, and flowers
Malabar spinach	Leafy green
Nira	Chinese chives
Santoh	Chinese cilantro
Shiso	Leaf and stalk vegetable

Specialty of the House

The vegetables profiled in the next few sections might be completely unfamiliar to you, or they might be things you grew up with. Most of these are not available everywhere all the time, so they might be special to you.

Growing Oysters in the Garden

Salsify, also known as oyster plant, is an old root vegetable that, according to his garden diaries, was a favorite of Thomas Jefferson, who imported the seeds from Europe. It looks a little like a parsnip, only longer and thinner.

Salsify got its "oyster plant" name because it does actually taste like oysters. Some gourmet food markets occasionally offer salsify for sale, but generally, if you crave this unusual root vegetable, you'll have to grow it yourself.

Salsify is grown in much the same way as other tap-rooted root vegetables, including parsnips and daikon radishes. They need the soil to be deeply cultivated, well drained, with a pH of 6.0 to 6.5, and rich with organic matter. Salsify takes up to 150 days from seed to harvest and should be planted as early as the soil can be worked. Sow seeds 1 or 3 inches apart and then thin out the weaker seedlings, leaving a space of 3 or 4 inches. You can use the green leaves of the thinnings for salad or cook them like beet greens.

Garden Guru Says

Salsify goes by other names. If you can't find it or "oyster plant," try *Tragopogon porrifolius* or vegetable oyster.

You can also plant salsify as a fall crop in warm zones because it's very cold tolerant. Some gardeners say it tastes better if the plant experiences a heavy frost. Harvest by pulling up the entire plant.

Tomatillos: Not Green Tomatoes

Nearly 30 years ago when I lived in Mexico, I was introduced to the tomatillo (*Physalis philadelphica*) or husk tomato, an essential for salsa and enchiladas verdes. Today, you can find tomatillos in many grocery stores in areas with a large Latino population.

A tomatillo is not a tomato, or even a close relative, but a completely different plant. The tomatillo does look a lot like a tiny green tomato, but it is firmer, has a thicker skin, and is covered in a husk that has the thickness and texture of tracing paper.

Start tomatillo from seeds using the same methods you would for tomatoes. Tomatillos are warm-weather plants, so wait until all danger of frost has passed. Allow about 100 days from seed to harvest, although some varieties require less growing time.

Tomatillos are large plants that have a tendency to sprawl all over the place. Using tomato cages or wire and stake supports might help keep them under control. Harvest tomatillos when the outer husk splits open.

Say Hello to Broccoli Raab

Yet another *Brassica*, *B. rapa* or sometimes known as *B. ruvo*, broccoli raab is a cool-weather plant popular with those who like Italian cuisine. The stems, leaves, and tiny unopened flower buds are all edible.

Broccoli raab, which is also called rapini, likes rich, well-drained soil with lots of organic matter mixed in and a pH of 6.5 to 8.0. It can be directly seeded in beds or grown from transplants placed about 6 to 12 inches apart.

This fast-growing plant bolts if exposed to hot weather, so get it going in early spring for a late-spring harvest or in late summer for a fall harvest. In places like California and Arizona, broccoli raab is a winter crop.

Okra Is A-Okay

Okra, or *Abelmoschus esculentus* or *Hibiscus esculentus*, is a relative of the ornamental hibiscus, and interestingly enough, cotton. With its big white flowers, okra can be a very pretty plant. Try using it in an ornamental bed as well as the vegetable patch.

Okra is pretty easy to grow, requiring a neutral soil, lots of sun, and warm temperatures. You can start seeds outdoors about 2 weeks after the last frost or start them indoors about 6 to 8 weeks before that date. To give the seeds a head start, place them between a couple wet paper towels overnight before planting. Sow the seeds about $1/2$ inch deep in medium-size hills placed about 2 feet apart. Okra gets pretty tall, sometimes up to about 5 feet.

> **Compost Pile**
>
> The leaves and stems of okra plants contain tiny hairs that can irritate your skin, so wear gloves and long sleeves when you're harvesting or working around them.

While most vegetable plants like well-drained soil, okra is particularly picky about it. It's better to underwater than to overwater this plant.

The edible part of okra is the immature seed pod. Harvest when the pods are no more than 6 inches long, but try to get them when they're even smaller—around 2 or 3 inches.

Growing Heirlooms

Heirloom plants are those open-pollinated varieties introduced more than 50 years ago. More specifically, heirloom varieties are the resurrected varieties of plants that were grown by farmers and gardeners before the mass production and mass distribution of seed, and before farming became big business.

Growing heirlooms is another step you can take to make your garden more Earth-friendly. Using heirlooms preserves genetic traits and a larger gene pool for future generations. A reduced gene pool can lead to increased susceptibility to diseases and pests. Also, unlike seeds of hybrid plants, heirloom seeds reliably produce plants with the same traits as their parents.

Here, we look at some specific heirlooms that are particularly interesting and fun to grow, including tomatoes, corn, squash, and peppers.

Terrific Tomatoes

Among the most fascinating heirloom plants are tomatoes, many of them throwbacks to the turn of the century. One of the joys of these old-fashioned plants is that they retain the true tomato flavor that's often lacking in the new varieties that have been bred for disease resistance, uniform size, ripening qualities, and long shelf life, often at the expense of flavor.

Heirloom tomatoes are grown using the same techniques as modern tomatoes. Some might need careful staking, others are not particularly prolific, and a few might be a bit more susceptible to diseases. But if true tomato flavor is one of your favorite things, growing heirloom varieties will be worth the effort.

Check the following table for a few other varieties to look for.

Variety	Color	Fruit	Size
Aunt Ruby's Green	Green with gold centers	Very large	Tall
Big Rainbow	Gold with red highlights	Very large	Tall
Brandywine	Pink-red	Beefsteak-type	Upright plant
Cherokee Purple	Purple-red	Extra large	Large plant
Green Grape	Gold-green	Cherry-type	
Rutgers	Tomato red	Traditional shape	Tall
Super Italian Paste	Red-orange	Elongated, lumpy	Large plant
Yellow Pear	Bright yellow	Pear-shape, small	Prolific

Food for Thought

In his 1942 Victory Garden in Long Beach, California, Prof. Price grew the relatively new Rutgers tomato that had been introduced in 1934. That tomato became the standard for decades until plant scientists developed newer varieties to meet the demands of the canned food industry.

Crazy About Corn

Corn is another one of those vegetables that has been extensively hybridized to the point that some purists find ridiculous. Today, mass-produced corn has been bred to stay sweet days after picking, which is a boon for those who can't grow their own and don't live near enough to a farm to buy it fresh. But that sweet taste, some would argue, is a far cry from the true corn taste that's so dear to our American heritage. Heirloom varieties, including some hybrids developed around the turn of the century and even earlier, allow gardeners to step back in time.

Heirloom corn is grown the same way new varieties are. The big difference is that these old varieties tend to lose their flavor soon after picking, so get that pot boiling before you head to the cornfield.

Super Squash

Old-fashioned squash varieties are, for the most part, a pretty funny-looking bunch. Many of them are winter types, including pumpkins, and a lot of them have strange shapes and lots of lumps and warts.

One particularly interesting one is Long Island Cheese squash. It's shaped sort of like a wheel of cheese, is tan on the outside like a butternut squash, and is bright orange inside. And each fruit can weigh as much as 20 pounds! Another old beauty is the Blue Hubbard. The Burpee heirloom catalog says it might have originated somewhere in the Caribbean and was brought to Massachusetts in 1798.

Other wonderful old varieties include the Native American scallop squash, Sibley, which was popular in the 1840s, Amish pie squash, the Georgia candy roaster, and Turk's turban, a favorite from France, pre-1820. Heirloom squash are grown using the same planting methods as modern varieties of squash.

Perennials—They Keeping Coming Back

Most vegetables are grown as annual plants. We harvest them when they fruit, and generally the plant dies and we replant the next year. A few vegetables are *biennials*, but we still harvest them in the first year and ignore their 2-year life cycle.

A few vegetables are true perennials and go through the fruit-production cycle year in and year out. Artichokes and asparagus are the best-known and most-often grown perennial vegetables. Another plant, cardoons, are popular in Europe but still don't have a large following in this country.

> **Prof. Price's Pointers**
>
> **Biennials** are plants that develop roots, leaves, and stems in their first year but do not flower and produce fruit or seed until the second season.

Globe Artichokes

Globe artichokes are huge, beautiful plants (Latin name *Cynara scolymus*) that produce flower buds treasured by gourmets and gourmands all over the world. And although they're considered a delicacy, artichokes aren't all that difficult to grow, as long as you provide them with a hospitable environment.

For the most part, artichokes prefer relatively cool weather. According to the Reimer Seed Company, they need 250 hours of below 50 degrees Fahrenheit to set their buds. That's only about $10^1/_2$ days. If you grow artichokes from seed, start them indoors about 6 to 8 weeks before the set-out date that's after the last predicted frost. In warmer climates, plant artichokes in the late fall for a spring harvest. But be advised: artichokes really don't like very hot weather. And they do require regular irrigation.

Globe artichokes are reliably hardy in zones 8 to 10. In zones 6 and 7, they might survive milder winters with a good layer of mulch.

Place artichoke plants about 2 or 3 feet apart. To harvest, pick the immature flower buds along with a couple inches of stem using a sharp knife. Harvest baby artichokes before they develop the prickly choke that must be removed from the mature flower bud before you eat. The baby form is ready to harvest when it's about 3 inches across, or about $^1/_3$ the size of the mature bud.

Artichoke plants die back in colder zones but grow year round in places like Castroville, California—the artichoke capital of the world. California artichokes produce from March through May and again in October through December. Some artichoke growers cut plants back after the first harvest and allow them to send out new growth for the second harvest.

From the Asparagus Patch

Asparagus is another highly prized gourmet vegetable that's an essential for Easter dinner in our family. This is a relatively demanding plant to grow, only in that you have to wait a year after planting to get the first sparse harvest. Asparagus pays you back for your efforts, however, because the plants continue to produce for 10 or even 15 years.

Home gardeners rarely grow asparagus from seed. Instead look for 1-year-old crowns.

Reserve an area in your garden for your asparagus patch, keeping in mind that each asparagus crown will produce about $^1/_2$ pound asparagus each year and that crowns

Garden Guru Says

When you buy asparagus crowns, insist on male plants. These are hybrids that have developed in recent years and don't produce seeds the way the female plants do. Plants that grow from these seeds could become a weed problem in your asparagus patch.

should be planted about 18 inches apart in rows about 5 feet apart. You can do the math to figure how many crowns and how much space you'll need.

Dig furrows about 5 inches deep and add a dose of triple superphosphate to the soil at the bottom of the furrow, working it into the soil. Asparagus likes soil with a pH of 6.0 to 7.0. Then put the crowns in the furrow, cover lightly with soil, and water well.

Although the asparagus produces a few spears its first year, leave them alone and let them die back. The second year, you'll have a small harvest, with a full harvest in the third year and after.

Asparagus grows in zones 4 through 10.

Ever Heard of Cardoons?

These Mediterranean favorites are a close relative of artichokes. And although cardoons still haven't made much of an inroad in the United States, adventuresome gardeners eager to try new things are beginning to give cardoons a small presence here, particularly in the Pacific Northwest where the climate conditions seem to be especially hospitable.

Cardoons are very large perennial plants with massive leaves that can be as long as 5 feet. Young new leaves and the immature flower stalks are the edible part of the plant.

Cardoons do not tolerate frost and prefer moist, cool conditions. They like rich, well-drained soil that's deeply cultivated to ensure good root formation. They also require regular irrigation.

Plant seeds outdoors after all danger of frost, spacing them about $1^{1}/_{2}$ to 2 feet apart. Or purchase stem suckers, which are commercially available rooted offshoots, and plant them with the same spacing.

Cardoons grow in zones 7a to 9b.

Garden Guru Says _____

According to a University of Oregon Extension Center publication, cardoons need to be blanched (*blanche* is French for "white") starting about 1 month before harvesting. This is usually done by tying up the leaves at the top and wrapping them with burlap or paper. The leaf stalks are the parts that are blanched.

Exotic Roots

Some foods that we think of as root vegetables are actually the thickened stems of the plant rather than actual roots. Kohlrabi and fennel are two such exotic fat stem plants that we'll look at in this section. We'll also cover Jerusalem artichokes and horseradish.

Cabbage + Turnip = Kohlrabi

Kohlrabi is another member of the *Brassicas* (*Brassica oleracea var. caulo-rapa*) and one of the easiest of that family to grow. *Kohlrabi*, which means "cabbage-turnip" in German, is considered a root vegetable, although the round, rootlike part we eat is actually a swollen stem that forms above the ground.

As with many of the *Brassicas*, kohlrabi likes cool weather. You can sow seeds directly 1 to 1¹/₂ inches deep in the garden in early spring and in the late summer for a fall crop. In warm zones, plant in late fall for a winter crop.

Provide them with a rich neutral soil that's been amended with plenty of organic matter. Allow 4 to 8 inches between plants. You can also start seeds indoors allowing 5 or 6 weeks for seedlings to develop before set-out time.

It's very important to keep weeds out of the rows where you grow kohlrabi, or you risk misshapen, stunted vegetables. Take care when weeding because the kohlrabi has shallow roots. Mulch helps considerably; just keep it away from the round stems.

Harvest when the stems are about 2 or 3 inches across by cutting through the roots just below the stem.

Food for Thought

Kohlrabi plants that have grown quickly are said to have the best flavor. To grow at a substantial rate, they require regular watering and every-other-week applications of a quick-release fertilizer.

Aw, Horseradish!

Did you ever wonder where that white, grainy pickled stuff that you add to ketchup to make cocktail sauce comes from? It's horseradish, a wonderful root vegetable that's pretty easy to grow.

Horseradish grows in cool to cold weather and is usually planted in the early spring or late fall. Plant roots in furrows 1 foot deep, spacing the roots about 1 foot apart. Be sure the soil is well drained, and avoid overwatering.

Harvest horseradish in the late fall, usually after a hard frost. This plant is a biennial that's generally grown as an annual. To collect seeds, leave one or two plants in the garden and allow them to die back. They'll grow back the following spring. Allow them to mature, and they'll produce seeds. The root will probably be too tough and woody for consumption.

Fennel (the Vegetable, Not the Herb)

It's important to differentiate between fennel, the herb, and fennel, the garden vegetable. Here we're talking about the vegetable, *Foeniculum vulgare var. dulce.* It's a particularly beautiful plant and can be used as a decorative foliage plant in an ornamental garden—with the added bonus that you can eat it later.

Fennel is generally grown from seed and planted outdoors after the last predicted frost. Space fennel about one every foot or so.

Harvest fennel about 70 to 80 days after the seeds have been sown, usually when the bulb, which is actually thickened stems that grow in an overlapping pattern, is about 3 or 4 inches across. You can blanch the bulb, which sits up in the soil above a taproot, by mounding soil up around it for a couple weeks before harvest.

Bulb fennel, which is sometimes called finocchio or Florence fennel, prefers a pH of 5.0 to 6.8, frequent watering, and cool weather. Keep the soil moist but not soggy to avoid having the bulb split, which will ruin the flavor.

Celeriac (a.k.a. Celery Root)

Celeriac, one of my new favorites since I was introduced to it by my CSA, is also called celery root. It's far better known in Europe, where it's served au gratin or julienned, than it is in the United States.

If you'd like to try growing this esoteric veggie, you'll most likely have to start it from seed, as it's not generally available as a seedling.

Celery root takes 100 to 120 days from seed to harvest, so start the seeds early. Grow it as you would a turnip.

Chapter 17: Exotic and Unusual Edibles **199**

Artichokes from Jerusalem

Jerusalem artichoke is a giant plant, Latin name *Helianthus tuberosus* (which tells you they are related to sunflowers), that grows up to 8 feet tall. The fleshy tubers are another example of a swollen, underground stem. They're eaten like potatoes, harvested in the fall, and can remain in the ground until just before or just after the first frost.

Grow these plants starting with pieces of tuber in a rich, sandy loam, planting them in early spring. Allow at least 2 feet between each plant.

They don't like hot weather.

Prof. Price's Pointers

The Jerusalem artichoke stores carbohydrate as insulin, instead of starch. Insulin is metabolized as fructose instead of glucose when eaten—this quirk makes Jerusalem artichoke a starch substitute for diabetics.

Baby Vegetables

Some of what we call baby vegetables are just that: they are the plant's fruit picked when it's still in its early stage of development—far enough along to look and taste like that vegetable but with a milder flavor and tender texture. Other so-called baby vegetables are actually varieties that have been bred to be tiny versions of the original.

Harvesting baby vegetables is done using the same techniques as for mature vegetables (see Chapter 24); it's just done earlier. (You'll also find some hints about when to harvest baby vegetables in Chapter 24.)

Here are some vegetables that can be harvested when very young and tender:

Artichokes	Fennel
Asparagus	Potatoes
Beets	Scallions
Bok choy	Spinach
Carrots	String beans
Crooked neck squash	Zucchini
Eggplants	

Vegetable plants with varieties that are bred specifically for their mini size include the following:

Beets	Potatoes
Cabbage	Pumpkins
Carrots	Radishes
Cucumbers	Squash
Eggplants	Tomatoes
Onions	Watermelon
Peppers	

The Least You Need to Know

◆ Don't be afraid to try new and unusual plants. They're often as easy to grow as the basics.

◆ Grow old-fashioned heirloom vegetables for authentic flavors and to contribute to a healthy gene pool for plants.

◆ Harvest some veggies early as babies, or try some specialized dwarf or mini varieties of your favorite vegetables.

Chapter 18

Growing Fruits

In This Chapter

- ◆ Tricks for raising strawberries
- ◆ Grow-your-own melons
- ◆ Reintroducing rhubarb
- ◆ A bowl of (ground) cherries

Many gardeners like to grow small fruits along with their vegetables. It's not hard to understand why. If you've ever harvested a basket of strawberries in the afternoon for your strawberry shortcake at dinner, you know the sublime pleasure of growing your own fruit. And what's a summer picnic without juicy slices of watermelon?

In this chapter, we learn more about growing small fruits, including strawberries, rhubarb, and melons. And in case you haven't met yet, we introduce you to ground cherries.

Sweet, Sweet Strawberries

According to the U.S. Department of Agriculture, Americans consume 4.85 pounds of strawberries per person per year. California, which is the country's largest producer of strawberries, grows 1 billion pounds every year. Think about it. Strawberries are huge! I don't have enough room in my garden to grow my own, so I rely on my CSA and a few pick-your-own farms in my neighborhood because the flavor of fresh-picked strawberries is unequaled. And I like to have enough to put up a dozen or so half pints of strawberry jam.

Prof. Price's Pointers

To grow strawberries in very cold climates, follow the advice of the experts at the University of Maine Cooperative Extension: plant strawberries on a slight slope to allow cold air to float away from plants rather than settle in with them. The slope has the added advantage of improving drainage.

Strawberries can be grown in every state in the country, but they do best in places where they can have a full 90 days of warm days with full sun, cool nights, and regular watering.

Strawberries prefer well-drained, deeply cultivated sandy loam with a pH of 5.8 to 6.2 and plenty of organic material worked in thoroughly. Strawberries are heavy feeders, so you'll be doing them a favor by adding a 10-10-10 fertilizer to the bed before planting. For about 250 square feet of strawberries (about enough room for 100 or so plants), you'll need about 5 pounds of fertilizer. (See Chapter 20 for more information about fertilizers, including organic options.)

Weeds are a real problem for strawberries; they just don't do well with competition. So if you've turned a lawn into a planting bed, wait a year until you plant strawberries, and be diligent about removing weeds during that time. (And if you're going to allow that extra year, why not bring in a truckload of manure to welcome those strawberry plants?)

There are three basic types of strawberries:

◆ June or spring bearing

◆ Everbearing

◆ Day neutrals

Generally, home gardeners work with everbearing or day neutral varieties, both of which produce over a longer period of time versus the June or spring bearing types.

Plant strawberries as seedlings as soon as you can work the soil. Just barely cover the roots with soil and take care not to cover the crown or it will rot.

You can use one of three different spacing techniques with strawberries:

♦ Matted row

♦ Space matted row

♦ Hill

The matted row is good for June or spring bearing types. With the matted row, runners form 15 to 18 inches of mat "daughter" plants spaced 4 to 6 inches apart. Allow 3 or 4 feet between the rows and 18 to 20 inches between the plants.

The space matted row is good for all types of strawberries. Here, runners are limited to 2 to 4 daughter plants spaced 6 to 12 inches apart. Allow 3 or 4 feet between the rows and 18 to 20 inches between the plants.

Finally, hills are best for everbearing and day neutral plants. Here, all runners are removed. The rows are 2 or 3 feet apart, and plants are spaced 12 to 15 inches apart.

Strawberry plants generally last several years, with the runners supplying new plants. The hill system of planting, however, quickly tires the plant, so you'll have to replant every couple years.

Strawberries do best in zones 4 through 8, depending on the variety.

Get a Load of Those Melons!

Melons come right after tomatoes on my list of favorite summer garden crops. These sweet, juicy fruits can be a challenge to grow because they need a lot of room, warm temperatures, and plenty of water. But they are also great fun, especially for kids.

Melons are members of the *Curcubitacea* family and are relatives of cucumbers and squash. They originated in the Middle East, where they remain a very important part of the agricultural scene.

In addition to cantaloupe and watermelon, the two most commonly grown melons in the United States, some gardeners enjoy growing these other melons:

Butterscotch	Dudaim Ogen
Canary	French Charentais
Casaba	Galia
Crenshaw	Honeydew

Muskmelon   Prince

Persian   Santa Claus

Most melons are vining plants that can take 6 or more square feet of garden space per plant. So to grow them, you need to have lots of room to let them sprawl. That said, plant breeders have been developing more compact bush varieties. Look for these if your space is somewhat limited.

If your garden is really small, you could try growing melons on a sturdy trellis or in a wire cage. But because melons are pretty heavy, you'll need to support the fruit as it matures.

Garden Guru Says

Here's a reuse tip that not only helps in the garden, but keeps out at least a little of the 3.9 million tons of textiles that enter the waste stream every year: fashion inexpensive supports for heavy melons with slings from pantyhose legs. Ease the stocking over the fruit, cut off a section, and make slits to form a pair of ties. Then tie the sling to a trellis or stake. The material expands with the growing fruit, keeping it supported above the ground where it might rot. This trick works for squash, too.

Unless you garden in a warm zone, start melon seeds indoors, and transplant the young seedlings on to large hills well after all danger of frost has passed, as they need warm weather to thrive. If you live in a warm zone, you can start your melons from seeds outdoors. If you live in a cooler zone, you can warm up soil temperatures early and keep it warm by using black plastic mulch in your melon patch.

The Summer of Watermelons

These giant, improbable fruits are the essence of summer. They don't ask for too much besides plenty of space, lots of sun, warm weather, and loads of water.

Watermelons, unlike their close relatives, do best in soil that has not been amended with compost or manure. They actually prefer a poorer soil and will thank you for not fertilizing them during the growing season.

Plant one watermelon on top of each planting hill and allow 6 to 8 feet in every direction.

Watermelons generally take from 75 to 100 days to mature, so be sure to leave them on the vine long enough to ripen. In zones with short summer seasons, leave the melon on the vine until just before the first frost. Harvest by cutting the stem with a sharp knife or garden shears.

> **Food for Thought**
>
> Huge watermelons are just the thing for big family gatherings, community picnics, or summer buffets for a crowd, but for small families, one of the mini varieties make much more sense. Most are round, many are seedless, and a few have yellow flesh. All are as delicious as their mammoth cousins.

Growing Cantaloupe

The cantaloupes we are most familiar with in the United States are actually muskmelons (*Cucumis melo 'reticulatus'*). The "true" cantaloupe (*Cucumis melo 'cantaloupensis'*) has a much different skin that's "rough and warty," according to the North Carolina Cooperative Extension Service, as opposed to the smoother, "netted" skin of American 'lopes.

You can plant as many as three cantaloupe seedlings on a large hill. Just give them plenty of organic matter in the soil, and feed them every 2 or 3 weeks with a high-nitrogen liquid fertilizer like a manure tea. To avoid the fruit rotting before it's ripe, some gardeners put a small piece of plywood under each fruit to keep it off the soil.

Updating Old-Fashioned Rhubarb

Have you ever tasted pie made from fresh rhubarb? It's one of those old-fashioned treats that stays vivid in your memory.

Rhubarb does seem like an old-fashioned fruit, but many up-to-date gardeners grow it with enthusiasm and success. As with most fruits, growing rhubarb requires some patience because you can't harvest it until the second or even third year after you plant it.

Rhubarb, which originated in Asia, is grown for its green, red, or pink stalks that are shaped like celery, only longer. These stalks are used to make pies, jams and jellies, stewed desserts, and sometimes punch (that's really old fashioned!).

Compost Pile

The leaves of the rhubarb plant contain oxalic acid, which is poisonous. Although a few bites of leaf aren't likely to kill a healthy adult, it can still make you quite sick. And someone in ill health, or small children, might become very sick indeed from ingesting even a small amount. Remove the leaves immediately upon harvesting the rhubarb stalks.

The stalks of the rhubarb plant look like beautiful red celery. Raw stems are tart when they are young and thin, but as they mature they're remarkably bitter.

©iStockphoto.com/Stefan Fierros

Rhubarb likes well-drained soil with plenty of organic matter worked in thoroughly. Although it's not all that fussy about pH, a range of 5.6 to 6.5 is best. Plant crown divisions, which are available from garden centers, nurseries, and online vendors, in the early spring or late fall, placing the crowns about $2^1/2$ to $3^1/2$ inches below the soil. Allow about 3 or 4 square feet per plant. Rhubarb is a heavy feeder, so plan on a regular fertilization schedule. Apply a high-nitrogen fertilizer a month after the leaves first appear and then about every 3 weeks after that.

To harvest, cut individual stalks a few at a time, over the course of a month or two, usually starting around mid-May.

Rhubarb is grown in zones 5 through 8.

Food for Thought

Rhubarb plants will last for years, but they do best when they're divided every 3 or 4 years (unless the plants aren't thriving). To make divisions, use a sharp spade to cut straight down through the crown. Dig up the two halves and, using a sharp, clean knife, further divide the crowns, being sure each small piece has one bud, or eye. Plant the divisions as individual new rhubarb plants.

Getting to Know Ground Cherries

My first experience with these marble-size orange- or yellow-colored fruits was when a vendor at New Hope's farmers' market offered me a handful to try. After enjoying their taste—a cross between strawberries and pineapple—I bought a pint of this hard-to-find treat and have been a fan ever since.

The Latin name for ground cherries is *Physalis pruinosa*, but they are also called husk tomatoes (not to be confused with tomatillos) and cape gooseberries.

Ground cherries are grown in much the same way as tomatoes, although some people like to plant them on mounds. You can start them from seed indoors 3 to 6 weeks before the last frost, but they like the soil to be quite warm before they're set out.

Ground cherries should never be allowed to dry out but must have good drainage. They like a rich, moist soil, so mulching is helpful. As with many plants, it's best to water them at the root level, rather than from above.

The plants grow like small bushes, up to 3 feet high and equally wide, and they sometimes need staking or caging. You'll know the ground cherries are ready to be harvested when the fruit, covered in a papery beige husk, drops from the plant. Be sure to get to them before the birds do!

The Least You Need to Know

- Most backyard fruit plants grow best with good drainage.

- Strawberry plants require about 90 days in warm, sunny conditions to produce ripe fruit.

- Mulch your strawberry plants heavily for higher yields, to keep weeds down, and to help retain moisture.

- Melons take a long time to reach maturity, so start them early.

- Rhubarb plants will produce for many years, especially if they are divided every three or four.

Part **5**

Keeping It Growing

Let's face it—the next few chapters aren't about the fun stuff. There are chores to be done. Someone has to water and weed. Pests and diseases won't go away just because you don't want to deal with bugs. Don't skip Part 5 if you want to make the most of your garden.

Go ahead, plow on in. It's good for you, and your garden, to know these things.

FUNGICIDES   PESTICI[DES]   WEED EATERS

BARR

Chapter 19

Weeding and Watering

In This Chapter

- Identifying and eliminating weeds
- Why plants need water
- Strategies for conserving water
- Irrigating your garden

This is the decidedly dreary part of gardening. Weeding and watering are time-consuming, boring, and tedious tasks. Weeding is particularly onerous, especially when it's hot and buggy. It's a lot like housework (which I loathe) because it never ends. Just as there are always dirty dishes and laundry, unmade beds, and dust and dirt in the house, there are always weeds in the garden. These are dirty jobs, but someone has to do them.

In this chapter, we analyze this essential garden work and look at ways to make it easier. Along the way, we identify the worst weeds, talk about mulch and herbicides, and explore various irrigation systems. We also look at some practices that will make your efforts more Earth-friendly.

What's Wrong with a Few Weeds?

You've probably heard the expression "one man's trash is another man's treasure." That's sort of the case with weeds. One gardener's *weed* is another's wildflower. Many of the worst *noxious weeds* were introduced at some point by gardeners who thought they were pretty.

Native wildflowers can be beautiful in a meadow but a royal pain in the neck in the vegetable patch. Some really invasive plants like kudzu and purple loosestrife were initially planted because someone liked the way they look. But then they ran amok, with sometimes devastating results.

Prof. Price's Pointers

A **weed** is a plant that grows in a place where it isn't wanted or a plant with unacceptable qualities. A **noxious weed** is one that grows rampant in places where it's not wanted and is resistant to efforts to remove it.

Although a few weeds in the garden are inevitable, gardeners should strive to eliminate as many of them as possible. Weeds compete with your edibles for water, nutrients, growing space, and sunlight. They also provide hiding places for insects and can be a contributing factor in the spread of disease. Weeds can and will reduce the quality and quantity of your harvest.

Even though we hate weeds, they can serve an interesting purpose for the home gardener. Some are known as *indicator weeds* because they start to appear with certain soil conditions. If you begin to see a big crop of chickweed, for example, it might indicate that your garden has a problem with poor drainage. The following table lists some indicator weeds that show up with certain soil conditions.

Soil Condition	Indicator Weeds
Compacted soil	Crabgrass, chickweed, goosegrass, knotweed, dandelion, quack grass
Low fertility	Red sorrel, henbit, Johnson grass, peppergrass, crabgrass, smartweed
Poor drainage	Chickweed, goosegrass, dock, thistle, hedge bindweed, bindweed
High acidity	Horsetail, dandelion, sorrel, dock, knotweed
High alkalinity	Peppergrass
High nitrogen	Horse nettle
High salt	Creeping Jenny, crabgrass

Weed ID

Far too many weed plants plague American gardens to allow us to profile all of them in this limited space. Fortunately, a number of excellent websites with well-designed weed identification formats show you photos of the plants and identify them by name, type, and growth habit. Some of the sites also provide eradication advice.

Check out these websites:

> njaes.rutgers.edu
>
> www.weeds.iastate.edu
>
> www.garden.org/weedlibrary
>
> www.css.cornell.edu/WeedEco/WeedDatabase
>
> www.ppws.vt.edu/scott/weed_id/cropweeds.htm
>
> www.ipm.ucdavis.edu/PMG/weeds_common.html

Some of these sites are specific to regions or states, but many of the weeds profiled are found all over the country, so you should be able to identify the culprits in your garden with only a few site visits.

Here are a few of the most common weeds:

Weed	Species	Description
Bedstraw (clingers)	*Galium* species	Broadleaf; perennial
Bindweed (creeping Jenny)	*Convolvulus arvensis*	Broadleaf; perennial; invasive vine with aggressive root system
Bitter cress	*Cardamine* species	Broadleaf; annual; prolific seeds that pop out of pods and spread profusely; often infiltrate the garden via nursery pots
Blackgrass	*Alopecurus myosuroides*	Grass; annual
Canada thistle (creeping thistle)	*Cirsium arvense*	Broadleaf; perennial; very invasive; aggressive root system

continues

continued

Weed	Species	Description
Carpetweed	*Mollugo verticillata*	Broadleaf; annual; shallow root system; easy to remove with light cultivation
Common chickweed	*Stellaria media*	Broadleaf; annual; problem for strawberries
Crabgrass, hairy	*Digitaria sanguinalis*	Grass; annual
Crabgrass, smooth	*D. ischaeum*	Grass; annual; grows close to ground; spreads with runners
Cut-leaf evening primrose	*Oenothera laciniata*	Broadleaf; perennial
Dandelion	*Taraxacum officinale*	Broadleaf; perennial; flowers distract bees from pollinating less-showy vegetable and fruit flowers; deep tap root
Dodder	*Cuscuta* species	Perennial; parasitic annual; sucks out chlorophyll; problem for blueberries
Goosegrass	*Eleusine indica*	Grass; annual; grows close to ground; difficult to pull out
Hedge bindweed	*Calystegia sepium*	Broadleaf; perennial; aggressive vine; problem for corn
Henbit	*Lamium amplexicaule*	Broadleaf; annual
Horse nettle	*Solanum carolinense*	Broadleaf; perennial; sharp, nasty spines; difficult to control; aggressive roots; poisonous berries; related to potatoes
Ivy-leafed morning glory	*Ipomoea hederacea*	Broadleaf; perennial; vine; looks like bindweed
Jimsonweed	*Datura stramonium*	Broadleaf; annual; toxic hallucinogen in seeds and leaves

Weed	Species	Description
Johnson grass	*Sorghum halepense*	Grass; perennial; very tall; aggressive roots
Kudzu	*Pueraria lobata*	Broadleaf; perennial; very aggressive vine in southern zones
Lamb's-quarter	*Chenopodium album*	Might have medicinal properties
Mexican bamboo (Japanese bamboo)	*Polygonum cuspidatum*	Broadleaf; annual
Mugwort (wild chrysanthemum)	*Artemisia vulgaris*	Broadleaf; perennial; very invasive; spreads with rhizomes
Pennsylvania smartweed	*Polygonum pensylvanicum*	Broadleaf; annual; extremely invasive
Pepperweed	*Lepidium* species	Problem for strawberries
Pineapple weed	*Matricaria matricarioides*	Broadleaf; annual; problem for spinach and other vegetables
Poison ivy	*Toxicodendron radicans*	Broadleaf; perennial; vine; invasive creeping stem and seeds; causes rashes
Prickly lettuce	*Lactuca serriola*	Broadleaf; annual
Prickly sida	*Sida spinosa*	Broadleaf; perennial; sharp spines
Purslane	*Portulaca oleracea*	Annual; broadleaf; fleshy stems
Quack grass (couchgrass)	*Bytrigia repens*	Grass; perennial; very invasive; spreads by rhizomes
Quickweed	*Galinsoga*	Broadleaf; perennial; very quick to germinate; reseeds many times during growing season
Roundleaf mallow	*Malva neglecta*	Broadleaf; perennial
Shattercane (wildcane)	*Sorghum bicolor*	Grass; annual; tall; looks a little like corn

continues

continued

Weed	Species	Description
Shepherd's purse	*Capsella bursa-pastoris*	Broadleaf; annual
Smartweed	*Polygonum* species	Broadleaf; annual; many types; some a problem for blueberries
Sorrelwood (sourgrass)	*Oxalis stricta, O. cornicula*	Broadleaf; perennial; spreads by popping seeds
Wirestem muhly	*Muhlenbergia frondosa*	Grass; perennial
Witchgrass	*Panicum capillare*	Grass; perennial

Not every one of these weeds will appear in your garden, but some inevitably will. Be prepared.

Saying Good-Bye to Weeds

The best defense against weeds is a good offense. You can gain the upper hand by starting out with a well-prepared bed. If the bed is thoroughly and deeply tilled, with all the old vegetation removed, you have fewer seeds to start with.

Food for Thought

Weeds aren't a huge problem in my small Pennsylvania garden because the beds were established a long time ago, and I spent a lot of time early on preparing the beds and keeping them weed free. I removed unwanted plants (weeds) before they had a chance to go to seed so new crops never became established. A few weed seeds do blow in on the wind or are deposited by a visiting bird, but these are incidental and don't require much effort to keep under control. The only time I have real weed problems is when I reclaim a bit more lawn for a new bed.

Weed Between the Lines

Even with a strong weed-free start, you still have to deal with any weeds that crop up. Weeding is an age-old chore that doesn't take a lot of skill. Just effort. In a small garden, you can probably manage by hand-pulling weeds. This isn't such an awful task if you do it in the cool of the early morning or in the evening. Wear your gloves and pull out the invaders. Or scratch lightly along the surface of the soil with a hand cultivator. But be wary of tap-rooted weeds. Get out your weeder tool for them. (This is the one that has the V-shape point on the end.)

If the weeds you've pulled have gone to seed, dispose of them in the trash or in a place far from your garden rather than on your compost pile. There's a good chance the seeds will survive in the compost, so when you add the compost to your garden soil, you'll simply reintroduce the weeds, only more of them.

In a larger garden, weeding by hand isn't a practical option, unless you don't do anything but garden all day and night. Instead, use some kind of cultivating tool like one of the hoes described in Chapter 4.

You need to attack weeds between rows as well as in the rows, but use different techniques for each space. Between rows you can be pretty aggressive and just whack away at the weeds. But when you're working around plants, you have to be really careful. Overzealous weeding with a cultivating tool can damage vulnerable roots and stems. Just scratch the surface lightly to loosen the weed and pull it away from the planted row. For good garden hygiene, remove the uprooted weeds.

The Beauty of Mulch

Mulch goes a long way toward reducing weeding chores. It provides a barrier over the surface of the soil that prevents seeds from working their way into the soil, and it also keeps out light, which is essential for any seeds that have somehow managed to germinate. Mulch has the added benefits of keeping moisture in the soil (so you may be able to use less water) and preventing soil from overheating.

Generally mulches are inorganic or organic. Organic mulches are those that are made of plant material. Here are some examples:

Aged manure	Pine needles
Compost	Sawdust
Grass clippings	Seaweed
Ground corn cobs	Shredded newspaper
Hay (without seeds)	Shredded or chunked bark
Leaves	Straw
Peat moss	Wood chips

When applying organic mulch, lay it on thick, but don't let it touch stems or leaves. Always leave a little space around the stem, and be sure to lift any leaves laying on the ground so you put the mulch on top of the soil, not on top of the leaf.

When using organic mulches, you might risk lowering the nitrogen levels in your soil because the soil uses existing nitrogen in the decomposition process. You might have to add more nitrogen to compensate.

Using rich compost as mulch not only helps retain moisture and keeps weeds down, but also adds important nutrients to the soil as it breaks down.

©iStockphoto.com/Sebastian Cote

The most common inorganic mulches are plastic sheeting and mulch cloth. Thousands, if not millions, of gardeners, including Prof. Price, have used black plastic mulch successfully.

Garden Guru Says

Some vegetables work in the garden as a sort of living mulch. These are the plants that sprawl across the ground and wind up shading and crowding out weeds. Melons, squash, potatoes, sweet potatoes, pumpkins, and large tomatoes do this.

Clear plastic sheeting helps retain moisture but won't inhibit weed growth—in fact, just the opposite. Weeds thrive in the moist, warm environment created by the plastic and get plenty of sunlight, much like in a greenhouse. Black mulch cloth keeps weeds in the dark so they can't photosynthesize and, thus, cannot thrive.

A 2002 study done by scientists at Pennsylvania State University Plasticulture Center showed that the use of different colors of plastic mulch resulted in increased yields for some plants. For example, tomatoes and eggplants prefer red mulch, peppers like silver, cantaloupes responded better to green or dark blue, as did cucumbers and summer squash, while potatoes did well with red, silver, or black. Although not available everywhere, some gardeners are beginning to use these new colored plastic mulches to boost production and hasten ripening. Virginia's Cooperative Extension office offers a list of sources for colored plastic mulch at www.ext.vt.edu.

Killing Weeds with Chemicals

Some gardeners won't touch herbicides with a 10-foot pole, and I tend to stay away from most of these chemicals. But I do admit that if it weren't for Brush-B-Gon Poison Ivy Killer, I'd be an itchy wreck all summer.

Herbicides may have their place. When used properly, some may not have a negative impact on the environment, and they can greatly reduce the time you need to remove unwanted vegetation. The most important role herbicides play is in the development of new beds. You can use an herbicide to kill a large section of grass before you till it. And spot applications on really difficult-to-remove weeds, especially those with taproots, is sometimes the only way to be sure you really kill the blasted things.

Three basic kinds of herbicides are used by home gardeners:

- All-purpose herbicides kill any plant they touch
- Selective herbicides kill specific plants
- Preemergents prevent germination

Roundup, Kleenup, and Kleeraway are three of the better-known all-purpose herbicides. The active ingredient in many of the all-purpose herbicides is glyphosate. According to a water conservation bulletin from the Arizona Cooperative Extension, glyphosate decomposes quickly, so you can use it in an area where you plan to put a new bed and plant a week later.

Dacthal is one of the best-known selective herbicides, with clorthal-dimethyl (DCPA) as its active ingredient. This one is a preemergent designed to kill annual grasses and broadleaf weeds. It's used on planted beds, whether they're seeded or if seedlings have been planted. Very specific usage instructions spell out when to use, how much to use, where it can be used, and how far from vines, stems, and leaves it can be used. Follow the directions exactly.

Treflan is another popular preemergent. It's used on prepared beds before planting. According to the label, it's a selective herbicide that prevents the germination of specific broadleaf and grass weed seeds, including such pests as Johnson grass, crabgrass, carpetweed, chickweed, lamb's-quarters, and pigweed. It also kills purslane, so if you plan to grow that particular type of fancy lettuce, don't use Treflan in your garden.

If you plan to use commercial herbicides, do so with extreme caution. Keep children and pets away from treated areas, and store the containers in a secure place.

Food for Thought

A number of organic herbicides have begun to appear in garden centers in the past few years. Most are made with a combination of ingredients such as vinegar, acetic acid, yucca extracts, citric acid, mineral oil, and clove and garlic oils. A study done by the University of Minnesota Extension found that, after doing initial damage to the weed plants, the products tested had little to no lasting effect and most of the plants recovered. So it appears that the greenest method of dealing with weeds is the old-fashioned one—weeding.

Why Plants Wilt

Why do plants wilt? The simple answer is that they don't have enough water. But the scientific answer is that they lose turgor. Prof. Price gives us a complete explanation:

Think of a tomato plant as a balloon filled with a salty solution and attached to a tube (the roots) that's sitting in a bucket (the soil). A filter (the osmotic membranes) in the tube allows water but not salts to pass through.

The activity of the water is decreased by the presence of salts. Because the activity of the water in the bucket (the soil) is greater than that in the balloon (the plant), water will try to move from the bucket into the balloon. The result is an increase in water pressure (osmotic pressure) within the balloon (the plant), causing it to fill up and stiffen (become turgid).

So if the balloon (the plant) develops holes and leaks, the balloon collapses. This collapse would also happen if salt were to build up in the water in the bucket. The collapse is the loss of turgor, or wilting.

Now you know why plants wilt, but why it is so devastating to a plant? It's not really that complicated. Remember in Chapter 10, you learned that to photosynthesize, plants had to be able to pull carbon dioxide from the atmosphere. And they did that through the tiny holes in the leaves called stomata. But these thousands of holes also lose water. It's like a catch-22 for plants. They need those holes to make chlorophyll (photosynthesize), which is essential for their growth. But they lose a lot of their precious moisture through those same holes. To survive, plants must have a continuous supply of water.

Irrigation 101

Plants can't survive without a continuous supply of water. In a perfect world, we would have enough rainfall during the growing season to provide just the right amount of water to meet the needs of all our garden plants.

But it almost never works out that way. Here in Pennsylvania, we have had a series of severe droughts for several summers in a row. Our droughts have been so bad that local and state governments have instituted emergency water restrictions on several occasions. Conscientious gardeners have had to develop strategies for irrigating their gardens while honoring the restrictions. This means careful attention to water conservation techniques.

Compost Pile

Avoid watering your planted garden with a light sprinkling. The water does nothing more than moisten the surface of the soil. None penetrates to the roots, and the plants will die of thirst.

The University of Georgia Cooperative Extension Office has prepared some very useful water conservation tips. These recommendations, along with suggestions from other experts, include the following:

- Use mulch to hold in moisture.

- Add organic matter to the soil to aid in moisture retention.

- Make individual plant waterers to direct water directly to plant roots using milk jugs or soda bottles. (Find directions for making these online.)

- Remove weeds thoroughly.

- Use a drip irrigation system to avoid loss of water through evaporation of surface moisture.

- Settle newly tilled soil with a light application of water so future waterings will conduct the moisture properly.

- Water before 8 A.M.

◆ Keep hoses, hose bibs, and nozzles in good repair.

◆ Pay attention to weather reports, and turn off automatic timers if rain is predicted.

◆ Don't irrigate areas of the garden that have been harvested.

Drip or Trickle Systems

Drip or trickle irrigation systems are a relatively new technology that helps conserve water while providing garden plants with just the amount of moisture they need to thrive. Essentially, the system is a set of hoses with emitters (holes that allow a spray of water out) or a set of *soaker hoses*, that you snake through the garden, The emitters are set intervals that match the spaces between plants. Usually drip systems are connected to timers. The initial investment is relatively high, and there is a fair amount of effort needed to install a system.

Prof. Price's Pointers

Prof. Price uses **soaker hoses** in both his California and his Massachusetts gardens. Soaker hoses look more or less like regular hoses except they're usually black and are made of a squishy porous material that allows water to seep out slowly, rather than drip irrigation hoses with emitters that release water at intervals. One end of the hose is attached to the hose bib, and the other is capped. Soaker hoses are best used where plants are relatively close together, such as in a row of vegetables.

Look for excellent instructions for installing a drip irrigation system in your garden from the Colorado State University Cooperative Extension at www.ext.colostate.edu/mg/files/gardennotes/714-irrigating. Cornell also has a very useful article at www.nysaes.cornell.edu/pubs/ask/irrigation.html.

Overhead Sprayers

Many gardeners rely on overhead sprayers. Some are as simple as a sprinkler head set up on a pole with a hose attached to it. Others are more elaborate systems with heads that pop up out of the ground. All can be attached to timers. You can use rotary heads, which require high water pressure, or spray heads that require less pressure.

This may be the easiest way to irrigate your garden, but it has its issues—mostly, but not exclusively, waste. Sprinklers are difficult to target so they wind up watering everything, including paths, fallow areas, and even the lawn along side your garden bed. With rising concerns over water conservation, this practice is coming under increasing scrutiny.

Another serious problem with spray irrigation is that the water lands on leaves, flowers, and fruits, which can promote rot, attract insects, and invite disease.

Important considerations include the size and shape of the area you want to irrigate, your water pressure, and the patterns of irrigation you want to use. The University of Rhode Island offers a wealth of information, including a helpful schematic and advice on spacing formulas, system designs, and more, at www. uri.edu/ce/healthylandscapes/dripirrigation.

Prof. Price's Pointers

In warm weather, most edible plants require 1 to 1½ inches of water per week. In very hot weather, plants might need as much as 2 inches of water per week. A good rule of thumb is that 1 inch of water equals about 60 gallons per 100 square feet. Use this to help you plan your irrigation schedule.

Watering by Hand

A very small garden or a container garden of edibles can be effectively watered by hand using a hose with a wand or with watering cans. The wand helps you reach farther in the garden and is usually fitted with a nozzle that allows you to adjust flow and choose from multiple spray options. Look for one with an on/off latch so you can have complete control of the flow.

If you like watering cans, be sure to use one with a good rose on it. The rose is the part of the spout that has little holes in it to form a fine spray of water. You don't want to water tender little plants with a blast of water from the can.

When watering by hand, be sure to target the root zone and avoid splashing leaves, stems, and fruit as best you can.

Turn Off the Tap

Even without drought conditions, environmentally concerned gardeners make an effort to use as little water as possible. There's no getting around the fact that plants need water and the gardener must provide it if Mother Nature is being stingy, but drawing water from a private well or community source must be done with the knowledge that there isn't an endless supply. Savvy, conscientious gardeners look for ways to use water that might otherwise go down the drain or run off into uncultivated areas.

A growing number of people, particularly those in drought-prone areas, are using rain barrels placed at downspouts to collect water for irrigation. Many rain barrels available now come equipped with filters and spigots and are very efficient. According to an article on HarvestH2O.com, the U.S. Environmental Protection Agency says that a rain barrel has the potential to save 1,300 gallons of water during peak summer months. The barrels are commercially available, or you can find plans for making your own at HarvestH2O.com or www.cityofbremerton.com/content/sw_makeyourownrainbarrel.html.

Collecting water runoff from your roof and gutters for use in the garden is an Earth-friendly way to conserve water.

©iStockphoto.com/Suzanne Carter-Jackson

If you decide to use a rain barrel, be sure to use a childproof lid. Also, if you live in a high-traffic area, have a copper or asphalt roof, or have treated your roof with chemicals to deter moss or algae growth, you may want to have the runoff water tested to be sure it doesn't have a dangerous level of contaminants. In addition, the University of Rhode Island website suggests that rain barrel water not be used for overhead spray watering, not be used just before harvest, and that all fruits and vegetables watered with rain barrel water be washed with potable water prior to eating.

Look for opportunities to collect water in other places as well. What about the shower water that usually runs down the drain while you wait for it to heat up? The dehumidifier collection container? Water from flower vases? The water you use to clean vegetables and fruit prior to cooking or serving? Pot water from cooked vegetables and pasta? Even the condensation lines from your air conditioner. Don't, however, use the gray water from the washing machine or from bathing.

The Least You Need to Know

- Keep garden beds well weeded to ensure healthy plants and a good harvest.

- Use mulch to conserve water and keep weeds at bay.

- Provide your plants with plenty of water.

- You have many options when it comes to irrigation.

- Look for ways to save and store water so you can conserve this valuable resource while meeting your plants' needs.

Chapter 20

Feeding

In This Chapter

- ◆ The nutrients your plants need
- ◆ NPK and other fertilizers
- ◆ Side dressings versus top dressings
- ◆ Feeding your garden organically

People have been fertilizing plants since the beginnings of agriculture, but we've only really known why we do what we do since the early nineteenth century. It was then that the first systematic studies took place on the requirements of plants for nutrients—nitrogen, phosphate, potassium, and so on.

In this chapter, we have another important science lesson. This time it's about the nourishment plants need to prosper and how gardeners can respond to those needs, including so-called organic approaches. All the substances are essential for every cell in every plant, but given nutrients might play a larger role in certain plant organs and developmental processes.

In this chapter, we also take a close look at the famous NPK trio: nitrogen, phosphorus, and potassium. We get familiar with some of the other important macronutrients and micronutrients, and we find out about the best ways to deliver these essentials to our garden plants.

What Plants Want

Keeping plants properly fed is all about balance. Just as humans and animals need a balanced diet, so do plants. In addition to adequate supplies of water and air, plants require generous portions of nitrogen, phosphorus, and potassium to produce leaves, grow roots, set fruit, and make seeds. And they need these things in specific amounts.

As plants grow, they draw nutrients from the soil. Some of the nutrients are plentiful, with more than enough to keep providing what plants need indefinitely. Other nutrients become depleted. In a natural setting, depleted nutrients are replenished when plants die off and decompose. But in a garden, the plants are harvested and dead plant material is generally cleaned up, so that natural process is short-circuited. It then becomes the gardener's job to replenish the supply of used-up nutrients.

Prof. Price's Pointers

We can now name 17 elements essential to the growth of plants, starting with carbon, hydrogen, and oxygen (air and water); then nitrogen, phosphorus, and potassium (the famous *NPK*); followed by the familiar calcium, magnesium, sulphur, and iron; through the lesser-known nutrients, including boron, manganese, and zinc; also copper, chlorine, molybdenum, and finally nickel, whose essentiality was confirmed only about 15 years ago.

A Short Course on NPK Fertilizer

The trio of NPK—N = nitrogen, P = phosphorus, and K = potassium—is the basis of all fertilizers. After you commit the following information to memory, you can officially call yourself a gardener.

Just about all commercial fertilizers have labels that give a series of three numbers like 5-10-5 or 10-10-10. These numbers represent the percentages of N (nitrogen), P (phosphorus), and K (potassium), respectively. But the numerical representations are not consistent, logical, or universal. Bear with me. You need to know this stuff.

In the United States, the numbers represent the percentages of elemental nitrogen, phosphorus as phosphate, and potassium as potassium oxide. The fertilizer labeled 5-10-15 contains the equivalent of 5 percent nitrogen, 10 percent phosphate, and 15 percent potassium oxide.

Prof. Price's Pointers

The percentages are equivalents because the nitrogen could be present as ammonium, nitrate, or urea, not as elemental N, which is nitrogen gas; the phosphorus as phosphate, bone meal, or other organic form; and the potassium would certainly not be present as potassium oxide, which is caustic.

Are you thoroughly confused? Well, don't go away. It gets worse. The percentages of nutrients, and especially of nitrogen, are only part of the story. Plants regulate themselves in terms of the balance of vegetative growth and reproduction, but too much nitrogen in a readily available form—ammonium or urea—can cause "fertilizer burn" or even turn off fruit set and push excessive vegetative growth.

Give Me an *N*

Eventually every gardener must become familiar with nitrogen. The big *N* is one of those really important factors in the health and prosperity of most plants. Nitrogen comes in several common forms.

Nitrate occurs as the mineral sodium nitrate. It's highly soluble, can be used immediately by plants, is the most expensive form of nitrogen (it comes from mines in Chile), and can be taken up by the plant and stored harmlessly.

Ammonium (similar to household ammonia) is instantly available to the plant, and the plant must convert it to a storage form, which requires an investment of starch. If the plant runs out of stored starch, the ammonium will kill it.

Compost Pile

Like nitrates, most ammonium salts are highly soluble and, like nitrates, ammonium nitrogen is readily available to the plant. In fact, the problem with ammonium salts is that they're too available to plants. If ammonium nitrogen isn't converted to organic nitrogen, it can become highly toxic.

Urea is the most common nitrogenous constituent of urine. Most plants convert it rapidly to ammonium nitrogen, so it has the same dangers. Urea is relatively inexpensive.

Organic nitrogen is made of complex organic compounds that contain nitrogen. These are ideal in that the nitrogen only becomes available as it's slowly decomposed by soil microorganisms. Urea (which is itself organic) can be converted to less-available forms by various chemical tricks.

Finally, there's *atmospheric nitrogen*. Eighty percent of the atmosphere is N_2 or nitrogen gas. Gaseous nitrogen is not normally available as a nutrient to plants, but nitrogen-fixing bacteria can convert gaseous nitrogen to ammonium, and certain of these bacteria live symbiotically with peas and a few other plants, supplying ammonium to their host in exchange for carbohydrates and other nutrients.

Give Me a *P*

The chemical symbol for phosphorus is P. Plants absorb this essential as phosphate ion (PO_4). Phosphorus is a significant factor in the storage and distribution of energy in plants, so it's especially important for root development.

Sometimes plant specialists recommend a shot of superphosphate for certain plants. This stuff (a mixture of calcium phosphate and calcium sulfate) is a less-soluble form of phosphate, which makes it available for a longer period of time. It won't wash away when it rains or when the irrigation system turns on.

Give Me a *K*

The chemical symbol for potassium is K. Potassium is the third element in the fertilizer formula. Unlike nitrogen and phosphate, potassium does not make strong bonds with other molecules, so it's always floating around as a free ion. It moves around inside plants to wherever it's needed most. And because it's a free ion in the soil, it leaches out easily, especially in sandy soil.

It's rare to have too much potassium in garden soils, but there can be deficiencies. This often shows up as problems with older leaves. Roots are also susceptible to potassium deficiencies. A soil test can point out whether you need to add potassium.

Most of the K found in commercial fertilizers comes in the form of potassium chloride. Old-time gardeners might still refer to potassium as *potash*, although this term is somewhat outdated.

Macro and Micronutrients

N, P, and K are the *macronutrients* plants require in the largest amounts. The other macronutrients are carbon, oxygen, calcium, magnesium, hydrogen, and sulphur. But plants need these *micronutrients*, too:

Boron	Manganese
Chlorine	Molybdenum
Nickel	Zinc
Copper	
Iron	

It's important to understand that plants require only tiny amounts of these nutrients. But if one element is out of balance, it can affect the availability (the ability of the plant to take in or use) of another one of the elements. For example, if there's too much magnesium, the plant might have difficulty with calcium uptake. This can result in poor growth, a reduction in seed production, and other symptoms. Conversely, too much calcium can interfere with magnesium absorption.

Most of the micronutrients plants need are present in soil in adequate quantities. However, the combination of high pH and high calcium levels can make a number of the heavy metals unavailable to plants.

Where micronutrients and trace metal deficiencies are common, as in the Southwest, you have a couple options when it comes to getting them to your plants. You can lower the soil pH with gypsum to about 6.0 to 7.0. Or you can add or spray with chelates.

Many commercial fertilizers also include micronutrients.

Compost Pile _____

One of the leading causes of eutrophication, or the overgrowth of algae in aquatic and marine environments, is fertilizer runoff. The contribution from home gardeners is relatively insignificant when compared to that from agriculture, but it's still important for home gardeners to mix and apply commercial fertilizers carefully and according to the manufacturer's directions. Gardeners who work in sandy soil should take extra care, as fertilizer runoff is generally worse from these soil types.

Natural Foods for Plants (the Organic Approach)

When it comes to organic fertilizer, the natural perspective has undeniable advantages. The nutrients from manure, compost, fish heads, and other organic matter are released slowly, which avoids some of the real dangers of overfertilization. There are a number of methods for feeding the garden organically. (Note the earlier cautionary point on urea, which is organic.)

Prof. Price's Pointers

Here's an easy equation for converting commercial fertilizer to organic types:

25 pounds commercial 10-10-10 fertilizer roughly equals:

50 pounds cotton seed meal + 15 pounds lambeinite + 50 pounds rock phosphate

60 bushels cow or horse manure

24 bushels chicken, sheep, or rabbit manure

Manure Tea, Anyone?

This is clearly not the tea to serve the ladies! Manure tea is a concoction made from—you guessed it—manure that's been steeped in water to create a liquid plant fertilizer. The best recipe I've found for manure tea is from *The Victory Garden Kids' Book* (Globe Pequot Press, 1994). (My good friend Alison Kennedy did the design for the book, and it's one of my most favorite gardening books.)

To brew your own manure tea, put a shovelful of well-rotted manure in a 5-gallon bucket and fill the bucket with water. Let it stand for a few hours. And then, ta da. It's ready to use. You can make larger quantities in a big plastic garbage can. Just use the same proportions.

Manure tea is great as a starter food for new seedlings or as an all-purpose fertilizer for the regular feedings you do every 2 or 3 weeks.

Sounds Pretty Fishy

The Wampanoag Indians of Massachusetts, as well as many early Native Americans, dropped a fish head in each planting hole when they sowed their corn, beans, and squash. They were following age-old traditions that were most likely based on someone's observation that plants grown near dead fish grew better than ones without the fish.

Compost Pile

There's been concern about a toxic form of the Escherichia coli (E. coli) bacteria that's caused serious health issues in recent years. The problem is related to the manure of ruminating (cud-chewing) animals, but it's usually caused by contamination of irrigation water, especially where there are high concentrations of animals, like in feed lots. The home gardener who uses well-rotted manure to amend soil is unlikely to risk that kind of contamination. But carefully wash all produce, from any source, before you eat it.

The scientific reason why decomposing fish might be good for crops is because in the breakdown of organic matter like dead fish, there's the slow release of nutrients like ammonium, nitrogen, phosphate, and potassium that, of course, are the principal nutrients plants require.

Today, instead of stocking up on dead fish, you can use fish emulsion to feed your garden plants. Don't try making your own unless you have large quantities of fish guts hanging around the house. Instead, look for commercial preparations at garden centers and nurseries.

The Poop on Poop

Manure is one of the best, and of course one of the oldest, organic fertilizers known to man. Cow pies, were, after all, free for the taking down on the farm. Manure from cows, horses, goats, chickens, and rabbits and, more recently, alpacas and llamas is the most commonly used.

Try to use manure that's free of straw. The microorganisms that help decompose the straw will convert nitrogen to organic forms that would only become available over time. This natural time-released nitrogen is typically a good thing for gardens, but sometimes you want just enough at once to meet plants' needs.

Avoid using fresh manure on your vegetable garden because the acids in it will actually burn the growing plants. As mentioned earlier, well-rotted manure can be used as a fertilizer. *Well-rotted* means it's been allowed to sit and age for several months. If you don't have your own source of manure, look for bags of processed manure at garden centers and nurseries.

While most herbivores produce suitable manure for gardening purposes, some purists say that stuff from horses works best. The form of nitrogen found in horse manure (called hippuric acid) is released more slowly than that in, say, cow, or sheep manure. But horse manure is more likely to contain viable seeds that could introduce weeds to your garden.

Never use waste from dogs, cats, or humans as a fertilizer. Although human waste (sometimes referred to as night soil) is still commonly used in some parts of the world to fertilize crops, it's a dangerous practice contributing to some really ugly diseases. Also avoid the use of processed sewage sludge as a fertilizer for edibles. It is a rich food for ornamental plants, but it might contain heavy metals that are toxic.

> **Garden Guru Says**
>
> You can add fresh manure to garden beds in late fall or early winter after everything has died back. Use a pitchfork or a big shovel and pile it on. Then spread it out as evenly as possible. You can either leave it on the surface or give the whole bed a quick till. In the spring, till it thoroughly.

When you use large quantities of cow, sheep, llama, alapca, or goat manure to fertilize your garden, keep in mind, while your garden beds will be rich and friable, there might be a phosphorus deficiency. Cud-chewing animals enlist the aid of microorganisms to extract phosphate from phytins and phytic acid, which can represent most of the phosphate in the plants that cows and others eat. Do a soil test to be sure. If your soil is low in phosphorus, add some superphosphate (0-45-0 fertilizer). About 4 pounds per 1,000 square feet of garden should be enough to get the levels up to par. Or you can use organic bone meal, acidulated bone, or rock phosphate.

The University of Florida IFAS Extension has a valuable publication on organic gardening that includes extensive information on organic fertilizers. The tables on NPK levels in various manures, as well as availability and acidity, are particularly useful. Find it at www.edis.ifas.edu.MG323.

Compost

If ever there were a product that warms my thrifty soul, it's compost. I love the way we can take otherwise useless kitchen garbage and garden debris and turn it into one of the richest plant foods possible.

I've already discussed how to make your own compost in Chapter 8 so I won't repeat myself here. Turn back to that chapter for a refresher if you need to.

Leaf Mold

This kind of organic fertilizer is a little different from compost. Essentially, it's the leftovers of big piles of leaves that have been left to rot. Eventually the leaves decompose, leaving behind a rich, fluffy organic material that makes a terrific plant food.

Leaf mold, especially from oak leaves, tends to have a very low pH (which means it's very acidic), so it's best used on plants that prefer a more acidic than alkaline soil.

Lay It On

There are several methods for applying fertilizer:

◆ Broadcasting

◆ Banding

◆ Side dressing

◆ Foliar feeding

Each one has its place in the home gardener's repertoire.

Broadcasting Fertilizer

If you've ever used one of those little spreader contraptions to fertilize or lime the lawn, that's broadcasting. In the vegetable garden, this kind of broadcasting is the uniform spreading of fertilizer over the whole surface of soil. Usually this is done just before you till so you can then turn the fertilizer into the soil. You can use the same spreader you use on the lawn; just be sure there's no lime left in it.

> **Garden Guru Says**
>
> Most gardeners don't refer to an overall application of manure or compost as broadcasting, although technically, it probably is.

Generally, you don't want to apply commercial fertilizers until you've had your soil tested so you know what formula to use.

Strike Up the Band

Applying fertilizer using the banding method is a highly reliable way to deliver nutrients to young plants, but it does require a fair amount of labor. Banding is done at the same time you plant seeds and at transplant time.

The amount of fertilizer you use depends on the results of your soil tests and what crop you plan to grow.

Here's how to band fertilizer:

At seed planting:

1. Dig two furrows parallel to, on either side of, and 3 to 6 inches from the seed furrow. Make them twice as deep as the seed furrow.

2. Add the fertilizer in the furrows and cover with soil.

Or …

1. Dig a furrow 3 to 6 inches deep.

2. Add the fertilizer and cover with soil.

3. Plant the seed in the furrow.

At transplant time:

1. Make two furrows 6 inches long and 3 inches deep on either side of each transplant. The furrows should be 4 to 6 inches from the transplant.

2. Add the fertilizer and cover with soil.

Or …

1. Dig a circular trench around each plant 3 inches deep and 4 to 6 inches away from the stem.

2. Add the fertilizer and cover with soil.

Or …

1. Dig a hole twice as deep as you need for the transplant.

2. Add the fertilizer and work it into the soil at the bottom of the hole. Fill the hole with soil to the level needed for the transplant.

3. Plant the transplant.

After all the furrows or holes are dug and filled and the seeds or transplants are planted, water thoroughly.

Banding fertilizer allows plants to have easier access to the phosphorus they need for good root development.

"I Like My Dressing on the Side"

This application method is done when young plants have reached a certain size. It's done by taking a small amount (1 or 2 tablespoons per plant) of a dry fertilizer and sprinkling on both sides of the row of vegetables or in a circle around individual plants. Allow 6 to 8 inches of space between the fertilizer and the plant. Then gently work the fertilizer into the soil with a cultivating tool and follow with a thorough watering.

Not all vegetables like getting a side dressing of fertilizer. Those that do like it at different times. The following table helps you know when to side dress some of your favorite vegetables.

> **Garden Guru Says**
>
> When a side dressing is not worked into the soil but simply left on top of the soil, it is called a top dressing.

Plant	When to Side Dress with Fertilizer
Broccoli	3 weeks after transplanting or when heads begin to form
Tomatoes	When first flowers appear or when first fruits appear
Peppers	When first flowers appear
Eggplants	When first flowers appear
Kale	4 weeks after transplanting
Onions	4 to 6 weeks after planting, or when 6 inches tall; then again every 2 weeks until bulb is nearly full size
Cabbage	3 weeks after transplanting or when head starts to form
Potatoes	6 or 7 weeks after planting; do it before adding more soil
Leeks	When plants are a foot tall
Corn	When 2 feet tall; again when silk forms
Cauliflower	5 or 6 weeks after transplanting
Squash	Just before plants start to form vines
Spinach	Just before blooms appear

Some perennial plants like asparagus and artichokes benefit from a side dressing of fertilizer, too.

Foliar Feeding Frenzy

If you read *foliar* and thought it sounded a lot like *foliage*, you're right. And you've probably also figured out that foliar feeding is a way of applying fertilizer to the leaves of a plant. Right again.

Applied as a spray, foliar feeding is a quick fix for plants and helps them absorb the nutrients they need. Generally, foliar feeding is done when there hasn't been enough fertilizer added to the soil before planting; when micronutrients, especially iron and zinc, aren't being released adequately; or if the soil is too cold to allow the plants' roots from taking up the existing fertilizer in the soil.

A phosphorus foliar spray can also help new transplants get off to a good start in cold soil.

The Least You Need to Know

- Well-rotted manure is an excellent alternative to commercial fertilizers. Never use waste from dogs, cats, or humans as manure.

- Avoid contributing to fertilizer runoff by only using the amounts recommended by the manufacturers.

- Look for Earth-friendly organic fertilizers as an alternative to synthetic options.

- Water thoroughly after applying all fertilizers, except foliar types.

- Apply a foliar fertilizer spray to give plants a quick feeding, especially when the soil is too cold for the plants to take up fertilizer from the soil.

Chapter 21

Pests, Diseases, and Blight

In This Chapter

◆ Your garden's worst nightmares

◆ Which insects like what plants?

◆ Natural and organic techniques for pest control

◆ Deterring pests

No matter how meticulous you are about planning, planting, and maintaining your garden, you're going to have problems with pests. It's inevitable. And it can be frustrating.

In this chapter, I introduce you to some of the most common insect pests, along with a few of the predatory insects that eat them. We also look at some insecticides and pesticides that are effective against the invaders. We consider some organic or natural approaches as well. And along the way, we figure out what to do with warm-blooded pests who can make a mess of the garden.

And before we proceed, I'd like to suggest that you use common sense when dealing with pests in the garden. Most experienced gardeners put up with a certain amount of damage. They accept the fact that there will be losses and that some produce will be less than perfect. The most successful gardeners are smart enough to plant more of the most troublesome things to get at least a small harvest, or to give up that item altogether.

Bad Bugs

Maybe I should have called this section "Icky Insects" because educated gardeners try not to use the word *bug*—kind of like *dirt*. Anyway, the number and diversity of insects that can cause damage to a garden is staggering. Different insects are sometimes more of a problem in different parts of the country and certainly create difficulties with some plants more than others.

The following table lists some of the most common insect pests and their favorite meals.

Pest	Favorite Plant(s)
Aphids	Corn, cucumbers, beans, squash, melons, peppers, potatoes, eggplants, beets, peas, broccoli, cabbage, brussels sprouts, cauliflower, kale, lettuce, okra, parsley, spinach, chard, tomatoes
Cabbage root maggots	Cabbage, broccoli, cauliflower
Cabbage worms	Cabbage, broccoli, cauliflower, corn
Carrot rust root maggots	Carrots, radishes, parsnips
Colorado potato beetles	Potatoes, eggplants
Corn earworms	Corn, beans, cabbage family plants, lettuce
Cucumber beetles	Zucchini, summer squash, winter squash, cucumbers, melons, beans, corn, eggplants
Cutworms	Corn, cucumbers, onions
Flea beetles	Corn, potatoes, eggplants, beets, carrots, beans, parsley, tomatoes
Japanese beetles	Raspberries, grapes, beans
Leafhoppers	Beans, potatoes, carrots, peas
Mexican bean beetles	Beans, peas
Red spider mites	Beans
Leaf miners	Cucumbers, beets, spinach, turnips, cabbage family plants
Slugs	Lettuce

Pest	Favorite Plant(s)
Spider mites	Eggplants, carrots
Squash bugs	Squash, melons
Stink bugs	Beans, beets, corn, cucumbers, okra, peas, chard
Thrips	Beans, corn, cucumbers, melons, peppers
Tomato hornworms	Tomatoes, beans, cabbage family plants, cucumbers, lettuce, melons, spinach
Vine borers	Zucchini, summer squash, winter squash, cucumbers, melons
Whiteflies	Beans, tomatoes, melons

As you can see, many insects are a problem for more than one type of plant. Frequently, the problems run in families. The *Brassicas* have trouble with cabbage root maggots and cabbage worms. Squash and cucumbers, which are members of the *Cucurbita* family, are troubled by cucumber beetles and vine borers. When you know how plants are related to each other, it can help you deal with their potential pests.

Food for Thought

One of the best sources for information on insect pests is a publication from the Texas A&M University Agricultural Extension Service called *Managing Insect and Mite Pests in Vegetable Gardens*. Find it online at insects.tamu.edu/extension/bulletins/b-1300.html. This thorough document contains descriptions, including drawings, of a host of pests; lists of plants and the insects that attack them; and the pesticides that will kill these insects.

Although no garden will be completely pest-free, it is possible to keep the damage to a minimum. The best defense is good horticultural hygiene. This means removing any insects found on seedlings before transplanting, thorough and regular weeding, removal of damaged leaves and other plant parts, and harvesting on time so rotting fruits don't attract more insects.

Also, keep in mind that healthy plants are more able to withstand the occasional insect attack. Conversely, plants that are compromised because of poor soil, lack of water, or too much or too little fertilizer will be more susceptible.

Good Bugs

I know people who find all insects disgusting and frightening. That's not a good attitude for gardeners. Some insects are absolutely essential for the very survival of plant species (especially the pollinators), and others spend their entire lives devouring the insects that can cause so much damage in the garden (the predators) or helping keep your soil in top shape (the aerators).

The following table offers a list of the good bugs. You can make friends with them if you want. (Look for illustrations of many of these pollinator and predator insects at www.ca.uky.edu/agripedia/agmania/insectid/BENEF.asp.)

Benefit	Good Bug
Pollination	Bees, wasps, butterflies, moths
Aeration	Dirt mites, earthworms
Extermination of bad bugs	Lady beetles (ladybugs), dragonflies, damselflies, praying mantis, assassin bugs, braconid wasp larvae, predacious mites, bigeyed bugs, hover fly maggots, green lacewings, minute pirate bugs, ichneumonid wasps, rove beetles, soldier beetles, spined soldier bugs, spiders

Food for Thought

As helpful as praying mantis are at keeping aphids and other pests in check, they have voracious appetites and will be just as happy chomping on beneficial insects like ladybugs or lacewings. Praying mantis can deliver a nasty bite to unsuspecting humans as well. I found that out one day when a granddaddy mantis attached himself to my ankle. Ouch!

As you can see, many insects are beneficial to your garden, and unless you've studied them, you might have difficulty telling a good bug from a bad one. That's why it's just not a good idea to use insecticides and pesticides indiscriminately. If you just go out and spray like crazy, you'll wind up killing every insect out there.

Take bees, for example. Bees are essential pollinators, but they're in trouble, with as much as one third of all honey bees in the United States having disappeared due to colony collapse disorder. Recent scientific studies may have identified the culprit—a class of pesticides called neonicotinoids. Even if you're inclined to use commercial pesticides, try to avoid products that contain neonicotinoids. Also, never apply pesticides when bees are around. They work during the day, so if you must spray with a pesticide, do it in the very early morning or late in the day after bees have returned to their hives. Better yet, look for products that aren't toxic to bees.

If you think you would like more bees living in or near your garden, think about offering to host a beehive on your property. Many professional (and amateur) bee-keepers are looking for good homes for their beehives. You'll have to promise not to use chemicals that are toxic to bees, and you may need to have the support of neighbors to do the same. But your garden will love it, and you'll probably be treated to some free honey. Get in touch with your local county extension office for a list of area apiarists (beekeepers).

Insecticides and Pesticides

Insecticides and pesticides are products that kill insects and other pests. To clarify, pesticides are products that kill pests; not all insects are pests and not all pests are insects.

Hundreds of chemical compounds are used as pesticides, some utterly lethal to everything and anything they touch. Their selection and use is too important and complicated an issue to be covered adequately in this small space. So before you use any commercial pesticide, read the labels carefully and thoroughly and follow the directions exactly. Be sure to identify the insects that are causing the damage so you can pinpoint the insecticide you need to use. If you have any doubts, consult your county extension office. The sales staff at garden centers, nurseries, and hardware stores won't necessarily know enough to help you make the right choices.

When you do elect to use a pesticide to control an infestation, make a thorough application, especially to the undersides of the leaves. Liquid pesticides are generally easier to apply than powders.

> **Garden Guru Says**
>
> A few pesticides are available that have a relatively low environmental impact, including insecticidal soaps and vegetable oil–based sprays that use pyrethrins and other plant extracts to kill aphids, mites, whiteflies, thrips, leafhoppers, and a few other pests. Milky spore, a bacterium, can be used against Japanese beetles, and iron phosphate–based baits kill slugs.

The Argument for Organic

Many gardeners grow their own food expressly to reduce their exposure to pesticides. Naturally, these gardeners want to take an organic, or at least Earth-friendly, approach to dealing with insect pests. A number of options are available, including barriers, natural repellents, and hand removing.

Prof. Price's Pointers

Integrated pest management is an approach to disease and insect control that uses environment-friendly methods that reduce the use of chemical agents while maintaining and promoting a healthy garden. Other natural ways to prevent disease and pest infestation include mechanical and barrier controls, good garden hygiene, crop rotation, the use of resistant plant varieties, adequate irrigation, and good soil preparation.

Floating Row Covers

Floating row covers are one of the best barrier methods for pest control in the edible garden. Also called agricultural fleece, floating row covers are lengths of lightweight fabric (usually spunbonded polyester) that are draped like a blanket over rows of plants. The fabric allows sun and water to penetrate and even provides some frost protection, but it keeps out insects. The covers are held in place by burying the edges in soil.

Food for Thought

Just what we need, more plastic, right? But the protection against insects that polyester covers provide makes using plastic seem like a reasonable trade-off. Good-quality floating row covers, if used and stored with care, can last many seasons. And perhaps, one day, someone will figure out how to make them out of recycled materials.

Floating row covers are usually installed at seed planting or transplanting time and kept on during the early stages of growth. As soon as the first flowers appear, the row covers must be removed or pollinating insects will be unable to do their work.

Floating row covers are particularly effective for protecting against the following:

Aphids	Corn earworms
Bean beetles	Cucumber beetles
Cabbage loopers	Leaf miners
Cabbage root maggots	Squash bugs
Cabbage worms	Whiteflies

If the soil under the row covers is infested with plant-eating insects, the row covers might do more harm than good because you won't be able to see much of the damage until it's too late. Rotating crops every year helps prevent soil infestation.

Cutworm Collars and Maggot Mats

Cutworm collars are insect barriers I first learned about back in the late 1980s from *The Victory Garden Kids' Book*. You can make your own or buy commercial versions.

The collars form a circular barrier around the stem that prevents nasty chomping or boring insects from climbing up the stems of young seedlings. You can use a paper cup with the bottom half cut off for a small collar. Or use an empty tomato sauce can with the bottom removed. Plastic soda bottles and milk cartons with the bottoms and the narrow parts cut off also make effective collars.

The collars work best on young seedlings, but you can make larger versions. Put the collar in place when you plant the seed or seedling, and leave it there as long as it doesn't interfere with the growth of the plant.

Maggot mats are like little carpets around the stem of young plants that prevent cabbage maggot flies from laying their eggs in the soil near the young plants. *The Victory Garden Kids' Book* gardeners used actual pieces of leftover carpet to make the maggot mats. The carpet is cut into 5-inch squares, and a slit is made from one edge to the center with a small hole right at the center. When the seedling is planted, the maggot mat goes on top of the soil around the stem and then the slit is taped closed.

If you don't have carpet remnants, use tar paper, cardboard, or even aluminum foil.

Pick a Peck of Pests

Removing the offenders by hand can be a very effective method of pest control. This works well for some and is almost impossible for others. Slugs, Japanese beetles, cabbage worms, tomato hornworms, and Mexican bean beetles are a few that are relatively easy to pick off plants by hand.

Pests like these slugs can be picked off by hand. It's not a particularly pleasant task, but it's preferable to chemicals in an organic garden.

©iStockphoto.com/Dieter Hawlan

Garden Guru Says _____

Slugs are nocturnal, so to catch them, you'll have to go into the garden at night. Use a flashlight, and follow their slimy trails. You can put them in a jar with alcohol, soapy water, or salt to kill them right away. You might want to wear gloves or use large tweezers; otherwise, you'll get their slime on your hands, and it's hard to get off.

A hard spray of water is another way to remove insects from leaves and stems. Of course, you can't do this on tender young seedlings. And if you see suspicious-looking eggs on the backs of leaves, try to wipe them off with a paper towel or even scrape them off with your fingernail and then put them in an airtight bag in the trash.

Organic Sprays

Although not always helpful, some organic sprays do provide some relief from pests. Many of them are made from essential plant oils that allow the spray to adhere to the plants' leaves.

Oils from mint, cedar, garlic, pepper, citronella, cloves, rosemary, tansy, and many more herbs are sometimes used to repel insects.

Anti-Bug Plants

Some plants have the ability to either attract or repel certain pests. By making the correct planting combinations, you might be able to reduce some of the pest problems in your garden by planting some anti-bug plants in with the plants you know bugs like.

The following table provides a few of the plants you can use to repel or deter harmful insects, or attract beneficial insects.

Plant	Benefit
Basil	Repels thrips
Catmint	Deters fleas, Japanese beetles, squash bugs, aphids
Chervil	Repels aphids near lettuce
Coriander	Deters aphids, potato beetles, carrot rust flies
Dill	Deters aphids; attracts tomato hornworm (use as bait)
Garlic	Deters rabbits
Marigolds	Attracts slugs (use as bait)
Mint	Deters flea beetles, cabbage worms, aphids; attracts predatory wasps, hoverflies
Nasturtiums	Deters aphids, whiteflies, squash bugs, cucumber beetles
Onions, chives	Deters aphids
Parsley	Repels slugs; attracts hoverflies
Sage	Deters cabbage moths, ants, carrot rust flies, slugs

Moles, Voles, and Other Small Critters

First let me say that I am an animal lover. I still stop the car to gaze at a herd of deer at sunset—it's a beautiful sight. I get a kick out of watching young groundhogs standing on their hind legs as they survey the countryside. And there's something so gentle and sweet about a wild rabbit nibbling in the lawn.

But critters in the garden are anything but cute. I'll never forget the sense of rage I felt when, after waiting weeks for the tomatoes to ripen in my New Jersey garden, I ventured out to harvest the first beautiful fruits and every one of them had huge gashes—courtesy of our neighborhood groundhog!

In this section, we look at some of the worst warm-blooded pests, and look at ways to, well, dissuade them. We also discuss some lethal approaches, and I hope any animal rights activists among you will forgive me. I've always used the nonkill methods. (Well, I used to have cats that liked to kill voles and the occasional mole.) But I wouldn't be doing my job if I didn't offer you as much information as possible.

Voles and Moles

Voles, also called meadow mice, are particularly insidious, and I might add, odious creatures. They are small rodents, ranging from about 3 to 5 inches long. They feast on just about every part of plants, consuming several times their weight every day. Voles can girdle young trees (eat the bark all the way around—a death sentence), devour an entire row of tubers, polish off leaf crops, and generally decimate a garden in a matter of weeks.

Voles live underground but spend a lot of time carrying out their destructive marauding along little aboveground runways. They reproduce at prodigious rates, and the amount of damage they do becomes worse as their numbers increase.

Moles are a different animal altogether, and they are nowhere near as hateful. They range from mouse-size to as much as a foot long, depending on the type. Moles are almost always carnivores. They eat worms, grubs, beetles, ants, and the larvae of other insects. They generally leave plants alone.

In the garden, moles aren't much of a problem except for the tunnels they dig all over the place that can be used by voles and mice after the moles have left.

Although voles are a real nuisance in the garden, moles aren't usually such a big deal. Because they eat grubs that will mature into Japanese beetles and other pests, moles can actually perform a service to the gardener.

Food for Thought

I have had some success in discouraging voles and moles from sticking around my garden, although my technique is somewhat gross. I use very soggy and smelly nonclumping kitty litter (with the solids removed). Using a trowel, I pour the litter into the vole and mole holes until I can't add any more. You can never really fill the holes because the burrows go deep and far. The smell of cat pee must be too much for the voles and moles, and they take a hike. This isn't a permanent solution, but it can discourage them long enough to keep your crops safe until harvest.

Poison and kill traps are the only sure-fire way to eliminate moles and voles. If you have children or pets, or if your neighbors have children or pets, I would stay away from using poison. Mouse traps work pretty well on voles. Unbaited traps in the runways reduce the population pretty quickly. But again, you won't want to do this if pets or children spend time in your yard. Special mole traps go deep inside their tunnels. They're gruesome but effective.

Groundhogs

I know people who think that the only good groundhog is a dead one. I don't belong to that group. I have nothing against groundhogs … until they come into my garden. That's when I get out my Havahart trap.

Groundhogs, which are also called woodchucks, marmots, and whistle pigs, are not very bright, so they're relatively easy to trap.

We trapped an entire family several years ago using a technique suggested by an old timer in the area. We located the main hole of the burrow (in this case it was under our neighbor's driveway), and placed a trap baited with half an apple directly outside the hole. We set it up so the trap was running in the same direction as the groundhogs when they left their burrow. We caught them one by one over the course of a few days. My husband carted them off to a large meadow a few miles away. (We probably unwittingly broke several laws doing that, but I'm hoping the statute of limitations has passed by now.) By the way, groundhogs smell really bad. It took days for my husband's car to lose that pungent odor.

Compost Pile

Before you set out to live-trap a wild animal, find out what the animal-control regulations are in your area.

Other ways to deal with groundhogs include shooting them, using kill traps, and fumigating (placing carbon monoxide canisters in the burrows). Most groundhogs do their damage during daylight hours, so some people leave their dogs outside to scare off intruders.

Cute as a Bunny

Admit it, rabbits are really cute. But when they attack your lettuces or go after the spinach, you want to wring their cute little necks. If rabbits are the only pests in your garden, keeping them out isn't such a difficult task: just put up a fence.

It only needs to be about 2 feet high, and you can use simple wooden stakes and chicken wire around the perimeter. Be sure to tack it down with steel pins, stones, or bricks, or Peter Cottontail and his relatives will find a way to go under.

Here Kitty, Kitty

We are a family of cat lovers. But even the most fanatic of feline fans might take issue when Kitty poops in the garden. It's just plain disgusting.

If neighborhood cats use your garden as a toilet, you have a couple options. First, keep the hose handy and give Kitty a shower when she sets paw in your space. Cats hate that, and they learn quickly. If she persists, sprinkle cayenne pepper on her favorite spot and she won't visit again. Neither method will hurt a cat, by the way.

You might also try a diversionary tactic: plant catmint well away from your vegetable garden in a place where visiting cats won't be a problem. Then watch them get silly.

Deer: In a Class of Their Own

My friend Ian McNeill wages a never-ending war against the deer that invade his backyard garden. On a recent visit to see his intensively planted raised beds, Ian discovered a gaping hole in the netting he'd just installed. The deer were so desperate to get at the young beets that they tore into the netting with their hooves until it split open! Boy, does Ian hate those deer.

And so do most gardeners. At least gardeners who attempt to grow things in the same neighborhood a herd of deer calls home.

But there are solutions. One, of course, is to hunt them. That's not always an option in the case of suburban communities or in other places that don't allow hunting, or it might not be a solution that appeals to you. People have also tried …

- Tying aluminum pie pans to poles so they bang against each other in the wind.

- Placing net bags filled with shaved soap or human hair in strategic spots around the garden.

- Spraying the ground around plants or the perimeter of the garden with bobcat, lion, coyote, or fox urine. (I want to know whose job it is to collect that stuff!)

- Playing a recording of shotgun blasts.

- Installing motion detector–activated sprinklers.

- Playing a recording of the *1812 Overture*.

- Rigging huge spotlights to shine on the garden all night.

- Spraying a mixture of garlic, cayenne pepper, and canola oil on every last leaf.

- Spreading lion dung around the base of plants.

There are also some commercial products like hot pepper wax and garlic oil spray, along with special dispensers for the coyote and lion urine. Some of these strategies work some of the time. But the truth of the matter is if deer are hungry enough, they will put up with things that scare them like the noise and the predator urine, and with things that smell bad like the cayenne pepper and the garlic oil.

The only really good solution is a barrier, which is almost always in the form of a fence. The key to a successful deer fence is height. Deer are remarkable jumpers, especially if they can get a running start.

I remember a garden in Princeton, New Jersey, with a deer problem that made national news. This garden had two chain-link deer fences, one running parallel to the other but inside the perimeter. The owner of the estate found that a single fence wasn't enough to keep out the local herd, but that the deer couldn't cope with the second fence because they couldn't get that running start. Unfortunately, the place looked like a prison camp.

Dave Benner, whose shade garden in Pennsylvania has been featured in many magazines and books, had such a problem with deer that he developed his own line of plastic mesh deer fencing. It can be up to 10 feet high and is strung between metal

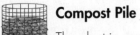

Compost Pile _____

The electric current that runs through electric deer fencing is not particularly high, but it can hurt a young child. Keep that in mind before you have an electric fence installed.

stakes. Combined with cattle gates at the driveway entrance, it has kept his garden deer free for a decade or more.

The other alternative is an electric fence. This really does keep Bambi and his family out of the garden. Electric fences have become less expensive as demand has increased.

The Least You Need to Know

◆ Identify the insects in your garden before you take any action.

◆ Encourage beneficial insects to take up residence in your garden.

◆ Give organic or natural approaches a try before using commercial pesticides.

◆ You can use fencing and a number of other tactics to keep warm-blooded animals from destroying your garden.

Chapter 22

Trimming, Deadheading, and Closing Up Shop

In This Chapter

- Your pruning toolkit
- What to cut and when
- Putting your garden to bed
- The benefits of planting "green manure"

Previous chapters have covered nearly everything you need to know about plotting and planning your garden, deciding what to plant, planting, weeding and watering, and feeding. You've put a lot of work into your garden, but you're not done yet.

In the next few pages, we look at the ways you can keep your plants healthy and productive by trimming and deadheading, with some specific information on how to trim herbs to maximize their potential. You also learn a little about dividing plants to multiply them. And finally, we go through the steps for putting your garden to bed for the winter.

Pick a Pruning Tool

Some gardeners get funny about tools. They may have a shed full of them, but they reach for the same two or three every time. You don't need a big selection of *pruning* tools, but a couple basic items are essential, including a versatile hand pruning tool and some small snips.

Basic Pruners

The pruner, held in one hand, is used for cutting plant material up to about $1/2$ inch in diameter.

Most hand pruners have metal blades and some sort of plastic-coated handles. A few have foam-covered or molded handles that have a comfortable feel. Blades can be chrome-plated steel, stainless steel, Teflon-coated steel, or carbon steel. The cutting mechanism is either a scissors action where a thin blade cuts against a thicker blade, or an anvil cut where a sharp upper blade cuts against a broad, flat blade.

Prof. Price's Pointers

Pruning is the cutting back of plant material to remove dead, diseased, or damaged parts; to alter the shape of the plant; to encourage new growth; and to improve the quality or quantity of the fruit or flowers.

My favorite pruners are the Felco #7 bypass style with anvil blade, spring action, and signature bright red rotating handle. I've owned several pairs over the past 30 years (they don't wear out; I just lose them), and I've never found a style of hand pruners I like better. A few years ago, I gave Prof. Price a pair, and he enjoys using them, too. What makes the #7s different is the way the rotating handle swivels in your hand—it's very comfortable and easy on the muscles, which is especially helpful when you have a lot of pruning to do.

Garden Snips

Garden snips are handy tools to have around for all kinds of garden tasks. You can use them to harvest herbs and vegetables that are cut from their stems (eggplants, peppers, okra, some squash, and so on). You can also use them to trim out dead or diseased herbaceous (as opposed to woody) plant material. And once in a while, you'll probably need them to cut twine or open a bag of mulch (but don't do that too often because it will dull the blade).

You'll find lots of different garden snips on the market. I have a pair that were a birthday gift 15 years ago, and I use them almost daily during the gardening season. (I also sometimes use them when I can't find my kitchen scissors, but don't tell my family that—they'd think that's disgusting.)

> **Garden Guru Says** _____
>
> Keep all your pruning tools well sharpened so they deliver a clean, smooth cut every time. And if you have any suspicion that a plant you're pruning is infected with disease, between every cut, wipe the blades clean with gauze soaked in alcohol.

Herbs All Year

If you've already had some experience with growing herbs, you know how easy they are to care for. And if you've been using your fresh herbs in your cooking, you'll not want to give them up. Isn't it nice to know that you can keep many of your herbs going all year long, even if you live in a cold climate?

Herbs are relatively easy to bring indoors when the summer growing season is over. And although they might not grow as well as they did outside, you could still have enough to harvest throughout the winter until it's time to take them outdoors again.

These are the best herbs for growing indoors:

Coriander	Parsley
French tarragon	Rosemary
Mint	Sage

From Outdoors In

In Chapter 16, we learned about growing herbs. But keep in mind that when you bring plants in from the garden, you'll have to acclimate them to the changes in temperature, light, and most importantly, humidity. Our homes tend to be a lot less humid than the great outdoors, and this can cause major stress on plants. Use a mister to make the plants feel at home.

It's a good idea to use fresh potting soil when you bring plants indoors. Never bring in soil from the garden; that's just asking for trouble. And be sure to inspect the plants for insects. Even if you don't see any, they might be there. One way to deal with that possibility is to spray the plants with an insecticidal soap before bringing them in.

You can suffocate insects on outdoor plants that are making the transition to indoors by putting the plants in a plastic bag, closing it with a twist tie, and putting the bagged plant inside another sealed plastic bag. Leave the shrouded plant in the bags for a few days. The plant must be dry when you do this, or it can rot. But the lack of oxygen might be enough to kill any lingering insects.

Pruning and Trimming Herbs

Herbs are pretty easygoing when it comes to keeping trim. Only the perennials need pruning, but some of the annuals require an occasional "haircut" to prevent them from going to seed or to help renew growth.

When the weather gets hot and the plants have been around for a while, some herbs are tempted to put out flowers. With most herbs, that's not a good thing. With all the energy plants need to produce flowers, there's less left for the leaves, and that's where the flavor typically is. Herbs may become bitter after they've flowered and their leaf production slows down.

With herbs such as basil, dill, mint, coriander, fennel, and most others, pinch out the flower buds as they appear. Simply squeeze the bud gently, just where it meets the stem, between your thumb and index finger and break it off with your fingernails.

If you have a lot of herbs growing in your garden, staying on top of this task takes some diligence.

Food for Thought _____

You might want to allow some herb flowers to bloom because they're attractive or even edible. Chives, rosemary, dill (to add to dill pickle jars as a garnish), nasturtiums (not technically an herb, but often grown with herbs), and chamomile are a few. And if you want to collect herb seeds, allow some of your herbs to go to seed so you have them to collect.

If your herb plants get really scraggly looking, go after them with your pruners. (You should do this anyway with your perennial herbs to keep them thick and compact.) Just cut away, even up to half the plant. Do your cutting in the late afternoon when the sun isn't so strong, and give them a good watering after. But don't do heavy pruning within a month or so of an expected frost. The new growth will be especially tender and the cold will most likely kill it.

Annual herbs can be cut back drastically, especially those that had an early start. Just don't expect them to grow back quickly. Allow a few weeks or even a month for them to grow enough foliage to start harvesting again.

The Best and the Brightest Veggies

When I was a young child, Prof. Price grew tomato plants in his garden at our home in New Jersey. I have a particular memory from that time of watching him pick the flowers off the tomatoes. When I asked him why he was doing that he patiently explained to me that it would make the plants produce bigger, better tomatoes.

Many fruiting annuals can benefit from the removal of some of the flower buds so more of the plant's energy can go into the remaining flowers and, thus, into the fruit. Try this not only with tomatoes, but also peppers, eggplants, cucumbers, melons, pumpkins, and squash. (By the way, this is one of the tricks some gardeners use to win the blue ribbon for the biggest tomato or pumpkin at the county fair.)

> **Prof. Price's Pointers**
>
> Seeds and fruits have the highest priority for a plant's resources. That's why the leaves of heavily fruited plants can sometimes look half-dead. Removing some of the flower buds, blooms, or very young fruits can help divert more goodies to the remaining fruits.

Deadheading

No, this has nothing to do with the Grateful Dead! Deadheading is the practice of removing dead blooms from plants. Most deadheading is done on ornamental flowering annuals and perennials and shrubs to encourage future bloom production. But some deadheading is appropriate for vegetable plants.

You should do this if the plant flowers but you don't want it to produce fruit or seeds. Use the same technique as you do for pinching out unwanted blooms described earlier.

Take Out Your Dead

Death is an inevitable part of the life cycle. With many, if not most gardens, death comes every year. You sow your annual plants, they grow, they reproduce, and they die. So what do you do with all those dead plants?

After the first heavy frost, just about all the leaves and stems of herbaceous plants will have curled up and died. The annual plants will be dead, and the perennials will go into dormancy. You should clean up all the dead plant material (unless you plan to do a tilling; see the next section), and get rid of it. The debris from healthy plants can go on the compost pile. Any with obvious disease problems should be disposed of.

If you have some late-harvest plants like turnips or kale, just clean up around them.

> **Compost Pile**
>
> It might be tempting to just walk away from the dead garden after a long season of working in it, but resist that temptation. Old plant material is a disease and infestation habitat waiting to happen. By maintaining good garden hygiene, even after the growing season, you'll be better able to avoid using harsh pesticides and herbicides in the future.

Not Dead; Just Asleep

Pulling up all the dead plants is the shortened version of the process of "putting the garden to bed" for the winter. Fastidious gardeners will do more.

For some gardeners, this extra work prolongs the time they get to spend in the garden. For others, it prolongs the time they have to spend in their garden. Either way, the more you do at the end of the season, the less you have to do at the beginning of the next gardening season.

Tilling and Fertilizing Encores

If you have the time and the inclination, you might want to give your garden a good tilling before you close it up for the winter. If you do plan to till, you won't have to pull out dead plants; you'll simply till them under. Just be sure to remove any diseased plants and dispose of them safely.

Before you till, you might think about adding a truckload or two of manure. When you fertilized earlier in the growing season, you used well-rotted manure, but this time you can use fresh manure because you're putting it on an unplanted bed where it can't burn tender plant parts.

Bedding Down Perennials

If your garden is in a colder zone, you might want to invest a little time in mulching the perennials. Strawberries, asparagus, and especially artichokes might need that extra protection.

For berries, use straw or wood chips 3 to 6 inches deep. Add this after the first hard frost.

Bed down asparagus with straw, wood shavings, compost, or leaf mold about 4 inches deep. Add the mulch after the first hard frost.

Artichokes do best with straw, leaves, or plastic mulch about 4 inches deep. Add the mulch before a frost. Artichokes won't survive long, cold winters; this protection is for marginal areas that sometimes experience a cold snap.

The Great Cover Up

Now that you have a beautifully retilled garden bed with nothing in it, why not plant a special crop of plants called a *cover crop* that will work to improve the soil while you do nothing at all (well, almost nothing)?

Cover crops, which are sometimes called *green manure*, help reduce soil compaction by loosening heavy soils at the root zone, reduce the leaching of nitrogen and other nutrients during winter rains, and, when tilled under, add organic matter to the soil. Legume cover crops add nitrogen to the soil because they fix nitrogen in their roots.

Some of the plants used for cover crops include the following:

Annual ryegrass	Hairy vetch (legume)
Buckwheat	Oats
Crimson clover (legume)	Sweet clover (legume)
Fava beans	Winter wheat
Field peas (legume)	

Most cover crops are planted in the late summer or early fall, although in parts of California this can be done as late as early December. For more information on how to sow your own cover crop, visit these websites:

www.gardening.cornell.edu/factsheets/ecogardening/impsoilcov.html

casfs.ucsc.edu/publications/gardenideas/cover_crops.pdf

hgic.clemson.edu/factsheets/HGIC1252

The Least You Need to Know

◆ Keep your pruning tools sharpened and clean.

◆ Disinfect pruning tools between cuts if you suspect your plants are diseased or infested.

◆ Pinch back flowers on herb plants to keep them going in hot weather.

◆ Use mulch to protect artichokes, asparagus, and strawberries in cold weather.

◆ Plant a legume cover crop to reduce soil compaction, protect loss of nutrients from runoff, and to help return nitrogen to the soil.

Chapter 23

Troubleshooting

In This Chapter

◆ A look at some diseases that could affect your garden

◆ Diagnosing fungus on your plants

◆ Addressing germination and seedling problems

◆ What leaves can tell you

A lot can go wrong in your edible garden. I don't want to sound like an alarmist, but even the most seasoned gardeners have had disappointing seasons or even disasters. It goes with the territory.

But to put your plant problems into perspective, it's important to keep in mind that thousands of plant pathologists, agricultural experts, and farm bureau agents have made plant pathology and the detection of diseases and problems their life's work. For our purposes here, there's only so much that can be covered in one chapter. The next few pages are designed to be an overview and a starting point for spotting and diagnosing problems in your garden.

In this chapter, we look at some of the major plant diseases, teach you to identify them, and help you handle them. We also look at a few of the more common symptoms of a distressed plant and some of the possible causes of the problems.

When Your Plants Are Sick

Most plant diseases are viral, bacterial, or fungal (not unlike human diseases). A few are related to nematodes. Then there are some *abiotic* problems that can occur because of nutrient deficiencies, too much or too little sun, or too much or not enough water.

Prof. Price's Pointers

Abiotic means that the problem is of nonliving or nonbiological origin.

Not every garden plant gets every disease. Some plants seem to get more than their fair share, whereas others are rarely bothered. The following table gives you a quick glance at some of the problems facing a few of your favorite garden plants.

Plant	Disease
Asparagus	Fusarium root rot, fusarium crown rot, asparagus rust, botrytis blight, Cercospora blight, purple spot, branchlet blight, asparagus virus, tobacco streak virus
Beet	Leaf spot, damping off, pocket rot, root rot, curly top, powdery mildew, downy mildew, cyst nematode
Lettuce	Downy mildew, leaf drop, turnip mosaic virus, bacterial leaf rot, corky rot, southern blight rust, sow thistle yellow vein virus, anthracnose, lettuce mosaic virus, cucumber mosaic virus, beet western yellow virus, big vein, powdery mildew
Okra	Fusarium wilt, root knot, leaf spot, blossom and fruit blight, cotton root rot, southern blight
Potato	Black dot disease, fusarium dry rot, early blight, late blight, black scurf fungus, silver scurf fungus, powdery scab, pythium seed rot, pythium rubber rot, ring rot, spindle tuber, fusarium wilt, verticillium wilt
Tomato	Anthracnose, tomato mosaic virus, curly top virus, blossom end rot, cucumber mosaic virus, root knot, bacterial speck, bacterial spot, bacterial canker, late blight, fusarium crown rot, fusarium foot rot, phytophyhora root rot, tomato powdery mildew, fusarium wilt, verticillium wilt

As you can see, the lists of diseases are pretty long. Some diseases are peculiar to a specific plant, whereas others attack a long list of victims. Don't be totally put off by this, though. Your garden isn't likely to be invaded by every disease listed here. But the more you grow, the more likely your chances of learning firsthand about these things. The following sections might help you get to the bottom of what's troubling your plants.

> **Garden Guru Says** _____
>
> If you're having trouble identifying what's wrong with an ailing plant, talk to an expert. But don't expect even the most experienced plant professional to make a diagnosis without seeing the problem firsthand. Put the evidence (leaf, stem, fruit, insect, whatever) into an airtight plastic bag for your own little show and tell. County agents and master gardeners are sometimes available to help. And some garden centers and nurseries have their own garden gurus on staff.

Dealing With Viral Diseases

As they can with humans, viruses cause mayhem, turning healthy plants into diseased ones in a matter of days, if not hours. There are hundreds of viruses that attack plants. Some of the more common ones include the following:

Beet curly top

Cucumber mosaic

Pepper golden mosaic

Pepper mottle

Potato virus

Tobacco mosaic

Tomato spotted wilt

Some symptoms of viral infection include curled or twisted leaves, mottled or mosaic patterns on leaves, brown or yellow spots on leaves, stunted growth, and small flowers that might be brown or otherwise "off."

Many plant viruses are spread by insects; aphids, leafhoppers, mites, and whiteflies are the worst offenders. Infected tools and equipment, infected mulch, and even a person's hands or clothing can also spread plant viruses.

> **Compost Pile** _____
>
> The tobacco mosaic, a virus that's deadly for tomatoes, can be spread by smokers. The tobacco in cigarettes can actually carry the virus and the smoker can become the vector (carrier) of the disease. As if you didn't need another reason to give up smoking!

Unfortunately, viral infections in plants are not treatable by methods available to home gardeners. The best thing to do if you suspect that a plant has a viral disease is to remove it immediately and dispose of it. Keeping weeds and insects under control helps, too.

Never put diseased plant material on the compost pile. Dispose of it by bagging it and putting it in the trash, incinerating it (if that's allowed in your area), or burying it far from the garden. The quicker you are to react to problems, the less you'll have to depend on less-than-earth-friendly practices.

When Bacterial Diseases Attack

There are lots of bacterial diseases, but three are of particular concern to vegetable gardeners:

◆ Bacterial wilt

◆ Bacterial canker

◆ Bacterial spot

In the following sections, we cover each of these diseases in detail so you can help keep them out of your garden.

Bacterial Wilt

Anyone who has ever grown cucumbers, zucchini, or pumpkins has probably had experience with this major bacterial plant disease. Bacterial wilt, which is also called *vascular wilt*, causes buildup of the bacteria within the vascular (water-carrying) system of plants. When the waterways become completely clogged, they can no longer carry water throughout the plant, and it wilts and dies. The disease is systemic, meaning it's carried throughout the plant, rather than localized, or limited to one part of the plant.

Bacterial wilt primarily attacks members of the cucurbit family, especially cucumbers, squash, pumpkins, cantaloupes, and muskmelons. It tends to leave watermelon alone.

Bacterial wilt is spread by cucumber beetles that have the bacteria living in their bodies. When they come up out of the ground in the spring, they start chomping on a healthy plant, making an opening or wound for the disease to enter. The bacteria is in the insects' waste and eventually finds its way into the wound. The plant can be dead in a matter of weeks.

When you first see your cucumbers or zucchini wilting, you'll probably suspect a water shortage. After watering, the plant might perk up a bit, but if it has bacterial wilt, it'll probably be wilted again the next day.

Some other symptoms include retarded growth and excessive blooms and branching. You might also see that the veins of pumpkins and squash plants turn yellow. This, however, doesn't happen to cucumbers with bacterial wilt.

Garden Guru Says

Squash borer produces similar symptoms to bacterial wilt. But with the insect infestation, you might actually find one of the caterpillars inside the plant, or you might find tunnels through the stems.

One way to help you determine whether your squash or cucumbers have bacterial wilt is to cut a piece of stem from an affected plant. Slowly squeeze the stem and see what comes out. If it's a white, slimy substance that pulls into a string, it's most likely bacterial wilt.

The best way to deal with bacterial wilt is to not have it in the first place. Keeping the cucumber beetle population down is key. But the chemicals that kill them also do a number on bees, and, of course, bees are essential for pollination. Removing infected plants, hand-picking insects, and rotating crops are good natural approaches. If the problem persists after several seasons, consider growing something else instead. Or call your county extension office to ask for some advice on using organic chemical controls that won't endanger bees.

Bacterial Canker

This nasty-sounding disorder is primarily a disease of stone fruit (which we're not interested in here) and tomatoes. It starts out locally with dark spots on the leaves or stems that look wet. The disease can also first appear with an overall wilting. Sometimes the stems split up and down, and you might see some dark brown sores (these are the cankers) with necrotic tissue (that's dead plant tissue). The wilting and splitting is evidence that the disease has entered the plant's vascular system and is, therefore, systemic.

Bacterial canker is caused by a bacteria that lingers in dead or dying tomato plants, or in *host plants* like eggplants, peppers, and other members of the *Solanaceae* family (the nightshade family). The disease is easily spread by splashing water, by small wounds made during transplanting (just a broken leaf is enough), or when the gardener prunes or removes stems while caging or staking.

Prof. Price's Pointers

A **host plant** is one that is susceptible to a certain pathogen (virus, bacteria, and so on). An *alternative host* is one in which a pathogen has taken up residence at some point in its life cycle. The alternative host might or might not be susceptible to the pathogen.

To keep the threat of bacterial canker to a minimum, buy certified disease-free seeds and seedlings whenever possible, disinfect pruners and snips between each cut, wash your hands before handling tomatoes, stay out of the garden when it's wet, and rotate your crops.

Bacterial Spot

This disease attacks tomatoes and peppers and affects every part of the plant except the roots, especially during periods of high humidity or rainy, wet conditions. Look for raised yellowish lesions (spots) on green tomatoes and on both ripe and immature peppers. The lesions turn brown or black and start to look like scabs. The leaves will develop spots, too, and often drop off. The plant will look absolutely awful, and you won't want to eat any of the fruit, even if some of it does ripen.

Garden Guru Says

Some gardeners use a copper-based fungicide to treat bacterial spot. The fungicide won't cure the plant, but sometimes it does keep the bacteria from spreading to the rest of your tomatoes and peppers. Although use of copper is approved for organic produce in the United States, it has been disallowed in Europe.

Bacterial spot spreads pretty much the same way as bacterial canker, and is just as, or more, difficult to treat. You'll probably wind up just pulling the diseased plants out and discarding them.

The best way to deal with this disease is to prevent it in the first place. Use certified seed, stay out of the wet garden, follow strict garden hygiene, and rotate crops.

There's a Fungus Among Us

Fungal diseases are another headache for gardeners. They're insidious, difficult to control, and frequently lethal. These are some of the most common:

◆ Anthracnose

◆ Various rusts

◆ Fusarium wilt

◆ Downy and powdery mildew

Anthracnose

Anthracnose is a pretty ugly plant disease with various forms that attack a number of vegetables, including tomatoes, beans, cucumbers, peppers, melons, squash, and pumpkins. It's caused by a fungus that lives in the soil over the winter and is spread by insects, rain, wind, watering, and by infected seeds or seedlings.

The symptoms start with large, round, soft spots on the fruits that might become black or brown and develop quickly into rot. The leaves and stems might develop lesions or spots.

You might find some relief if you spray with an antifungal spray. Other ways to deal with anthracnose include the following:

◆ Use pretreated seeds.

◆ Select resistant varieties.

◆ Practice good garden hygiene.

◆ Rotate annual crops every year.

◆ Avoid walking in the garden just after a rain or an overhead watering.

◆ Keep weeds to a minimum.

◆ Remove infected plants.

Anthracnose can affect other plants, too, including strawberries, corn, and lettuce. Providing good air circulation for your crops also helps keep anthracnose at bay.

Rust

Rust is another bad problem caused by a parasitic fungus. Rust attacks asparagus, corn, beans, and peas.

The first symptom is usually a blemish or lesion on the underside of lower leaves. Eventually it becomes more of a sore that opens and releases orange to red spores, hence the name.

There is no good cure. Commercial growers might use some heavy-duty fungicides, but home gardeners don't want to go there. Instead, cut your losses by digging up the infected plants and disposing of them. In your next attempt, plant in new or different beds and look for resistant varieties.

Fusarium Wilt

Fusarium wilt is tricky because the fusarium fungus can live in the soil for years without showing itself in plants. But when plants it likes, including members of the *Cucurbit* family, are planted in the infected soil, the fusarium fungus easily enters the plants through their roots.

Plants can be infected at several stages of their development, including just after germination when it results in damping off. Older plants might wilt, appear to recover, and wilt again. Later the leaves start to turn yellow or brown, and eventually the whole plant just dies. Sometimes, when conditions are particularly wet and humid, you might see a pale pink powdery residue on the leaves and stems.

There's not much you can do about the disease after the plants are infected. Prevention is the key. The only defense is a good offense—plant resistant varieties. If you have a crop of fusarium-infected plants, don't plant any more *Cucurbits* in that spot for a few years.

Mildew

The two major mildew diseases are caused by different fungal infections. Powdery mildew, which affects cucumbers, squash, and onions, tends to hit new growth and particularly blossoms, which often dry up, so no fruit is set. The mildew grows on the surface of leaves, which will look dark and dirty and feel kind of sooty.

Downy mildew is actually a parasite that grows inside plants, especially cucumbers, beans, and onions. It produces purple and black spots on leaves and a gray mold on fruits. Downy mildew weakens plants so they produce less.

A few mildew-killing fungicides on the market are marketed as safe for vegetable gardens. Most contain copper and sulfur. Be sure to read labels carefully before using. Both mildew fungi can live in old garden debris, so good garden hygiene is a must.

Compost Pile _____

It should go without saying, but always wash any fruits or vegetables that come from treated plants. You don't want to ingest any of the fungicide.

Coping With Germination Problems

When seeds don't grow, it could be because of a limited number of reasons:

- ◆ The seed is old.
- ◆ The seed is infected.
- ◆ It is planted too deep.
- ◆ It was washed away in the rain or by heavy irrigation.
- ◆ Birds got it.
- ◆ It was burned by fertilizer.
- ◆ Too much moisture.
- ◆ Not enough moisture.
- ◆ Too cold.
- ◆ Too hot.
- ◆ Residual preemergent herbicide in soil.

Sometimes it's a combination of things that prevents seed from germinating. But if you see a big flock of crows or starlings land in the garden right after you plant, and the seeds don't sprout, I think you'll know what the problem was.

Seedling Situations

So your seeds have all germinated and the little sprouts have gotten off to a fine start when, all of a sudden, they're failing to thrive or even dying. What happened? Following are possibilities for what might have gone wrong:

◆ Too cold or too hot

◆ Too much water

◆ Not enough water

◆ Not enough sunlight

◆ Too much fertilizer

◆ Not enough fertilizer

◆ Insect attacks

◆ Damping off

◆ Residual herbicide in the soil

Not all these conditions result in dead plants. But you need to correct those things that can be corrected—and quickly, if you want to save your newly planted crops.

Lousy Leaves

The appearance of a plant's leaves gives some pretty clear indications of its overall health. The occasional nibbled edge or a yellow leaf or two is not a sign that the plant is in deep trouble. If, on the other hand, all the leaves are turning yellow or if more leaves have holes than don't, you can be pretty sure the plant is in big trouble.

Any number of issues show themselves in the foliage—disease, insect infestation, lack of nitrogen or another crucial element. The trick is to make the correct diagnosis.

Yellow Leaves

Yellow leaves are one of the most common symptoms that indicate something is wrong with your plant. And diagnosis can be a little tricky with yellow leaves.

If many of the leaves are yellow, it can mean the plant isn't getting enough nitrogen, the weather is too hot, or there's not enough sunlight.

Food for Thought

Occasionally, too much sunlight can be the culprit that causes leaves to yellow. Although most edible plants want full sun all day, some plants might find themselves suddenly in a sunnier situation than they were used to. This might happen if, for example, you were growing corn next to some kale. If you've harvested the corn and the kale is no longer shaded by the corn, its leaves might turn yellow.

If only the newest leaves are yellow, it might mean that the plant is getting too much fertilizer or it has an iron or manganese deficiency.

When older leaves turn yellow, it could mean there's not enough nitrogen (or iron or manganese), the plant is being watered too often, or it has root rot problems. But sometimes yellow older leaves mean that the leaves are getting ready to drop off anyway. If the plant has plenty of healthy-looking newer leaves, it's probably fine.

Sticky Leaves

When you find black or brown sticky stuff on your plants' leaves, you know that you'll find some kind of insect infestation. That sticky stuff is called frass or honeydew, and it's basically insect poop.

Keep your eyes open for the insects that are leaving their calling cards behind. Then refer to Chapter 21 to find out what to do with your insect problems.

Other Problem Leaves

So many things can go wrong with plants, and much of it will show up in the leaves. The following table lists a few symptoms to look for.

Symptom	Possible Causes
Defoliation	Too much or not enough water, too much fertilizer, root rot, too cold, exposure to herbicide
Leaf ends are necrotic	Too much fertilizer, not enough water, damage from pesticides, bacterial wilt
New leaves are yellow	Too much fertilizer, iron or manganese deficiency
Wilted leaves	Too much or not enough water, too much fertilizer, too cold (frost damage), root rot

continues

continued

Symptom	Possible Causes
Yellow leaves	Low nitrogen, too hot, not enough light, sunscald
Yellow older leaves	Nitrogen, manganese, or potassium deficiency; too much water; root rot; normal loss of older leaves

We've described the seemingly endless things that can make your vegetable plants very sick, and even kill them, but don't be discouraged. Some plants do die quickly, and you'll have to replant or give up on that particular vegetable, but others will look terrible while continuing to produce prodigiously.

The Least You Need to Know

- ◆ Look for disease-resistant seeds and seedlings.
- ◆ Always buy certified disease-free seeds and seedlings.
- ◆ Avoid working in the garden when it's wet.
- ◆ Practice good garden hygiene.
- ◆ Rotate crops every year to avoid soil-born and insect-spread diseases.
- ◆ Consult a garden professional when you can't figure out what's troubling your plants.

Part 6

Reaping the Rewards

This is what it is all about—let's eat! There's nothing like picking crops you have grown yourself. In Part 6, we look at the end product. You learn how to determine when it's time to harvest and how to do it right. We include sections on canning, freezing, and drying food and there's also some information on how to share what you grow with those who are less fortunate.

In these last few chapters you also learn about seed saving, which has become a near cult with wildly enthusiastic followers. Also included is a section on tool care and repair. Finally, you get a chance to take a guided look back on what you've accomplished, to see what you did right and to figure out what you can do better next year.

Chapter 24

Harvest Time

In This Chapter

- ◆ When and how to harvest
- ◆ Tips for extending your harvesting season
- ◆ The basics of putting up foods
- ◆ What to do with 100 zucchini

It's finally here, what you've been waiting for all season: the harvest! It's the gardener's big reward.

In this chapter, we look at some of the ways you can determine ripeness and some techniques for harvesting. We also talk about how to preserve and store the fruits and vegetables you've grown so you can enjoy the bounty for weeks and even months after the harvest. And finally, we explore some of the ways you can spread the wealth by sharing the food you've grown yourself.

The Ripeness Test

Many factors contribute to the process of ripening. Plant varieties, soil and air temperature, day length, rainfall or irrigation amounts, stress, even insect infestation or disease can all make a difference on the rate of growth and ultimately ripeness.

Prof. Price's Pointers

The ripening of fruit involves many metabolic changes including the conversion of starch to sugars; the breakdown of cell walls and of chlorophyll; and the synthesis of other pigments, such as anthocyanins (red) and carotenoids (yellow and orange). Ripening in many (but not all) fruits is associated with a spectacular rise in the rate of respiration, or *cliacteric*. These metabolic and respiratory changes very strongly depend on temperature, which is why refrigerated fruits ripen very slowly.

Usually, we talk about ripeness with regard to fruiting plants such as tomatoes, eggplants, and peppers and for fruits like melons. It's actually pretty easy to figure out whether or not they're ripe. Common sense helps. But there are a few rules of thumb to consider before deciding whether something is ready to be picked.

Fruiting Vegetables

Tomatoes, unless they're one of the heirloom or exotic varieties, should be evenly red, with maybe just a little green or yellow at the top where the fruit meets the stem.

Eggplants and peppers should be shiny and firm, but not hard, with well-developed color. You can pick red, orange, or yellow peppers when they're still green. Green peppers won't change color but will eventually rot if you leave them on the vine too long. If you're growing several varieties of peppers, be sure to place markers so you'll know which plants are which.

Garden Guru Says

You can pick tomatoes before they're fully ripe. And if the weather turns very hot, you might want to do a thorough harvesting of unripe good-size tomatoes and let them finish ripening on a sunny windowsill. Or you can fry or pickle green tomatoes.

To harvest fruiting vegetables, use a pair of clean, sharp garden snips or kitchen scissors. Cut just a bit of stem with the fruit. Avoid sawing or hacking at the stem (which happens when using a dull tool) because that can cause damage, making it easier for insects or disease to enter the wound. Clean your snips with alcohol between each cut, or at least between each plant to minimize the risk of introducing disease.

Strawberries and Melons

Strawberries should be all red with little or no white at the stem end. Most people pick strawberries with a little thumbnail action. Take the entire berry stem, cutting it off where it meets the main stem. This helps the berries stay fresher longer.

Did you ever thump a watermelon in the supermarket to determine whether it's ripe? You chose one that "sounded" right only to find it was still hard as a rock inside? Even the experts recommend the thump test, but you'll have a better idea if you know more or less how many days the melon is supposed to take from seed to harvest and how large it's supposed to be at maturity. Add that information to the fact that ripe watermelons have a little patch of yellow on the skin where the fruit meets the ground and have that slightly hollow sound when you give them a thump.

Food for Thought

For more specific harvesting information on many of the plants we have covered in this book, go to www.urbanext.uiuc.edu/tog/harvest.html or aggie-horticulture. tamu.edu/extension/harvest/harvest.html.

Bigger Isn't Always Better

When I go to our local Grange and 4-H Fairs, I always visit the vegetable exhibits where area gardeners and 4-H kids get prizes for the biggest tomatoes and pumpkins. Sometimes bigger is better. But often, the smaller veggies have superior flavor. Of course, you can grow dwarf varieties or small versions of all kinds of vegetables, including cherry and grape tomatoes, carrots, patty pan squash, watermelons, and others.

Some standard-size vegetables can be harvested when they're still very tiny, yet fully formed, as mentioned earlier in the book. These tasty "baby" vegetables can command high prices in the produce department, but they won't cost you a penny more to grow in your garden. The following table lists some of the best vegetables for harvesting young and the best time and size to harvest them.

Vegetable	Minimum Size to Pick (Estimated)
Beets	Golf ball size
Carrots	2 inches or more
Cauliflower	Softball size (remember to blanch it)
Corn	Fully formed; 2 or 3 inches long
Eggplants	10 inches long
Leeks	2 inches across
Lettuce	Whatever size appeals to you
Okra	2 or 3 inches
Other greens	Whatever size appeals to you
Peas	Peas are fully formed; half the size of fully mature peas
Potatoes	Size of a medium egg
Scallions	As big around as a pencil
Snap beans	As wide as a chopstick
Summer squash	4 inches long; 1 inch across
Zucchini	4 inches long; 1 inch across

If you plan to harvest lots of "baby" vegetables, you might want to add extra plants. It takes many more tiny beets or eggplants to fill your dinner plate than normal-size ones.

Late Harvests

As you might have figured out after reading the chapters devoted to how to grow various edibles, some plants have a drawn-out harvest period.

If you've planted in relays (that is, made additional sowings of the same plant over a period of several weeks), or if you've made spring, summer, and fall plantings, you can probably count on a longer harvest period.

There are additional methods for giving the home gardener extended and late harvests of some of their favorite edibles, including the following:

♦ Use floating row covers, after the fruit has set, to hold in heat and protect plants from early frosts.

- Make mini-greenhouses over your garden rows with wire or wooden frames and plastic sheeting.

- Plant a crop of smaller things like lettuce, arugula, tender herbs, mini carrots, and radishes in a cold frame.

- Cover individual plants with cloches or bell jars when the temperatures dip. Remove them when it gets warmer.

- Bring a few things inside (especially herbs).

- Build a greenhouse.

Food for Thought

Garden writers Eliot Coleman and Barbara Damrosch grow organic vegetables year round in their tunnel-style greenhouse using only heat generated by the sun. And they do this in Maine! Coleman has written a book, *Four Season Harvest* (Chelsea Green Publishing Co., 1992) with details on how they have accomplished this amazing feat.

If you expect an unusually early frost and don't have the time or inclination to build shelters for your garden, you can improvise. I've covered the plants I wasn't willing to sacrifice to early frosts with sheets, blankets, beach towels, tablecloths, drop cloths, shower curtains, and even newspapers. On many occasions, I was able to add several weeks to my gardening season with my eclectic plant covers.

You can also extend your harvest by planting things that don't mind spending a little time in the cold. You might recall that some vegetables like brussels sprouts, kale, spinach, and chard can be harvested after the first frost, and some, like rutabagas, turnips, winter squash, and pumpkins actually have a richer flavor after they've been exposed to some cold.

Handle with Care

Some plants—cabbage, cauliflower, carrots, turnips and parsnips, radishes, leeks, onions in particular—are harvested whole. You either cut or pull them right out of the garden and discard (or, preferably, compost) the parts you don't want.

But many plants—beans, peas, tomatoes, peppers, eggplants, lettuce, zucchinis, and strawberries, to name a few—are harvested in stages. Many of these plants produce fruit over the course of several weeks, so the attentive gardener might have the opportunity for (or the chore of) daily harvesting.

Compost Pile

Always wash your hands before entering the garden to harvest, or any time for that matter. It's not a bad idea to wash again between visits to different types of plants. This might seem hypercautious, but it can help avoid spreading disease in your garden.

With this kind of extended harvest period, you must take great care not to damage the plants you pick from. Never yank or tug on a fruit to remove it from the stem. If the fruit doesn't release after a slight twist of the wrist, use your garden snips or kitchen scissors to cut it off. With peas and beans, use your thumbnail to cut through the tiny stem that attaches the fruit to the vine.

While you're harvesting, be on the lookout for signs of disease or infestation. Examine the undersides of leaves, pick off insects, and remove damaged leaves and fruits. In addition to carrying a basket for your harvest, take along a plastic bag, like the ones your newspaper is delivered in, to collect anything yucky. Then dump it in the trash after you've finished your picking.

Try to harvest on dry days and late enough in the day that the dew is gone. Harvesting in the early evening is a good time, too, especially right before you start making dinner. You'll have the very freshest produce that way.

Food for Thought

One way to harvest lettuces and other greens such as spinach, kale, chard, beets, and collards is by thinning young seedlings to the desired distances between plants in a row. You can use these tender young thinnings for salad. Later, you can continue to harvest individual leaves from plants without disrupting their growth. Just be sure to only take a few from each plant so it's left with enough foliage. You should never take more than about ⅛ or so of the leaves of an individual plant until it's time to harvest the whole thing.

Canning, Freezing, and Drying

There's something extraordinarily satisfying about having a pantry full of jams, jellies, relishes, and pickles you've prepared yourself from the bounty of your garden. In the summer of 1977, back when I had my really big garden in New Jersey, I took a course on canning at the Rutgers University Cooperative Extension. It was a half-day affair during which I learned how to "put up" foods.

That summer I made strawberry and cherry jams, mint and apple jellies, bread and butter pickles, and dill pickles, and I put up dozens of jars of tomatoes. It was glorious. I later learned from my mother, who had never in her life made jelly or pickles, that *her* mother had taken the very same kind of course from the cooperative extension in Connecticut back in the 1920s. I felt an incredible sense of connectedness to my roots.

In this section, we look at some of the options you have for putting up food. Keep in mind that whatever method you try, use only the best and fully ripe fruits and vegetables and those that are free of blemishes and signs of insect damage or disease.

Can It!

Canning fresh produce is a great way to preserve the bounty from your garden. And it's not all that difficult. The key is safety. You need to know what you're doing or you could wind up poisoning your family and friends. If you can't take a class at your local county extension office or adult education school, or if you don't have a friend or relative who is willing to teach you, go online for excellent step-by-step instructions. There's been an enormous renewed interest in this subject recently, so you should be able to find thousands of websites. The university county extensions are among the best bets.

There are several basic canning methods. With *cold pack*, you put uncooked food into canning jars and then process them. *Hot pack* involves putting cooked food into canning jars and then processing. If you're *pickling*, you combine cooked or uncooked food with a vinegar solution, then process. For *conserving*, you combine fruit products with sugar (and sometimes pectin) and then process.

The pickling process raises the acid level in the preserving jar to a level that's inconsistent with the growth of bacteria, yeasts, molds, and fungi that cause spoiling—and possibly illness. Because of their naturally high acid content, most tomatoes can be canned without adding anything to them, although some people add a little lemon juice or citric acid. They are usually processed in boiling water for a specific amount of time.

Food for Thought

Eating produce you've canned from your organic garden is about as green as you can get. Your food hasn't been trucked in from miles away, you haven't driven to the store to buy it, you've conscientiously avoided Earth-damaging products and practices, and you've packaged it in reusable containers. Good for you!

Some varieties of tomatoes have been bred to have reduced acid levels, which might be kinder on some people's stomachs. However, lower acid levels make these varieties poor candidates for canning. Know your tomato varieties before you can.

Canning vegetables other than tomatoes requires a different process—one that's done in a pressure canner. And even if you add as little as a garlic clove or a sprig of basil to your tomatoes, you'll need to do those in a pressure canner as well.

Freeze!

If you plan your garden well, you can freeze enough food to last all year in the freezer. And for those who are just a little afraid of the canning thing, freezing is the way to go.

Just about anything you grow can be frozen. Some things need to be cooked first, whereas other vegetables can be frozen after a quick blanching (which is basically a short boil in water, followed by a quick bath in ice water to stop the cooking process).

The following table tells you what you need to do before freezing some of the vegetables we've covered in this book.

Food	Prefreezing Prep
Asparagus	Blanch
Beans	Blanch
Beets	Fully cook
Broccoli	Blanch
Cabbage	Blanch
Corn	Blanch, fully cook
Eggplants	Fully cook
Garlic	None—freeze raw
Onion	None—freeze raw
Peas	Blanch
Peppers	None—freeze raw
Summer squash	Blanch, fully cook
Tomatoes	None—freeze raw, blanch, or fully cook
Winter squash	Fully cook

Most vegetables only need to be blanched for 1 to 3 minutes. To stop the cooking process, put the blanched vegetable in a bowl of ice water, drain, and dry before freezing. For a complete list with detailed instructions, visit www.ochef.com/617.htm.

All Dried Up

Humans learned to dry food very early in our collective history. For thousands of years, it was the only method we had to preserve food. You probably learned in grade school how Native Americans dried berries, corn, fish, and thin strips of meat to help them survive during difficult times.

Drying food became a lost art until the back-to-nature movement of the late 1960s. Since then, more people have been trying it. My old neighbor Frank Pinello made sun-dried tomatoes on racks on his terrace one summer. They were quite delicious.

Tomatoes and various fruits are among the easiest things to dry, but enthusiasts try drying just about any vegetable. It takes a lot of effort, and failure is common. The important elements to success are high heat, low humidity, and adequate air circulation. Open-air drying is the most difficult method and the most prone to failure. Simple solar dryers have more success, while electric dehydrators are probably the best way to go. If you're really interested in trying this method of food preservation, go online to find one of the many websites with details on how to do it.

Garden Guru Says

Root cellaring and cold storage are two more options for preserving food. To learn more, visit www.extension. umn.edu/distribution/horticulture/ DG1424.html. Check out the chart on vegetable storage requirements.

Sharing Your Bounty

There are lots of jokes about gardeners searching for ingenious ways to dispose of an overabundance of zucchinis or eggplants. That's a success problem we'd all like to enjoy. But sometimes we're blessed with more produce than we can manage to eat, can, freeze, or give to our neighbors and coworkers. So what do we do with it?

If you've given away fresh vegetables and fruits from your garden to everyone you know and you still have too much, think about donating some to a local food bank or homeless shelter. These places are often delighted to be able to offer fresh food to their clients, who usually subsist on canned or packaged items. Some food banks also accept fresh food that you've frozen yourself, especially if they know you and you've labeled the item with the contents and the date it was frozen.

Plant a Row for the Hungry, a national public service campaign started in 1995 by the Garden Writers Association of America, encourages gardeners to grow a little extra each year to share with needy neighbors. To find out more about this organization go to www.gwaa.org. Many organizations, communities, and states have their own version of this type of program. Look online to find such an organization near you, or your county extension office might know of a program in your community.

Compost Pile

No matter how much people like to receive a gift of fresh produce from a gardening friend, no one wants an overweight zucchini. Those huge green hulks that look like caveman clubs are best thrown on the compost pile. Then take a look at them as they rot to remind yourself to harvest early and often.

If you still have way too much harvest to handle, think about setting up a little roadside stand. Bill and Jane MacDowell, who have an extraordinary organic garden in my community, put their excess produce on a stand at the end of their driveway with an honor box for people to pay for what they take. Then Bill and Jane donate the proceeds to a local wildflower preserve.

And if your garden produces prolific amounts of gourmet-style vegetables and herbs, you could let some of your local restaurants, caterers, or specialty markets know about it. They might want to give you all kinds of money for your fancy fresh stuff.

The Least You Need to Know

♦ Know your varieties and their approximate maturity times so you can estimate a harvest date.

♦ Use clean, sharp garden snips or kitchen scissors to harvest stem fruits.

♦ Harvest when the garden is dry to avoid spreading diseases.

♦ By canning and freezing foods, you can enjoy your harvest for months.

♦ Think about sharing your harvest with friends, neighbors, and those who might not have enough to eat.

Chapter 25

Next Year's Garden

In This Chapter

- ◆ The fascinating world of seed savers
- ◆ Bringing herbs indoors safely
- ◆ The advantages of keeping a record of your gardening activities
- ◆ Getting a handle on tool care

If you're an obsessive planner like I am, you'll enjoy thinking about next year's garden and all the wonderful things you might be able to do in it. If you're the out-of-sight-out-of-mind type, you've probably already skipped this chapter.

In the next few pages, we enter the fascinating world of seed savers, who might very well have transformed an ancient agricultural practice into a cutting-edge horticultural trend. We also talk a little more about bringing herb plants indoors for winter enjoyment. And we look at why record keeping is not just for tax reasons. Finally, you learn how to take care of your pruners and other tools so they'll be ready to go in the spring.

Saving Seeds

Did you know there's a whole culture out there devoted to saving seeds? I'm not kidding. Seed saving is a worldwide phenomenon. There are seed saving clubs and associations, how-to books and handbooks, newsletters and magazines, websites, legislation, and meetings and conventions. One website starts out with the words this "tool is designed to empower individuals to participate in the creation of tomorrow." It's from an activist network dedicated to "protecting agricultural biodiversity and creating local food security."

Seed saving is a fascinating topic. But what does it have to do with you, you might ask? Well, if you're the thrifty type, you can save money by saving seeds. You can also be assured that you'll have seeds for the plants you want, without risk of disappointment should the seed company run out of them. Another advantage of seed saving is that you can do your own organic thing. And you could actually develop a new variety with traits that please you.

Prof. Price's Pointers

Hybrid plants are the offspring of two plants of different varieties (or species). A hybrid is a new variety with one or more genetic traits different from the parents. **Open-pollinated** seeds come from plants that have been pollinated by nature. Generally they produce offspring that are exactly like the parent plants, although it is possible for nature to produce a hybrid.

There are only a few basic things you need to know to start saving seeds. One of the most important is to know the kinds of plants you're planning to collect seeds from. You want to collect seeds from plants that were grown from *open-pollinated* seeds (meaning by birds and other natural pollinators) rather than from *hybrids*. The naturally pollinated seeds will be more true to the original plant.

It's very easy to save seeds from plants that produce seed pods or stalks. Simply allow the seeds to fully ripen on the plant, carefully cut the stalk or pod, place it in a paper bag, and shake it gently. Then remove the dried stalk and any vegetation, which leaves you with just seeds. Put the seeds in an airtight container like a baby food jar or a plastic zipper bag, and store them away from heat and light.

Saving seeds from fruiting vegetables is a little more complicated because you have to deal with the messy insides where the seeds develop.

I've read, although I have never tried it, that the way to save seeds from tomatoes is to take the squishy parts that hold the seeds and smear them on a piece of newspaper.

Let this dry, pick the seeds off the newspaper, and put them in a storage container. As messy a job as it is, I do think it's worthwhile, especially if you've just had a spectacular season with an unusual plant.

Be sure to label your seeds as soon as you put them in the storage containers. It's really hard to distinguish seeds, and you don't want to plant turnips instead of cabbage!

Food for Thought

I'm not a seed saver (I'm way too disorganized), but I used to collect seeds from pumpkins every year at Halloween. After my husband cut jack-o'-lanterns with our girls, I would take the scooped-out pumpkin innards and clean them, removing all the gunk. Then I toasted them, but had I wanted to save them for planting, I would have dried them with paper towels and put them on a drying rack in a cool dry place. After the seeds were completely dried, I would have sorted through them to eliminate any that had any mold or rot and then put them in an airtight container. Very simple, very easy.

Some gardeners save seeds as a generation-to-generation thing, and they enjoy knowing that the corn or beans they're growing is from the same stock as the ones their grandfathers planted. Other gardeners do it for the trading aspect. People swap seeds all over the country. Saving seeds is also a great hands-on science lesson for kids, and they might have fun with it.

Tool Care and Repair

You probably have a bit of investment in your garden tools, so you should take good care of them. I assume that during the gardening season you've been reasonably careful with your tools, taking care to clean off the soil and debris after each use. And you've always put them away at the end of the day. Right?

Well, even if you've been a little slipshod, you make up for it by giving all your tools a good cleaning and servicing before you hang them up for the winter.

Sharp as a Tack

Keeping pruning tools sharp is an essential task. You can have it done by a professional, which isn't usually very expensive, or you can do it yourself.

My good friend Steve Cooper, who managed one of my favorite nurseries, used to sharpen my pruners for me when I'd stop by for a visit during the off-season. He'd take out an ancient whetstone and, with just a few strokes, make my pruners razor sharp. It's a very old-fashioned skill, and one worth having.

Here's how to take care of your pruners:

1. Clean the blades with a solvent like paint thinner, turpentine, or nail polish remover.

2. Rub the blades with steel wool or emery cloth to remove any rust or plant residue.

> **Food for Thought**
>
> I've seen classes on tool sharpening offered at large garden centers, adult schools, and county extension offices. If there's one scheduled near you, go for it. Take all your pruners along and get them done while you learn the tricks of the trade.

3. Sharpen the blade with a sharpening stone (also called whetstone or honing stone) at the same angle as the blade and always going in one direction (away from the blade).

4. Lubricate the hinges and springs with WD-40 or other lubricating oil.

5. Rub all the metal parts with mineral or vegetable oil or some other lubricating oil.

6. Wipe clean.

7. Return them to their proper storage space.

Some experts suggest taking pruners apart to clean them thoroughly, but I'm not convinced. It would be just my luck to drop a screw or misplace a spring, and I would never be able to get the pruners back together again.

Other Tools

I assume you've cleaned all the soil off your spades, shovels, rakes, cultivators, and hand tools. That's a given. The last cleaning of the season should include a thorough buffing with steel wool or emery cloth on the metal parts, followed by a rubdown with some kind of oil.

Pay attention to any wood handles, too. Sand wooden handles that might have developed rough spots, chips, or splinters. If the tools are old, the wood might be dried out. You can use some liquid or spray furniture polish or linseed oil to put some moisture back in.

Hoses and Machinery

If you live in an area that gets really cold, you should put all your hoses away. First drain them thoroughly, especially if you store them in a place that isn't heated. Then roll them up. This simple step will save you money if you don't have to replace hoses that have split open because they froze with water in them. Also be sure to drain any outside faucets that aren't protected.

Of course you need to clean off any power equipment like a tractor or tiller, too. And you might want to think about having them serviced. But don't do it now. Instead, make an appointment now to have the servicing done a month before you usually open your garden. That way it will be taken care of when you want to be out there digging.

If you put off taking your equipment, you'll have to wait along with all the other gardeners who weren't smart enough to plan ahead.

Garden Miscellany

Gardeners always have lots of other things besides tools that need to be taken care of at the end of the season. Here are a few to keep in mind:

- ◆ Clean and stack tomato cages.
- ◆ Untangle, roll, and store bird and pea netting.
- ◆ Gather and bundle stakes, and throw away any broken ones.
- ◆ Pull up, clean, and put away row markers.
- ◆ Empty watering cans and put them away.
- ◆ Check irrigation timers for any needed repairs or replacements; clean, and store.
- ◆ Clean your wheelbarrow or garden cart, and check for needed repairs. Don't put it at the back of the shed because you might need it during the winter.
- ◆ Clean and disinfect pots and containers. Stack and store terra-cotta pots where they won't get wet. (They absorb water, which can cause cracks or disintegration when it freezes.)
- ◆ Review any containers of herbicides, pesticides, and fertilizers to see if they should be kept or disposed of. (Check with your local waste management department to find out the proper disposal methods.)

Keeping Records

I think the human race is divided into two basic groups: those who keep records and those who don't. The record-keepers always write down their ATM withdrawals; the nons don't. Record-keepers remember birthdays and anniversaries; the nons forget more often than not. I'm a non, and I keep lousy garden records—but that doesn't mean I'm not a good gardener, and it doesn't mean you aren't a good gardener either.

Keeping a record (or at least good notes) provides you with all kinds of valuable information that not only helps you plan future gardening efforts, but allows you to improve your gardening skills. When you keep a record of your efforts, you'll see patterns of successes and failures so you can change what you're doing when necessary or increase other activities that are going well.

Take notes on what interests you. These are some of the things you might keep records of, but don't limit yourself to the ones I've thought of:

◆ Plants, including the varieties and numbers you planted

◆ Sowing dates

◆ Weather details (temperature, rainfall, frosts, other conditions; include dates)

Food for Thought _____

Some of my favorite garden books are the elaborate written records of the authors' years of experience. *Thomas Jefferson's Garden Book* (University of North Carolina Press, 2001), a phenomenal collection of his garden notes, have been published in a book (a copy of which my parents gave me) that is more than 3 inches thick. It provides readers with a fascinating glimpse of the history of gardening in America.

◆ Germination times and success rates

◆ Set-out dates

◆ Flowering dates

◆ Fruit-set dates

◆ Maturity dates

◆ Harvest quantities and dates

- Insect information and dates they appear

- Disease problems and dates they appear

- Fertilizer use (types, quantities, dates)

- Expenses

- Tool purchases and repairs

It's fun to go back through your notes from previous years to compare the current year's weather or harvest details. And when you get old, you can impress your grand-children with your ability to "remember" that, on March 17, 2003, you planted 5 rows of peas and on August 1 of the same year, there was a huge hailstorm.

There are lots of pretty garden journals on the market. More often than not they are given to gardeners as holiday or birthday gifts; I don't think gardeners tend to buy them for themselves. You can use a ledger book, like Thomas Jefferson did. Some people like to keep their journals on wall calendars (although it's hard to find one with large enough squares), or in day planners. Having the dates right there makes it easier to keep track.

On my few attempts at keeping notes, I used a spiral-bound notebook. I liked the large pages, which gave me plenty of room to paste in seed packets, photos, and arti-cles cut from magazines or newspapers. I like those notebooks with little pockets built into the front cover. That makes it easier to keep handouts from the county extension office or receipts from garden centers.

Planning for Next Year

For passionate gardeners, planning next year's garden usually starts about the time the last seeds and seedlings have been planted this year. That's when they wish they'd ordered more arugula seeds or had planted five different types of eggplant instead of just two.

Thinking about next year's garden is one of my favorite off-season pastimes. I always have a stack of gardening books and catalogs beside my bed along with note cards and a pen so I can make lists (although I am a poor record-keeper, I am a world class list-maker).

Here are some resources for planning and reading up on next year's garden:

◆ Stock up on gardening books. You can find lots of them at the library, but I think most gardeners like to own them; perhaps that's the garden writer in me telling you to buy more books!

◆ Read and cut out magazine articles on garden topics that interest you.

◆ Send for gardening catalogs.

◆ Make lists of things you want to grow next year.

◆ Take classes and attend lectures. Community colleges, adult schools, and county extension offices offer courses and talks.

◆ Visit garden centers, nurseries, public gardens, and even friends' gardens to look for ideas and gather information.

You can also take time during the off-season to go through the copious notes you took in your garden book. This will refresh your memory and give you a little shot of reality before you place your seed orders in December or January.

Let's Rethink This

Did you make some really big mistakes this year? If you did, you're not the only gardener who needs to make changes in next year's effort. The biggest mistake many new gardeners make is that they started off with too much garden and it just got away from them.

Other mistakes include growing too much of one thing and not enough of something else. Some gardeners vow at the start of the season that everything will be done organically and naturally, but then they run into problems with severe infestations or diseases, or find out that the nitrogen deficiency isn't helped enough by the application of a natural fertilizer.

The important thing to remember when you realize that you've made a mistake is that all gardens are living things; they grow and change every season and every year. You can always learn from your mistakes, make changes and adjustments, try new plants, and look for new solutions.

The Least You Need to Know

- ◆ Think about saving the seeds from your most successful vegetables for planting next season.

- ◆ Keep good records of your gardening activities.

- ◆ Use fresh potting soil and check for insects when bringing herbs indoors.

- ◆ Use your downtime to repair your tools, replace those that are beyond repair, and add new ones that will make gardening easier or more fun.

- ◆ Don't be afraid to change the size of your garden or the way you work in it next year.

Appendix A

Gardening Resources

This short list of manufacturers and companies is just a starting point for finding gardening equipment, tools, seeds, and plants. Spend a few minutes online, and you're likely to find plenty of additional sources of your own.

Catalogs and Garden Guides

Cyndi's Catalog of Garden Catalogs
gardenlist.com
This site lists hundreds of well-known and obscure gardening catalogs, including dozens of catalogs featuring vegetable seeds and plants. It originates and has its focus in Canada but is a great site for all gardeners.

Garden Guides
gardenguides.com
This website calls itself "your guide to everything gardening." It includes links to blogs and forums as well as gardening dictionaries, directories, and guides; nurseries; garden centers; and other sources of information, products, and services.

Gardening Tools

Smith & Hawken

smithandhawken.com

Here you'll find extensive garden offerings, including tools, composting equipment, containers, and seeds. This is where my favorite poacher's spade came from, but they don't carry it anymore!

Kinsman Company

kinsmangarden.com

This company's retail store is located just a few miles up river from my home. The owners have assembled a terrific collection of tools and garden equipment, many imported from England. They offer tools, containers, gloves, plant supports and ties, and a section of "garden helpers and useful things," like composters, a sieve, and a mud boot holder.

Mantis Tiller

mantis.com

This company makes the tiny tiller.

Seeds and Seedlings

W. Atlee Burpee and Company

burpee.com

Burpee is one of the grand old seed companies with extensive offerings, specialty catalogs, growing guides, and much more.

Seeds of Change

seedsofchange.com

Seeds of Change, whose tag line is "Goodness from the ground up," is bio-diversity-oriented with gourmet greens, cover crops, and interesting veggie varieties. It now sells its 100 percent organic seed in reusable, recyclable envelopes.

Sand Hill Preservation Center

www.sandhillpreservation.com

Sand Hill offers more than 350 tomato varieties, 50 sweet potato varieties, lots of other vegetables, poultry breeds, and more.

Irish Eyes Garden City Seeds

gardencityseeds.net

Irish Eyes specializes in unusual potatoes (more than 80 varieties) as well as offering onions, shallots, garlic, and other veggies. It also provides some great online growers' guides.

Johnny's Selected Seeds

johnnyseeds.com

This is one of the best-known seed companies specializing in short-season crops. It offers a broad selection of everyday seeds, exotics, cover crops, and organic selections, along with tools and supplies.

Native Seeds/SEARCH

nativeseeds.org

This group, whose motto is "ancient seeds for modern needs," offers seeds of Southwest Native Americans. They also have valuable information on seed saving.

Oriental Vegetable Seeds

evergreenseeds.com

More than 350 varieties of Chinese, Japanese, Korean, and Thai vegetables are this group's specialty.

The Cook's Garden

cooksgarden.com

The Cook's Garden has culinary plants and seeds, an especially large collection of herbs, and some organic selections.

Park Seed Co., Inc.

parkseed.com

This company has a huge inventory with dozens of varieties of your favorite vegetables. Look for their Whopper hybrids of super-size vegetables.

Greenpeople

greenpeople.org/seeds.htm

This organization maintains a list of 168 companies, many of them small, that sell organic, heirloom, and untreated seed.

Equipment and Supplies

Benner's Gardens

bennersgardens.com

1-800-753-4660

This is my friend's family's company. They sell the mesh deer fencing and cattle grates that really do keep out deer. Also look for their groundhog/rabbit barrier. If you call, tell them I sent you!

Clean Air Gardening

cleanairgardening.com

This company has an incredible collection of compost bins, cans, tumblers, and pails, along with all kinds of interesting Earth-friendly tools, equipment, and supplies.

Planet Natural

planetnatural.com

Here you'll find compost bins, cold frames, soil test kits, organic fertilizers and pest controls, heirloom seeds, rain barrels, and more.

Natural Insect Control

natural-insect-control.com

I like this company's Earth-friendly tone. It sells beneficial insects, organic fertilizers, insecticidal soaps, and floating row covers. They also have some great birdhouses (remember, birds eat insects!).

Gardens Alive!

gardensalive.com

This company boasts "environmentally responsible products that work." It has organic fertilizers and insecticides, floating row covers, soil test kits, and a zillion other things organically minded folks will appreciate.

Books, Magazines, and Websites

Here is a short list of publications and websites where you may find answers and solutions to your gardening problems and issues.

Books and Magazines

Bagust, Harold. *The Gardener's Dictionary of Horticultural Terms*. London: Cassell Publishers Limited, 1992. This is a thorough dictionary with an English (as in England) focus, so you'll find words we don't tend to use in the United States.

Brenzel, Kathleen Norris, ed. *Sunset Western Garden Book*. Palo Alto, CA: Sunset Publishing Group, 2001. Prof. Price consults this book when he has questions related to his San Diego garden.

Creasy, Rosalind. *The Complete Book of Edible Landscaping*. London: Periplus Publishing, 1982. Rosalind Creasy also has a series of books on specific edible gardens, including: *Mexican* (2000), *Asian* (2000), *Italian* (2001), *Edible Flowers* (1999), *French* (1999), and *Edible Herbs* (1999).

Lovejoy, Sharon. *Sunflower Houses*. Loveland, OH: Interweave Press, Inc., 1991. You'll find whimsical and wonderful garden projects for children in this book. (I heard the author speak at a children's gardening conference many years ago, and she was inspirational.) Find tepee plans, tips for growing a zucchini in a bottle, and a personalized pumpkin in this book, along with a lot of other great ideas.

Nick, Jean, M.A., and Fern Marshall Bradley. *Growing Fruits and Vegetables Organically*. Emmaus, PA: Rodale Press, 1994. This small book covers all the basic techniques you need to grow fruits and vegetables organically.

Sunset Book Editors. *Vegetable Gardening Illustrated*. Palo Alto, CA: Lane Publishing Company, 1987. This book contains basic, how-to information for growing vegetables and small fruits with good sections on raised beds and container gardening.

U.S. Department of Agriculture. *USDA's Complete Guide to Home Canning*. Mineola, NY: Dover Publications, 1999. This is a no-nonsense guide to putting up food. If you take a course at your local county extension office, chances are you'll follow directions from this guide.

Waters, Marjorie. *The Victory Garden Kids' Book*. Boston: Houghton Mifflin, 1988. This charming book has been around for a few years, but its approach to gardening couldn't be more with it. My friend Alison Kennedy, who is the art director for the book, gave it to me when my kids were little. Its simple, step-by-step approach is just as helpful for grown-ups as it is for children.

Websites and Blogs

Besides the various websites referenced in the chapters, here are others you'll find useful as you plan, plant, and harvest your vegetable garden. A few others are just inspirational.

Historic

Monticello Gift Collection
monticello.org/shop
Go here for the Thomas Jefferson Center for Historic Plants at Monticello.

Gardening History Timeline
gardendigest.com/timegl.htm
This site offers a timeline of gardening, from ancient times to 1600.

Food Timeline
foodtimeline.org
This timeline is amazing. It includes dates when many foods were first introduced.

Garden History on the Web

gardenhistoryinfo.com

This site offers an extensive collection of articles on the history of gardening.

General

DIY Home Improvement Information

doityourself.com

Search this site for "gardening" for a lot of do-it-yourself gardening tips.

The Gardening Launch Pad

gardeninglaunchpad.com

Check out this site's links to more than 4,000 gardening sites.

The Best Extension Office Websites

Ohio State University Extension

extension.osu.edu

Here you'll find very detailed articles on plant and pest diagnostics, weed control, soil management, and specific growing information on a long list of plants.

Oregon State University Extension

extension.oregonstate.edu

I like the garden hints archives here.

Rutgers New Jersey Agricultural Experiment Station

njaes.rutgers.edu

Who can resist an article on the brown marmorated stink bug? This is one of my favorite extension websites. (Full disclosure: Prof. Price taught and did research at Rutgers for more than 40 years, and I am a graduate of Rutgers College.)

Texas A&M's Aggie Horticulture Network

aggie-horticulture.tamu.edu

This site's PLANTanswers section is top drawer.

West Virgina University Extension Service

wvu.edu/~agexten

Click on Horticulture & Gardening and then Our Favorite Gardening Links.

Index

Q-R